SOVIET JEWS IN WORLD WAR II
FIGHTING, WITNESSING, REMEMBERING

Borderlines: Russian and East European Jewish Studies

Series Editor:
  Maxim D. Shrayer (Boston College)

Editorial Board:
  Ilya Altman (Russian Holocaust Center
    and Russian State University for the Humanities)
  Karel Berkhoff (NIOD Institute for War,
    Holocaust and Genocide Studies)
  Jeremy Hicks (Queen Mary University of London)
  Brian Horowitz (Tulane University)
  Luba Jurgenson (Universite Paris IV—Sorbonne)
  Roman Katsman (Bar-Ilan University)
  Dov-Ber Kerler (Indiana University)
  Vladimir Khazan (Hebrew University of Jerusalem)
  Mikhail Krutikov (University of Michigan)
  Joanna Beata Michlic (Bristol University)
  Alice Nakhimovsky (Colgate University)
  Antony Polonsky (Brandeis University)
  Jonathan D. Sarna (Brandeis University)
  David Shneer (University of Colorado at Boulder)
  Anna Shternshis (University of Toronto)
  Leona Toker (Hebrew University of Jerusalem)
  Mark Tolts (Hebrew University of Jerusalem)

SOVIET JEWS IN WORLD WAR II

FIGHTING, WITNESSING, REMEMBERING

Edited by **HARRIET MURAV**
and **GENNADY ESTRAIKH**

Boston
2014

Library of Congress Cataloging-in-Publication Data:
A catalog record for this book is available from the Library of Congress.

Copyright © 2014 Academic Studies Press
All rights reserved
ISBN 978-1-61811-313-9 (hardback)
ISBN 978-1-61811-314-6 (electronic)
ISBN 978-1-61811-816-5 (paperback)

Cover design by Ivan Grave

Published by Academic Studies Press in 2014
28 Montfern Avenue
Brighton, MA 02135, USA
press@academicstudiespress.com
www.academicstudiespress.com

Table of Contents

Acknowledgments 6
Preface. Gennady Estraikh and Harriet Murav 7

Part 1: HISTORIES

Chapter 1. Mordechai Altshuler, "Jewish Combatants of the Red Army
  Confront the Holocaust" 16
Chapter 2. Joshua Rubenstein, "Il′ia Ehrenburg and the Holocaust
  in the Soviet Press" 36
Chapter 3. Oleg Budnitskii, "Jews at War: Diaries from the Front" 57
Chapter 4. Gennady Estraikh, "Jews as Cossacks: A Symbiosis
  in Literature and Life" 85
Chapter 5. Arkadi Zeltser, "How the Jewish Intelligentsia Created
  the Jewishness of the Jewish Hero: The Soviet Yiddish Press" 104

Part II: REPRESENTATION, DOCUMENTATION, AND INTERPRETATION

Chapter 6. Marat Grinberg, "Foreshadowing the Holocaust:
  Boris Slutskii's Jewish Poetic Cycle of 1940/41" 130
Chapter 7. Harriet Murav, "Poetry After Kerch′:
  Representing Jewish Mass Death in the Soviet Union" 151
Chapter 8. Olga Gershenson, "Between the Permitted and the Forbidden:
  The Politics of Holocaust Representation in *The Unvanquished* (1945)" 168
Chapter 9. David Shneer, "From Photojournalist to Memory Maker:
  Evgenii Khaldei and Soviet Jewish Photographers" 187
Chapter 10. Memoirs:
  a. Boris Slutskii, "The Story of Gershel′man, a Jew" 208
  b. Mikhail Romm, "The Question of the National Question, or
    A Rally for a Genuinely Russian Cinema" 219
  c. Anatolii Rybakov, "A Novel of Memoirs" 230
Chapter 11. Zvi Gitelman, "Afterword: Soviet Jews in World War II:
  Experience, Perception and Interpretation" 251

Index 264

Acknowledgments

We are extremely grateful to the United States Holocaust Memorial Museum, the Blavatnik Archive Foundation, and the Skirball Department of Hebrew and Judaic Studies at New York University for their sponsorship of the conference on which this volume is based. We would also like to thank the Fund for the Study of the Holocaust in the USSR, Center for Advanced Holocaust Studies at the United States Holocaust Memorial Museum, New York University, and the Program in Jewish Culture and Society at the University of Illinois at Urbana-Champaign for their generous support of the publication of this volume.

Preface
Gennady Estraikh and Harriet Murav

The Holocaust is commonly defined as the mass murder of millions of Jews by the German Nazis and their collaborators. This book, however, mainly discusses a concurrent phenomenon of World War II: the participation of Jews in combating the Nazis during the Great Patriotic War, as the period between June 22, 1941, and May 9, 1945 was known in the Soviet Union and as it is still called in many Russian-language sources. Approximately 300,000 to 500,000 Jews served as combatants; the estimate of non-combatant Jewish deaths is 2.5 million.[1] In the West, the Holocaust emerged as a unique and paradigmatic set of events, of singular significance for world history. The Holocaust occupies a privileged place in Jewish identity, especially in North America and Israel.[2] Beyond issues of identity, moreover, the Holocaust came to signify the limit case of representability, as in Theodor Adorno's famous dictum about the impossibility of poetry after Auschwitz. The same events, however, came to be understood and represented in different terms in the Soviet Union. For example, when the authors of *Eynikayt* (Unity, the newspaper of the Jewish Anti-Fascist Committee) used the term "khurbn" in 1942, they were doing so to reference a Jewish national disaster the way that Yiddish-speaking Jews, whether Soviet or not, traditionally referred to their national disasters. The term *khurbn* originally referred to the destruction of the first and second Temples. In a speech given in Moscow in May 1942, published in the first (June) issue of *Eynikayt*, David Bergelson used the term *karbones* when he asked the Jews of the entire world to respond to the call of the dead: "our victims [karbones] have not yet been counted and not even brought to their graves." Neither *khurbn* nor *karbones* is identical to the term Holocaust, which began to circulate in the late 1950s; however, both Yiddish terms link the events of the war to traditional Jewish forms of responding to catastrophe.[3] The term signified a Jewish understanding of the events as they were taking place, but without the same meanings that the term Holocaust eventually assumed. By probing the overlap and the differences between Western and Soviet narratives of the destruction of the Jews, we hope to make a contribution to the broader understanding of the war and the Nazi genocide.

In the 1940s, the topic of resistance was central in Yiddish publications, which appeared under the auspices of the Jewish Anti-Fascist Committee, established in 1942 as one of the propaganda units at the Soviet Information Bureau, or *Sovinformburo*. The Moscow publishing house Emes put out books about Jewish soldiers and resistance fighters, while *Eynikayt* featured articles describing the heroic deeds of Soviet Jews.[4] In the 1960s-80s, the theme of Jewish resistance continued to be discussed in Soviet Yiddish belles-lettres, particularly in the Moscow Yiddish journal *Sovetish heymland* (Soviet homeland).[5] One of the Yiddish novelists, Mikhail Lev (1917-2013), wrote almost exclusively about the war.[6] Some of these writings came out also in Russian, but very few of them appeared in English or any other translations.

The Cold War left a heavy imprint on the field of Soviet Jewish studies. In the Soviet Union, this field was nowhere in evidence, because its potential output might (according to the Kremlin's paranoid logic) provide fodder for Jewish nationalists. In the West, neither the general ideological atmosphere nor the sources of academic funding stimulated research projects on Soviet Jewish patriotism. Jewish veterans of the Red Army were often stereotyped as die-hard communists and anti-Zionists. It is known, for instance, that some Polish Jews, who fought against the Nazis as soldiers in the Red Army and later settled in America, would not reveal this part of their biography in their immigration papers, because they were afraid that it could jeopardize their chances of entering the United States. General David Dragunskii, twice decorated as the Hero of the Soviet Union, was scorned in the West for his role of chairman of the Anti-Zionist Committee of the Soviet Public.

During the last two decades, numerous books have been published—predominantly in Russian—about Soviet Jewish soldiers and partisans. The vast majority of the publications are memoirs and diaries, or studies by amateur researchers, often themselves veterans of the war. Some of the books are collections of material about Jewish soldiers of a region or city.[7] At the same time, professional scholars continue to pay relatively little attention to the participation of Soviet Jews in armed resistance.

This volume examines the role of Soviet Jews in the Second World War, not from the perspective of their destruction, but rather, by examining their role in the Red Army and in various domains of Soviet life of the time. We focus on Jews who fought and survived the war outside the zone of occupation, who served as soldiers, journalists and propagandists. Jews created the Soviet narrative of the war; they created the images that accompanied the text. Yurii Levitan, for example, became the voice of *Sovinformburo*, the centralized Soviet information agency during the war; Il'ia Ehrenburg was the most prominent Soviet journalist of the period. The same writers, including Ehrenburg and Vasilii Grossman, who could not publish a compilation of testimony about the fate of Jews under German occupation, *The Black Book*, in the Soviet Union, published reams of material about the Soviet war effort. Jewish intellectuals who served on the front lines subsequently rose to prominence as members of the Soviet cultural establishment, including the writers Anatolii Rybakov and Emanuil Kazakevich.

The volume is based on a conference, "Soviet Jewish Soldiers, Jewish Resistance, and Jews in the USSR during the Holocaust," held in 2008, jointly sponsored by the U. S. Holocaust Museum, the Blavatnik Archive Foundation, and the Skirball Department of Hebrew and Judaic Studies at New York University. It was, to a considerable degree, the brainchild of Dr. Kenneth R. Alper, who inspired the abovementioned institutions and organizations to turn their attention to a patent dearth of scholarship on the Red Army's Jewish combatants during World War II. Like the 2008 conference, this volume is not about the Holocaust proper, though the destruction of Jews affected and even determined the actions and outlooks of those Soviet people who were on or behind the frontline. The essays examine newly discovered and previously neglected oral testimony, poetry, cinema, diaries, memoirs, newspapers, and archives. This book is among the first to combine the study of Russian and Yiddish materials, reflecting the nature of the Jewish Anti-Fascist Committee, which for the first time during the Soviet period, included under the same institutional umbrella both Yiddish language and Russian language writers.

By August 1914, when the Romanov Empire entered the war (later called the First World War) with Germany and Austro-Hungary, Russian Jews represented a well-organized community, with numerous philanthropic, mutual-help, religious, cultural, and educational organizations and institutions, political parties and groupings, publishing houses and periodicals in Yiddish, Hebrew, Russian, and Polish, and intensive links with foreign Jewish communities. Jewish political and civic activists were able to restructure the existing institutional network into a shape that reflected the needs of wartime. The Central Jewish Committee for the Relief of Victims of War was backed by four influential organizations: the Society for the Propagation of Enlightenment among Russian Jews; the Jewish Colonization Society, the Organization for Rehabilitation through Training, and the Society for Health of Jews. As a result, Russia's Jewish civic society came out from the war as a strong, multi-functional institutional edifice, staffed by ambitious people, many of whom sought to build autonomous Jewish life in the multinational, federative republic they believed would replace the Romanov autocracy.

The reality of post-1917 transformations of the Russian Empire had little in common with these activists' blueprints. In the 1920s, the Soviet regime had destroyed or put under its tight control all existing independent organizations, and thus eliminated political and legal conditions for autonomous civil society. By June 1941, the Yiddish sections (based in Moscow, Kiev, and Minsk) at the Soviet Writers' Union were the only ostensibly-civic-society body that existed in the Soviet Jewish landscape, which still contained state-run cultural and educational institutions, most notably several Yiddish theaters, newspapers and journals, and Yiddish schools in Birobidzhan and the areas that fell under Soviet control according to the Molotov-Ribbentrop Pact. There was no institutional or organizational space left for real civic activism, never mind that the vast majority of pre-1917 activists had either emigrated or perished in the purges.

It is a small wonder then that when Stalin's ideologists decided to form a new ostensibly-civic-society organization called the Jewish Anti-Fascist Committee (JAC), the Yiddish sections at the Soviet Writers' Union and the stars of the Moscow State Yiddish Theater were almost the only people suited to work at this structural unit of the *Sovinformburo*. This bureau, established on the third day of the war, on June 24, 1941, was to realize the directive of the Soviet government and the Communist party's Central Committee "to bring into the limelight international events, military developments, and day-to-day life through printed and broadcast media." The only Soviet Jewish organization in the 1940s, the JAC played a marginal role in the wartime life of average Soviet Jews. Many or even the majority of them did not know about its existence. The only Yiddish periodical, the newspaper *Eynikayt* of the JAC, had a relatively insignificant circulation, and a small proportion of the younger generation could read a Yiddish text. Yet the JAC and its milieu have attracted the attention of students of Soviet Jewish political, social, and intellectual history and, together with studies of the Holocaust in Ukraine, Belarus, Moldova, and the Baltic countries, dominated scholarship on Soviet Jewish life during the war.

Topics related to the JAC and the Holocaust are discussed also in this collection of articles, but they do not occupy center stage. The protagonists of this volume are Jewish soldiers and officers, including writers and artists in uniform, who usually had little or nothing to do with collective forms of Jewish life and suffering. In contrast with the Holocaust victims, their Jewish experiences were usually individual, if typical. The Red Army did not have chaplains, Jewish or non-Jewish, and, apart from several military units, notably the 16th Lithuanian Division and the 308th Latvian Division, Jewish combatants were rarely concentrated in the same platoons or battalions. At the same time, Jewishness, often a marker of secondary significance in the pre-war phase of the lives of Soviet Jews, became for many very important during the war.

The war put conflicting pressures on the boundaries separating the Soviet and Jewish dimensions of the identity of the soldiers, evacuees, partisans, photojournalists, and poets who participated in and responded to it, and yet also fused these two dimensions together. The Soviet government encouraged greater ethnic identification during the war; Hitler's target was "Judeo-Bolshevism." Thus, the (im)balance between Jewishness and Sovietness is in the center of the chapters that follow.

We divide the essays into two parts. Part I includes histories: confronting the occupation, fighting the war as soldiers, officers, and partisans, evacuating from the front, and confronting the murder of Jews. Mordechai Altshuler's "Jewish Combatants of the Red Army Confront the Holocaust" describes the emotional response of Jewish soldiers to the aftermath of the mass killings. Fragments of Hebrew texts discovered in the rubble acquired particular significance for these soldiers, and as Altshuler observes, the Hebrew alphabet itself was a powerful symbol in letters and other documents the soldiers wrote. Yiddish writers of the time, including David Bergelson and Peretz Markish, used the leitmotif of Hebrew letters in their works to memoriale the destruction of Jews. In "Il'ia Ehrenburg and the Holocaust in the Soviet Press," Joshua Rubenstein shows Ehrenburg's importance, not only as the chief Soviet propagandist during the war, but as one of the very few public figures of the time who alerted the public to the massive destruction suffered by the Jewish community; Ehrenburg was one of the first to specify six million as the number of Jews killed. Ehrenburg also staunchly defended Soviet Jews against the charge that they failed to serve in active duty.

Oleg Budnitskii's essay, "Jews at War: Diaries from the Front," provides a fascinating glimpse of what he calls "Private Abram's" war. These diaries reveal the soldiers' ordinary, daily existence of sleeping, eating, and resting; occasionally the business of fighting turns into scenes of horrific violence. Budnitskii concludes that his subjects' Soviet identity was far more important to them than their Jewishness. Arkadi Zeltser shows in "How the Jewish Intelligentsia Created the Jewishness of the Jewish Hero: The Soviet Yiddish Press" that Jewish writers working for *Eynikayt* crafted a specifically Jewish type of hero, using references to Jewish history. They overfulfilled the brief created by the Soviet government at this time, which sought to mobilize the population with narratives that were both patriotic and ethnic. Itsik Fefer, for example, as Zeltser points out, relied on the traditional religious model of the martyr for the faith. Gennady Estraikh, on the other hand, reveals to what extent a new and unlikely form of interethnic cooperation emerged in Jewish literature about the war. In "Jews as Cossacks: A Symbiosis in Literature and Life," Estraikh argues that Jewish authors relied on the new phenomenon of Cossack-Jewish cooperation, fostered by the Soviet policy of the brotherhood of nations, in their portraits of Jewish wartime heroism. These writers used imagery associated with the Cossacks, the traditional enemy of the Jews, to depict feats of Jewish bravery.

Part II focuses on representation, documentation, and interpretation in poetry, cinema, and photojournalism. In this section of the volume, the Nazi destruction of the Jews appears as an explicit theme. As the authors of these essays point out, scholars have largely ignored the Soviet Jewish literary and cultural response to the Holocaust. Boris Slutskii (1919-1986), the subject of Marat Grinberg's essay, and Il'ia Sel'vinskii (1899-1968), the subject of Harriet Murav's essay, both served in the Soviet army and wrote about their experience and their encounter with the Nazi genocide. In "Foreshadowing the Holocaust: Boris Slutskii's Jewish Poetic Cycle of 1940/41," Grinberg refutes the argument that Slutskii's awareness of his Jewishness developed only as a reaction to the Holocaust. The 1940/1 cycle, written before the destruction of the Jews had taken place, reveals Slutskii's Biblical, messianic, and profoundly Jewish orientation at the very core of his poetics. Murav's essay, "Poetry After Kerch': Representing Jewish Mass Death in the Soviet

Union," explores three poems written and published from 1942 to 1947, all addressing what the Soviets did not call the Holocaust. The poems touch on the theme of the impossibility of representing the Nazi genocide, a central motif of Holocaust writing in the West, but also frame the poet's response to the German massacre of Jews in terms of revenge and victory over Germany, issues largely suppressed in Western Holocaust representation.

In "Between the Permitted and the Forbidden: The Politics of Holocaust Representation in *The Unvanquished* (1945)," Olga Gershenson discusses the first feature film on the Holocaust, made in the Soviet Union. Gershenson argues that the graphic and explicit representation of the execution of Jews outside a town is at the very core of the film's message. What makes the film even more remarkable, as her explanation of the film's reception reveals, is that it went against the grain of Soviet representations of the war, which emphasized the universality of suffering. David Shneer's essay, "From Photojournalist to Memory Maker: Evgenii Khaldei and Soviet Jewish Photographers," explores how the war shifted the difficult balancing act between the Soviet and Jewish dimensions of Evgenii Khaldei's identity. Khaldei was well-known for his photograph capturing the Soviet entry into Berlin—he took the picture of the "raising of the red flag over the Reichstag," as it came to be called. As Shneer points out, however, Khaldei also took photographs of Nazi atrocities committed against Jews, some of which did not subscribe to the Soviet policy of the universality of suffering. It is the afterlife of Khaldei's explicitly Jewish photographs that is at the heart of the story Shneer tells, a story about the shifting contours of memory and identity in the postwar and post-Soviet period.

During the entire Soviet epoch, Jewish intellectuals densely populated the world of literature, cinema, theatre, and other domains of creativity; many of them became household names among connoisseurs and even the general public. In pre-war society, they often did not have problems with forging their hyphenated Soviet-Jewishness (typically more Soviet than Jewish) identity. During and after the war, the veneer of internationalism showed cracks, revealing clear signs of antisemitism. The fragments that we include here from the memoirs of three leading intellectuals—the poet Boris Slutskii, the film director Mikhail Romm (1901-71), and the novelist Anatolii Rybakov (1911-98)—discuss various aspects of the change: Slutskii and Romm recall their experiences during the war, whereas Rybakov's piece of memoirs provides insight into the history of his 1979 novel *Heavy Sand*.

Finally, we end the volume with a set of reflections about the topics covered by the various essays and the essays themselves by a noted scholar of Russian and Jewish studies, Zvi Gitelman. Professor Gitelman's numerous publications on Russian-Jewish political thought and practice, and in particular, his groundbreaking work on the Holocaust in the USSR, make his an eminently qualified perspective with which to conclude our volume.

Notes

1. See Mordechai Altshuler, "Jewish Combatants of the Red Army Confront the Holocaust"; Oleg Budnitskii, "Jews at War: Diaries from the Front"; and Joshua Rubenstein, "Il'ia Ehrenburg and the Holocaust in the Soviet Press,» in this volume.
2. For a discussion, see James Young, *Writing and Rewriting the Holocaust* (Bloomington: Indiana University Press, 1988); Peter Novick, *The Holocaust in American Life* (New York: Houghton Mifflin, 1999); and Neil Levy and Michael Rothberg, *The Holocaust: Theoretical Readings* (New Brunswick, NJ: Rutgers University Press, 2003).
3. For a discussion, see David Roskies, *Against the Apocalypse: Responses to Catastrophe in Modern Jewish Culture* (Cambridge, MA: Harvard University Press, 1984).
4. Dov-Ber Kerler, "The Soviet Yiddish Press: *Eynikayt* During The War, 1942-1945," in *Why Didn't the Press Shout?: American and International Journalism During the Holocaust*, ed. Robert M. Shapiro (Jersey City: KTAV Publishing House, 2003), 221-49; David Shneer, "From Mourning to Vengeance: Bergelson's Holocaust Journalism," in *David Bergelson: From Modernism to Socialist Realism*, ed. Joseph Sherman and Gennady Estraikh (London: Legenda, 2007), 248-68.
5. Zvi Gitelman, "Soviet Reactions to the Holocaust, 1945-1991," in Lucjan Dobroszycki and Jeffrey S. Gurock, *The Holocaust in the Soviet Union: Studies and Sources on the Destruction of the Jews in the Nazi-Occupied Territories of the USSR, 1941-1945* (Armonk, NY: M. E. Sharpe, 1993), 16.
6. Hersh Remenik, *Shtaplen: portretn fun yidishe shrayber* (Moscow: Sovetskii pisatel', 1982), 323-32. See, e.g., Hersh Smolar, *The Minsk Ghetto: Soviet Jewish Partisans against the Nazis* (New York: Holocaust Publications, 1989) and Mikhail Lev, *Sobibor: A Documentary Story of the Sobibor Uprising* (Jerusalem and New York: Gefen, 2007).
7. See, e.g., S. Bass et al. (eds.), *Kniga pamiati voinov-evreev Dnepropetrovska*, 4 vols. (Dnipropetrovsk: Association of Jewish Veterans, 1999-2004); *Evrei Samary na frontakh Velikoi Otechestvennoi*, 2 vols. (Samara: Vozrozhdenie, 2002-2006).

Part I

HISTORIES

Chapter 1

Jewish Combatants of the Red Army Confront the Holocaust[1]

Mordechai Altshuler

In this essay, I examine how the direct encounter with the results of the Holocaust affected some of the Red Army's Jewish combatants. The focus here is on young Jews who grew up in the Soviet regime and were distant from Jewish religion and culture; I do not deal with Jews from the newly annexed territories, where they continued to lead traditional Jewish lives despite the brief period of Soviet rule.

During the Soviet-German War an estimated 300,000 to 500,000 Jews were drafted into the Red Army.[2] Some of them were among the liberators of cities and towns that had sizable Jewish populations before the war. For example, one account of liberation comes from a survivor who was a resident of the town of Kryzhopol[3] in Ukraine's Vinnitsa *oblast'*. The local Jews were imprisoned in a camp that was surrounded by Romanian guards. A Soviet tank broke into the city and rolled over the barbed-wire fence. One of the soldiers, who was a relative of the survivor, shouted from the tank, "Jews, don't be afraid—you can come out now."[4] These Jewish combatants were the first to come face to face with the aftermath of the Holocaust.

Most of the letters that soldiers sent to their families are short and laconic and do not display any expressions of feelings and thoughts.[5] Nonetheless, the few testimonies indicate that, for a fair number of Jewish combatants, the direct encounter with the Holocaust, on the one hand, and the eruption of anti-Jewish hatred, on the other, brought about a change in their attitude toward their own ethnic identity.

The father of Iakov Ravich (born in 1925) worked in the Soviet commercial mission in Berlin and was sent to the Gulag in 1937. Iakov lied about his age and volunteered for the Red Army. He wrote his mother the following in a brief letter: "A special portion was allotted to the Jews [in Kursk].[6] Hundreds of people were taken and put aboard trucks and gas cars [*dushegubki*]. They were transported to an area outside the city and none of them ever came back."[7]

Vulf Zelenyi expressed his empathy with the Jewish people in a typically Soviet fashion. Born in 1923 in Kharkov, he was evacuated to the city of Molotov (Perm') together with the factory in which he was employed. In 1942, he joined the Red Army and was sent to the front. He participated in the heavy fighting at Stalingrad, from where he wrote to his mother on February 20, 1943:

> This is a difficult hour for many nationalities of the Soviet nation, especially for the Jewish people. Hitler's bloody hands want to subjugate the Jews and, what is even worse, to wipe them off the face of the earth. However, that goal will never be achieved. The Jewish people will show him [Hitler] where true justice lies and will revenge the torture its sons and daughters have endured. Knowing all this, I am fighting the enemy courageously and heroically as a member of the Jewish people.[8]

For reasons of field security, Red Army soldiers were not permitted to keep diaries; however, this prohibition did not apply to poets and writers, who were allowed to express their feelings even while participating in the fighting. This is the case with two poems written by a Russian poet of Jewish descent, Iakov Khelemskii (born in 1914), who was one of the liberators of the Latvian capital. In the course of a few days, he wrote two poems, both entitled "Riga."[9] In the first poem, he describes the city's buildings with their northern European architectural style. Young girls with flowers greet the liberators: "They are running toward them with daisies in their hands/ They are running quickly, they are in a hurry, these girls with their multi-colored kerchiefs." The festive mood changes quickly when the poet turns toward the northern part of the city, where he feels:

> The dying ghetto…
> the Jewish quarter is cut off with barbed wire…
> Behind every door a human being once lived…
> Here they lived, loved and hated
> Here they prayed to God…

Here there is a smell of blood and of cruel pain.
Here each stone dies after being tortured.
Here every house becomes another Wailing Wall....
This sorrow cries out with all the power of their muteness...
and the searing heat of the tormented ghetto
you can feel with the skin of your body.

In the first poem, the city comes to life, whereas in the ghetto there is nothing but death and a heap of rubble. The poet hears and senses through the pores of his skin—physically—the mute cries of the murdered victims. The contrast between the unique fate of the Jews and the surrounding society is thus given emphasis. Vasilii Grossman expressed a similar feeling in a letter to his wife in early 1944:

> Yesterday I was in Kiev. It's hard to express what I felt and what I suffered in the few hours when I visited the addresses of relatives and acquaintances. There are only graves and death. I am going to Berdichev[10] today. My comrades have already been there. They said that the city is completely devastated, and only a few people, maybe a dozen out of many thousands, tens of thousands, of Jews who lived there, have survived. I have no hope of finding Mama alive. The only thing I am hoping for is to find out about her last days and her death.[11]

Although combatants were prohibited from taking notes, some of them clandestinely recorded their thoughts and impressions. One of those was Moisei Loifer, who wrote down anything that he considered important. Loifer was born in the town of Kanev in Ukraine.[12] The language spoken in his home was Yiddish, and his father was one of the organizers of a *kolkhoz* in the late 1920s. Although the family observed the Jewish holidays, Moisei openly demonstrated his negative attitude toward religion, even eating in public on the fast of Yom Kippur. He was drafted in 1939 and remained in uniform until the end of the war. In September 1943, his unit set up camp in the vicinity of Smolensk,[13] and the villagers in the area related how the Germans "gathered about 100 people from families that had members in the partisan groups, and that included Jews who had sought refuge in the forests.... Gasoline was poured on them and lit torches were thrown at them.

The people were burned to death."[14] Between December 13 and 17, 1943, he recorded the following in his diary:

> Along the way, we learned that, in an anti-tank ditch, in the town of Liady[15] ... the Germans collected about 3,000 Jews, who were residents of Liady and surrounding towns. The Germans "ironed" them in the ditch with the tanks; afterwards, they covered up [the ditch]. For several days, the earth in the ditch was in constant motion and you could hear groans.[16]

One of the few soldiers who made almost daily entries in a diary during the fighting, Gedalia Safian,[17] recorded on July 18, 1944:

> The first small town on the [now former] trans-Soviet-Polish border was Witkow Nowy.[18] The center of the town had been burned down. On one house two Stars of David had been painted ... [W]hite shells [of houses], without windows or doors, were still standing. Once there was life in those homes, happy and sad occasions took place there. Where are those people now? How hard it must have been for them in the last days [of their lives].[19]

A few days later, in the provincial capital of Radziechow, a festive rally was held to mark the town's liberation and ardent speeches were made from the podium; however, Safian visualized something entirely different:

> A strong breeze passing through the square was playing with the pages of ancient Jewish books that were being used to wrap cherries in the market. The letters of the ancient Aramaic language were shining brightly and it was so difficult to look at them. They had been looted from the houses along with the other possessions of the town's shoemakers, tailors, shopkeepers, the *luftmentshn* [people with no definite income] and the synagogues—people fanatically attached to their religion once lived in this town. They were annihilated and the ruins of their homes and the pages of holy books are the sole reminders that they ever existed.[20]

This same kind of deep emotional attachment to the "worn-out Hebrew letters," which many of these young Jewish soldiers had previously regarded with disrespect and scorn, can be seen in following passage from a letter written by a Jewish combatant to Il'ia Ehrenburg in 1945:

> The bloodthirsty looters shot to death 44 of my relatives, including my sisters and my parents. The members of my brother's family were buried alive.... I have passed through nearly all of Estonia, Lithuania and Poland without meeting a single Jew.... A short while ago, we took up a lookout position in the attic of a house in a Polish town that we had recently liberated. In this attic I found many Jewish books, which seemed to be weeping over the fate of their owners.... I am not religious but, when I held a Passover *Haggadah* in my hands, I began to weep.[21]

The Hebrew letters that many of the young Jewish soldiers had previously considered as representatives of the world of yesterday now acquired a new significance in their eyes and some of these soldiers tried to learn them in the frontline trenches. In 1943, Samuel Margolin was inducted into the Red Army. He was the grandson of Shraga-Feivel Margolin (1870-1942), the publisher of the Hebrew-language newspaper *Hazman*, which appeared in Vilna in 1910. In Samuel's last letter to his mother, which he wrote on September 14, 1943, he asked her, "Please send me the Jewish alphabet." However, before the 18-year-old soldier could begin learning this alphabet, he fell in battle in a village in the Smolensk district in early December 1943.[22]

Ber Mark (1908-1966), a Jewish historian from Poland who was at that time in the Soviet Union, detected this change in the attitude of Soviet Jewish soldiers toward the Hebrew alphabet and devoted an entire (semi-)documentary story (*ocherk*) to this topic, entitled "The Square Letters." He opens his story with the description of a chance meeting with a Red Army soldier in a railroad station close to the front. A wounded soldier, who did not look at all Jewish, got off the train at this station. However, when the soldier saw Mark holding a book written in "square Hebrew letters," he approached the narrator and introduced himself as a Mountain Jew. A friendship developed between Mark and the soldier, and Mark would regularly visit his new friend in hospital. During one of their meetings, the soldier told the narrator about the liberation of a town in which he discovered great suffering and destruction. When he asked "And where are the Jews?," he was taken to a place outside the town, where he saw scorched corpses. Beside the corpses,

> There was the scorched corpse of a child that was so full of holes it looked like a sieve. The boy was holding a book. A simple book that had been printed in square Hebrew letters was lying open on the ground. The book was slightly soiled by the mud and somewhat scorched.... [The soldier] picked up the book.... On one of the pages there was a large yellowing bloodstain.... Had the child opened the book at this page when he received the initial deadly blow from his murderer? [The soldier] tore out the page and kept it. Whenever no one was looking, he would take it out of his pocket, smooth it out and look at the yellowing print and the mute letters.[23]

The soldier recovered and continued to fight against the Germans with admirable courage in the Caucasus Mountains. In one of those battles, he was fatally wounded and the narrator one day received a letter from a hospital. The letter was accompanied by a "page from a Jewish book. There was a stain in the middle of the page. 'Guard this, my dear friend, in case I die.... This page is printed in those beloved square letters and has been sanctified by the blood of a holy child.'"[24]

Mark deliberately chose a Caucasus Mountain Jew as the hero of his tale. The language of these Jews had not been written in the letters of the Hebrew alphabet since the 1920s;[25] thus, Mark was alluding to the hundreds of thousands of Jewish soldiers in the Red Army who knew Russian but had no knowledge whatsoever of the Hebrew alphabet. Not only did the letters of the Hebrew alphabet draw Jews closer together during the Second World War, the letters acquired new significance because they became a symbol of the blood of the Jews murdered by the Nazis. Thus, the hero of Mark's story preserves a Hebrew text although he is unfamiliar with the language; moreover, the letters in that text are regarded here as holy.

The Soviet education system as well as Soviet propaganda continually stressed that there was no such entity as a Jewish nation, and that there never was and never could be a common destiny linking Soviet Jews who were engaged in building a socialist world with the Jews of capitalist countries. Many young Soviet Jews accepted this approach and even adhered to it with fervent conviction. This attitude of the Soviet Union did not change during World

War 2, even if for propagandistic and practical reasons they organized the Jewish Anti-Fascist Committee. However, when Jewish combatants of the Red Army came in direct contact with the results of the Holocaust, the emotional impact seriously undermined this belief, at least at the subconscious level.

In his memoirs, Anatolii Rybakov (1911-1998), who would later become a well-known Russian writer, describes his encounter with a Holocaust survivor whom he met in Berlin in the course of his duties as a Red Army officer:

> On the first day [of my stay in this city] I noticed a thin woman in a courtyard.... [H]er dress, coat and kerchief were all black. She stared at me intensely and then, in the evening, she was again standing in the courtyard and staring at me. The next day, she approached me and, with considerable hesitation, handed me a small piece of paper on which a *Magen David* (Star of David) had been drawn. It was obvious that she was Jewish, that she had been hiding and that, when the Russians came, she had decided to "expose herself" [that is, expose her Jewishness] to a Soviet Jewish officer.... [At headquarters, where the author of this memoir took the woman] she removed the kerchief from her head: Half of her hair was black, and the other half was white.... Here was a totally exhausted woman who was probably 35 or 40 years of age; yet she already looked like an old woman .... When she revealed her age, my tongue clicked against my palate—she was actually only 16 years old![26]

The Star of David—which, in caricatures and newspaper articles in the Soviet Union, was used to symbolize Jews in the capitalist world who, according to Soviet ideology, were so distant from the Jews of the USSR—now became a sign that led this Jewish Red Army officer to feel a kinship with a young Jewish girl from Germany whose language he did not even know.

The sense of solidarity that Soviet Jewish veterans felt toward Jews of other countries was expressed in various ways. Evgenii Khaldei (1917-1997) served as a military photographer, and his staged photograph depicting Red Army soldiers hanging the Soviet flag on the Reichstag became a symbol of the USSR's victory over Nazi Germany. Many years after the war, he described his chance meeting with a Jewish pilot serving in the U.S. Air Force. The military unit to which Khaldei was attached was in Romania at the time. When they sat down to eat, a rumor spread that an American bomber had been downed and its pilots had survived the crash. Suddenly, the Red Army soldiers saw the American pilots led by their commander walking toward them: "I was sitting beside my friend Grinia. I turned to Grinia and said to him, 'you see the captain over there?... I think he's Jewish.'" After the two Soviet soldiers had wagered as to the captain's Jewishness, Khaldei turned to the officer, asking him in Yiddish, "Du bist a yid?" ("Are you Jewish?"). Khaldei recalled:

> The officer jumped to his feet and gave me a big hug. I gave him a present: a hundred-ruble note with Lenin's picture on it. [To reciprocate, the Jewish officer gave Khaldei a ten-dollar bill and] wrote on it something from right to left.... I told him, "I can speak Yiddish, but I can't read Yiddish. What did you write?" He replied, "There is no place on earth where two Jews cannot find one another."[27]

In January 1945, the photographer reached Buda; the Germans still controlled Pest. Like all military photographers, Khaldei's job was to document the heroism of the victorious Red Army. However, when Khaldei saw an older Jewish couple wearing yellow Stars of David on their jacket lapels, he decided to record this fact. The photograph was never circulated in the USSR. In an interview, he described the situation in which he took that photo:

> I saw them walking down the street. I was in a black leather coat, and at first, they were afraid—they thought I was from the SS. I walked over and tore off their stars, first the woman's, then the man's. She got even more frightened. She said, "No, no, you can't do that, we have to wear them!" I told them that the Russians were here. I told them, "Ikh bin oykh a yid. Sholem aleykhem" (I'm Jewish too. Hello). Then she cried.[28]

Having grown up in a village in an area populated by Cossacks in the Taganrog district, Khaldei apparently had had no Jewish education except for a few Yiddish words he had picked up from the grandfather who raised him. Nonetheless, he was very moved by the encounter with the American Jewish soldier and by the words the latter had written on the ten-dollar bill; similarly, Khaldei reacted very emotionally when he was confronted with the yellow Star of David, which symbolized the Holocaust in which his father and three sisters had been murdered.

A similar, spontaneous emotional reaction was evident among the Jewish soldiers who liberated a village near Uman'[29] and who encountered a little Jewish girl there who said to them in Yiddish, "Don't forget what you have seen here with your own eyes."[30] Such expressions led the Jewish Red Army combatants to identify with the Jews they encountered and to sense the existence of a common Jewish destiny, just as was the case in the next example describing an encounter in the streets of Berlin after Germany's defeat.

After Germany's surrender, groups of Red Army soldiers wandered through Berlin's streets, where smoke was still rising from the ruins of some of the destroyed buildings. The soldiers sang and felt jubilant. When the Jews among them encountered Jewish soldiers from the Polish Army conversing in Yiddish, they left their comrades, and joined the Polish Jews. David Kahana, the rabbi of the Polish Army, testified about the atmosphere of the meeting as follows: "We mingled among them—and they drank a toast with us, shouting out *L'chaim*." A few minutes later, you could have sworn that all the persons standing there, beside Berlin's Brandenburg Gate, were old friends, even relatives, members of one large family.[31]

The change in attitude toward Jewish symbols and feelings of solidarity with Jews who had survived the Holocaust were sometimes expressed in letters by Soviet Jewish combatants that were sent to their relatives in ways that bypassed military censorship. The text of one such letter, which was received in Tashkent in October 1944, was included in a published book of memoirs. The mother of a Jewish combatant was very worried after not hearing any word from her son, who was on the front for two months. She finally received a letter from him. Her son wrote that, two months earlier, he had been wounded in battle in the town of Ponovich. Since the hospitals were full, those soldiers whose wounds were not serious were billeted in private homes. The soldier was happy to report that he was on his way to a full recovery. He wanted to do more than just dispel his mother's worries and therefore shared some of his feelings with her:

> I was lying on my bed...when I spied a small object affixed to one of the doorposts. It was a narrow rectangular box.... I had never asked before what it symbolized.... This time I asked the homeowner and her reply was: "This is not a cross, but rather it is a Jewish amulet.... In our communities, this amulet did not save the Jew-boys. We finished them off with some small measure of assistance from the Germans....

You must not pay attention to the traces that they have left here and there and which still emit a foul Jewish odor. Take it easy, we scoured the house thoroughly before we moved in." My blood boiled inside me! This is a *mezuzah* and I do not even know what it contains. Yet it has become a symbol for me, a symbol of my nation's suffering![32]

He closes his letter with the following words: "My dearest mother, when I married Nadia [who was apparently not Jewish], you asked whether I would remain loyal to my Jewish origins.... Today more than ever, I am yours and I know precisely to whom I belong."[33]

Whenever Soviet Jewish soldiers participated in the liberation of a city or town where they or their relatives had lived before the war, they sought out relatives who had survived the Holocaust. One Jewish soldier, who reached Kiev soon after its liberation, noted:

> There was not even one Jew left here.... I stopped an old man on the sidewalk and asked him what life had been like here under the Germans. "My son!" he cried out, "We lived, we served, because they were the ones who were in control." I asked him, "But where are all the Jews?" The old man closed one eye and looked at me with surprise. "What, you mean, you don't know?!" he sounded incredulous. "All those who didn't manage to flee—were murdered at Babii Iar.... Our strong young fellows worked hard to please the Germans." I just left the old man standing there and started to run.... I ran so that I wouldn't have to see anything or hear anything.[34]

Another Jewish combatant who reached Kiev,[35] where he had lived before the war, wrote to his family back home, "I returned to Kiev on November 6, 1943 [the day the city was liberated].... I was in Kreshchatik,[36] which lay in ruins, and, at 11 in the morning, at Babii Iar and the Luk'ianovka cemetery." In his letter, he noted that he simply did not have the strength to describe what he had seen with his own eyes; however, he stressed that the images he viewed would remain with him until his dying day.[37] Another Jewish combatant[38] returned to his hometown of Mariupol'[39] soon after its liberation, where:

> [He] learned that his entire family—his wife, his two children, and another 96 relatives—were [all murdered].... He went to see acquaintances and neighbors to learn what had happened to his

relatives and, in every apartment, he recognized their possessions: in one apartment, there was a clothes closet, in another a few chairs, and, in a third, one of his wife's dresses.... He could not bring himself to ask that these possessions be returned to him because they conjured up memories of the past, but that was the very last time he ever visited those neighbors.[40]

Quite a number of Jewish combatants who were granted an early discharge from the Red Army due to injuries hastened to return to their hometown or the hometowns of their relatives. These soldiers came into direct contact with their own personal tragedies and those of their families. One such combatant had escaped from a prisoner of war camp, joined the partisans, and ultimately fought as a member of the Red Army. Many years later, he wrote, "After my discharge from the army, I returned to my home in Cherkassy.[41] In every single [Jewish] family there, at least one member had perished. Of the 32 members of my own family, 16 had been murdered."[42] It is not too difficult to imagine the feelings and thoughts of Jewish combatants in such situations; however, it can be stated with a high degree of certainty that a wide gap developed between them and the neighbors with whom and in whose company they had spent time up until the war.

Several Jewish soldiers who were unable to reach their hometowns tried to discover the fate of their relatives through letters to other family members as well as to friends and acquaintances. One of those who corresponded with relatives in the quest for information was Major Moisei Shvartsman,[43] who, on July 22, 1944, posthumously received the Hero of the Soviet Union medal for bravery in battle. Born in 1911, he spent his childhood and adolescence in a village where there were very few Jewish families.[44] From an early age, Moisei was involved in political activity in his village and, in the early 1930s, he was sent to a pedagogical college in the provincial city of Vinnitsa. After his graduation in 1936, he returned to the district town not far from the village where he was born—Tyvrov—and, as an active member of Komsomol (the Communist youth movement), he was appointed director of the education department. After the German invasion of the Soviet Union, all members of Komsomol were called upon to join in the defense of the homeland. Moisei was conscripted on June 25, 1941, and he said goodbye to his wife Hannah (Nusia), his daughter Dusia, and his parents. Fighting in the battles that were waged in Smolensk, Moscow, and other parts of the Soviet Union, he had no knowledge of his family's fate. After considerable effort, he found his wife and father, both of whom had managed to flee to Kazakhstan; his daughter and his mother remained under the Nazi occupiers. On June 2, 1944, his wife informed him that the Nazis had murdered his daughter and mother. He then wrote the following to his brother:

> I saw entire towns and district centers where all the Jews, all of them, had been shot—not one Jew survived. When I read about the massacres in Kiev, Kharkov, and other cities in Ukraine, I began to have doubts whether either of our parents...were still alive.... I will remember June 2, 1944 for the rest of my life, because, on that day, I learned of the fate of our parent and relatives ... in short, I learned of the fate of Dusia and my mother.[45]

However, Moisei did not live a long life. On June 25, 1944, he headed a unit that established a fortification on the banks of the Western Dvina River in the Vitebsk region, and he fell in the battle that took place there.

Leon Shmerkovich, who served as a sergeant in the reserve battalion of the First Ukrainian Front, turned to neighbors soon after the liberation of Kharkov on February 16, 1943 in order to find out the fate of his parents. Leon and his sister were evacuated from Kharkov together with the employees of an engine factory, *Serp i molot*, where the sister worked. Their parents remained in their hometown. A few months later, he received a reply in which one of the neighbors described the mass murder of the Jews in this city. "The letter I received was read by all the soldiers in our battery," recalled Shmerkovich, and one of them wrote a poem about this letter, which included the following passages: "A father and mother stand beside the ditch/ And beside them stand thousands of Jews,/ Rows and rows of Jewish families."[46] Until his dying day, Shmerkovich preserved the letter and the poem, both of which he regarded as a monument to the memory of his parents' last moments.

A few years later, a career officer in the armored corps, Yosef Nudelman, wrote the following:

> In 1944, when I learned that the cities of Zhitomir and Novograd-Volynkii had been liberated, I immediately sent a query to Chervonoarmeisk, where my family had lived prior to the war.... The

fate of the family was clear from what had been written on a small piece of paper: "Your family perished at the hands of the fascist German occupiers." I was not at all surprised when I received that reply, although I cried all night just like a little child.[47]

Another Jewish combatant, a resident of the city of Nikolaev,[48] which was liberated in late March 1944, turned to a close friend, who informed him that his parents and brother had been murdered between September 15 and 17, 1941. In the correspondence between the two, she described the lives of her family and their return to a normal routine in Nikolaev.[49] Furthermore, in this correspondence, in which the friend emphasizes that she is still unmarried, one can easily distinguish the gap between, on the one hand, this Jewish soldier's loneliness and his situation as an orphan and, on the other, the life of his friend and her family.

One Jewish soldier who volunteered to serve in the army soon after the German invasion of the Soviet Union and who experienced all the hardships of the retreat, the city's encirclement, and the battle, wrote many years later: "I cried on more than one occasion. I remembered my mother, my father, my grandfather and my grandmother."[50] This same orphaned feeling is expressed in a letter written by a Jewish combatant who learned that all the members of his family had been murdered (apparently in Breslav and its environs). The letter ends, "Why I am even writing to you? After all, you are strangers! [...] This is a hard time for me and I must share everything I feel with someone—I have no one who is close to me, you must understand me!"[51] In a letter written on July 3, 1943 to the father of a friend who fell in battle, Boris Schwartzman, another combatant, concluded, "Two years have passed since I lost my family.... I once lived in Odessa. My father, my wife and my son, who would be now nine years old—I have lost everyone and now I have no one."[52]

This feeling of orphanhood, which was common among many Jewish combatants in the Red Army, stood in sharp contrast to the expressions of antisemitism they experienced from local residents and sometimes even among their own comrades. Concerning antisemitic incidents in the ranks of the army, it seems that a significant difference existed between the initial and the final years of the Soviet-German war. In the early period, Jewish soldiers apparently did not encounter crude expressions of antisemitism, even when they heard certain jokes that made them feel uncomfortable.[53] Such allusions were described in the autobiographical novel of the unrecognized Russian writer and poet[54] of Jewish descent, Aleksandr Sobolev (1915-1986). His novel *Yefim Segal: A Sergeant Who Suffered Shell-Shock*, first published in 1999, is based on the writer's experience in the army. Sobolev was conscripted in 1942 and served until his discharge in late May 1944 due to a serious physical injury and to his shell-shock. Describing the atmosphere in his military unit, he wrote:

> When the soldiers in the company where Yefim [that is, the author] learned that he was Jewish, they cried out, "But that's impossible! How can Segal be Jewish? Segal, you are a brave fellow, a machine-gunner, and you even went out on reconnaissance missions [behind enemy lines]. No, Jews don't act like that! They are all in hiding back home, and besides, your surname isn't Haimovich, Rabinovich or Abramovich. OK, so what if you have curly hair? A lot of us Russians have curly hair, too. Stop slandering yourself, you're not Jewish!" Yefim tensed up when he heard the mocking, scornful and disgusting tone with which they pronounced the names Haimovich, Rabinovich and Abramovich.[55]

The traditional Jewish stereotype was deeply rooted in the public's awareness and it was expressed in the ranks of the Red Army as well.

However, the situation changed as the war progressed. As the Red Army achieved victory after victory on the battlefield, feelings of chauvinism intensified among the Slavic peoples and found expression in the ranks of the Red Army as well. An additional factor was at play here. Whenever a place was liberated from Nazi occupation, its young people were inducted into the Red Army. These young people had been fed with widespread antisemitic propaganda; they had been witnesses to the mass murder of Jews and some of them may even have been indirect collaborators in that murder. Boris Potik (born in 1914) was one of the soldiers who liberated Kharkov. After bitter fighting, the soldiers of Potik's unit were sent to one of the villages to relax. While they sat together in one of the houses in the village, the farmer who lived there said, "Jewboys [*zhidy*] aren't fighters!" "This was the first time in my entire military career that I had ever encountered antisemitism," admitted Potik. His comrades-in-arms reacted sharply to the farmer's words and threw him out the window.[56]

Apparently, the increasing frequency of antisemitic outbursts in the ranks of the Red Army troubled Il'ia Ehrenburg, who was very sensitive to any expression of antisemitism. He raised the issue publicly, albeit indirectly, in the second general assembly of the Jewish Anti-Fascist Committee, which convened from February 18-20, 1943. In his unique, sophisticated way, Ehrenburg did not refer directly to antisemitic incidents in the army but instead called attention to their occurrence on the home front, and the resulting infiltration of antisemitism into the ranks of the Red Army. Furthermore, he noted the disastrous effect that this antisemitism was having on the fighting capacity of the Red Army:

> Many [of the soldiers] on the frontlines are not even aware that they are Jews. They have, however, begun to sense their Jewishness after receiving letters from relatives in Uzbekistan or Kazakhstan. In these letters they read, "Here people are saying that they don't see Jews on the front, that the Jews aren't fighters." When they [the Jewish soldiers] receive such messages, while they sit in trenches or while they are on the move, their peace of mind is disturbed.... In order to ensure that Jewish soldiers and commanders in the Red Army can fulfill their duties, we must report how Jews are fighting on the front.[57]

Anti-Jewish hatred in the ranks of the army was also expressed in private letters. For instance, one soldier on the Stalingrad front, who apparently was a prisoner in the Gulag before his induction into the army, wrote the following:

> It's really too bad that people are being killed because of the parasites and their control of the Russian people on whose bones socialism was built. These bones are now loudly sighing.... However, that is not enough for a [Russian] man, who has to be [beaten] again and again so that he will become meaner and will wake up to the fact that the Jews are very smart, very vicious, but also silent and very crafty parasites that shouldn't be allowed to gain entry anywhere.... We are all sick of moving around from place to place and fighting for a bunch of Jews.[58]

One Jewish combatant described a particularly crude antisemitic incident in the Red Army many years later. The incident took place during one of the bloodiest battles in the Zhitomir-Berdichev campaign (December 24, 1943-January 14, 1944). After several days of continued fighting, the soldier tried to get some sleep. He was rudely awakened by the shouts of the battalion commander, Labazov: "'Why aren't you reporting? I forbid any of my soldiers to sleep while a war is going on! You'd better watch your step around me, Jew-boy face [*zhidovskaia morda*]. This isn't your Palestine!'... I lost my self-composure and drew my pistol."[59] The Jewish soldier was punished for his reaction. However, the incident hurt him very much, as can be seen from the fact that, although the event took place many years earlier, he was able to describe it so precisely. In his diary, Gedalia Safian also recorded in early January 1945, "Sometimes I hear such crudely mocking antisemitic remarks."[60] These blatant antisemitic incidents, which took place even in the army, only served to intensify the sense of solidarity that the Red Army's Jewish combatants felt toward their coreligionists.

* * *

Of course, one cannot speak of a standard response to the Holocaust among the hundreds of thousands of Jewish combatants who served in the Red Army during the Soviet-German war. Many of them considered the massacre of Jews to be just one more expression of the atrocities of the occupiers.[61] However, there were also many cases where the direct encounter with the unique fate of the Jews during the Holocaust, combined with the hostility of their comrades-in-arms, produced among Jewish combatants a change—whether short- or long-term—in their attitude toward their Jewish ethnicity and its symbols and had a profound impact on their identity.

Notes

[1] This article is part of a comprehensive research study, "The Impact of the Holocaust on the Ethnic Awareness of the Jews of the Soviet Union," which is being supported by the Israel Science Foundation (650/05).

[2] No serious demographic study has yet been conducted on the number of Jews inducted into the Red Army during the Soviet-German War of 1941-1945. Most of the publications refer to 500,000 Jews, relying directly or indirectly on Jacob Kantor's article in a Polish Yiddish-language newspaper, "Yidn oyf dem grestn un vikhtikstn front," *Folks-Shtime*, 18 April 1963, 8-11. Kantor's article is flawed for the following reasons: (1) He uses Soviet declarations concerning the number of inductees in the Red Army during this war and, basing his conclusion on the percentage of Jews in the general population, arrives at the figure of about half a million; (2) he does not take into account the division between the sexes, which was different among the Jews and in the general population (women were not drafted); (3) he overlooks the different age

breakdown among the Jews and the general population; and (4) he fails to deal with the problem that, in a large number of the cities and towns that were captured in the first weeks of the war, almost no residents were conscripted.

3   On the eve of the war, Jews constituted more than one-third (37 percent) of the town's general population; see Mordechai Altshuler, ed., *Distribution of the Jewish Population of the USSR, 1939* (Jerusalem: Hebrew University of Jerusalem, Centre for Research and Documentation of East-European Jewry, 1993), 23.

4   Interview with Devorah Shaikovich (Lamdeman), born in 1925, which was conducted on June 20, 1989, Yad Vashem Archives, 03/5459, 18.

5   See, for example, Ilia Al'tman and Leonid Terushkin, eds., *Sokhrani moi pis'ma...: sbornik pisem i dnevnikov evreev perioda Velikoi Otechestvennoi Voiny* (Moscow: Tsentr i Fond "Kholokost": Izd-vo "MIK", 2007).

6   According to a 1939 census, there were 4,914 Jews living at the time in Kursk; they constituted 4.1 percent of the city's general population (Altshuler, *Distribution of the Jewish Population*, 35).

7   Al'tman and Terushkin, *Sokhrani moi pis'ma*, 231.

8   Ibid., 287.

9   Iakov Khelemskii, "Riga," *Znamia* (1945): 51-52.

10 On the eve of the war, there were 23,300 Jews in Berdichev, or more than a third (37.5 percent) of the city's population (see Altshuler, *Distribution of the Jewish Population*, 22). Concerning the general population's feelings about the Germans' entry into the city, one of the Jewish soldiers learned the following from a Ukrainian woman: "When the Germans appeared in the suburbs of Berdichev, loyal assistants rallied around them.... With great diligence they hunted down Jews, who they discovered in ditches and cellars" (Iakov Ben-Ami, *Vremia i pamiat'* [Tel Aviv: n.p., 1976], 128).

11 *A Writer at War: Vasily Grossman with the Red Army, 1941-1945*, ed. and trans. Antony Beevor and Luba Vinogradova (New York: Pantheon Books, 2005), 254.

12 The town's prewar Jewish population numbered 500 (Altshuler, *Distribution of the Jewish Population*, 22).

13 The city's pre-war Jewish population numbered 15,000 (Ibid., 32).

14 Moisei Loifer, *Niti vremeni* (Tel Aviv: Israel Press Center, 2000), 108-9.

15 The town's pre-war Jewish population numbered 900, constituting 39.2 percent of the total population (Altshuler, *Distribution of the Jewish Population*, 40).

16 Loifer, *Niti vremeni*, 112.

17 Prior to the war, Gedalia Safian (1920-1985) was a student in the faculty of history at the State University of Belorussia in Minsk. He left Minsk just before the Germans occupied it. After considerable wandering, when he spent some of his nights walking in the dark, he reached the district of Chernigov. There he was inducted into the Red Army, in which he served until November 1945. From November 24, 1944 until his discharge, he kept a diary, in which he would record his thoughts every few days.

18 On this town, see D. Dombrowska, A. Wein, and A. Weiss, eds., *Pinkas ha-kehilot. Polin: entsiklopedyah shel ha-yishuvim ha-Yehudiyim le-min hiyasdam ye-'ad le-aḥar shoat Milḥemet ha-'olam ha-sheniyah (The Register of Communities: East Galicia*, vol. 2 (Jerusalem: Yad va-shem, 1979-80), 186-87.

19 "A byl on lish' soldatom," *Mishpakha*, no. 6 (1999): 94. He writes about a visit to another town: "I took a walk over to that town. What a grim impression it made on me. The center [of the town] where the Jews had lived was in ruins. The houses were still standing but they had no windows or doors—only black holes. Everything had been dragged off. Even the windows had been torn off. All that remained was emptiness and death. The vitality and warmth that were the hallmarks [of these towns] are gone.... Stables have been set up in the synagogues, filth and dirt are everywhere.... I went to the cemetery.... Large, old tombstones dating from the Austro-Hungarian period are still standing.... On some of them our ancestors' pure ideas have been inscribed.... Here the tombstones are broken and potatoes have been planted atop the graves. The dead are not even allowed to rest now. I passed through the town of Lopatin, where 450 [Jewish] families had once lived; not many of them had survived. The houses were destroyed and had been looted. There were two large synagogues: One of them had been converted into a flour mill. How painful it was to see all this! My nation, how cruelly and unjustly has fate treated you!! And for what?"

20 Ibid. On August 19, 1944, Safian entered the following in his diary: "I came to the town of Turomichi.... The house [where we had taken up quarters] once belonged to the owner of a tavern [by the name of] Fisch, and a physician lived on the second floor. The Germans had shot to death the owner of the house and his tenant together with their families.... The local letter-carrier now threshes his wheat here. The entrance to the house is paved with tombstones from the Jewish cemetery. No matter where I go in this town, I am constantly reminded of the lives that have been snuffed out here."

21 M. Altshuler, I. Arad, and Sh. Krakovskii, eds., *Sovetskie evrei pishut Il'e Erenburgu* (Jerusalem: Prisma-Press, 1993), 202.

22 *Rakhel' Pavlovna Margolina i ee perepiska s Korneem Ivanovichem Chukovskim* (Jerusalem: Stav, 1978), 5-10, 55-56.

23 Ber Mark, "Di kvadratne oysies," in *Tzum zig: literarisher zamlbukh*, ed. P. Markish (Moscow: Der Emes, 1944), 327-32.

24 Ibid.

25 On the change in the alphabet used in the language of the Caucasus Mountain Jews, see my book *Yehude Mizrah Kaykaz: toldot ha-Yehudim ha-harariyim me-reshit hamah ha-tessha-esreh* (*The Jews of the Eastern Caucasus Region: The History of the Caucasus Mountain Jews from the Early 19th Century Onwards*) (Jerusalem: Hebrew University, 1989-1990).

26 Anatolii Rybakov, *Roman-vospominanie* (Moscow: Vagrius, 1997), 108.

27 Evgenii Khaldei, *Witness to History: The Photographs of Yevgeny Khaldei, with Biographical Essays by Alexander and Alice Nakhimovsky* (New York: Aperture, 1997), 10.

28 David Shneer, "Soviet Jewish Photojournalists Encounter the Holocaust," *The Holocaust in the Soviet Union: Symposium Presentations* (Center for Advanced Holocaust Studies, United States Holocaust Memorial Museum, 2005), 22. For more on Khaldei, see Chapter 10 in this volume.

29 In Uman', according to the census of 1939, there were 13,233 Jews, who constituted one third of its general population (Altshuler, *Distribution of the Jewish Population*, 20).

30 I want to thank Dr. Leonid Finberg, who permitted me to use documents from the Institute of Judaica in Kiev—over 100 interviews, which he conducted in the 1990s on the subject "Jewish Life in Ukraine in the Twentieth Century" (henceforth to be referred to as "Judaica"). Testimony of Mania Guralnik, who was born in 1931. (The interviews in "Judaica" are not paginated.)

31 David Kahana, *Ahare ha-mabul* (Jerusalem: Mossad Harav Kook, 1981), 39. In an interview, Rabbi David Kahana recalled: "There was a victory celebration at the Brandenburg Gate beside the statue of Kaiser Wilhelm. I can't remember whether it took place on May 10 or 20...." On that day, he turned to an officer who referred him to his assistant (*denschik*), "who was a Communist! He attended party meetings.... Yet he had a warm spot in his heart for any Jew he happened to encounter.... He did everything to provide bread for hungry mouths, to help people leave the village, where Jews had been murdered.... He was constantly risking his life ... He told me [in Yiddish], 'Do you know why I love Jews? My father was an important figure in his *beit midrash* [house of learning] in Minsk.' ... Suddenly, I saw a group of high-ranking officers ascending ... the stairs. I heard them starting to speak in Yiddish. They said 'Shalom Aleichem'.... One of the members of this group was a general. He was the head of the medical service of a certain brigade, Vovsi [between 1941 and 1947, he was the Red Army's Chief Medical Officer], and we began to converse and toast each other with the Hebrew expression 'L'chaim.' We talked in Yiddish and danced. It was clear that he considered Communism to be the only solution for Judaism. Nonetheless, he spoke very fondly of Jews and Judaism! And I saw that he was very happy to see a rabbi in uniform...." (The interview was conducted on July 2, 1963. Oral History Department, Institute of Contemporary Jewry, no. 4/15, 18-19.)

32 Israel Eichenwald, *Bi-derakhim uvi-gevulot* (Tel Aviv: Moreshet, 1989), 93.

33 Ibid., 94.

34 In his youth, the author, who was born in 1915 or 1916, had distanced himself from anything connected with Judaism and most of his friends were Russians. In 1932, he left his parents and his town, moving to Briansk and then to Leningrad. On the eve of the Second World War, he completed his studies in engineering. In the introduction to his book, the author wrote: "These entries have a documentary character; many of them are engraved in my memory of my distant adolescence and are based on notes that I recorded in the diary I kept when I was on the front" (Ben-Ami, *Vremia i pamiat'*, 125-26).

35 The author is Shimon Cherbinskii, who was born in 1906 and who lived in Kiev until July 1941.

36 Kiev's central boulevard.

37 "Iz pisem," in *Babii Iar, 1941-1961*, ed. Efraim Baukh ([Israel]: Izdanie Soiuza zemliachestv—vykhodtsev iz SSSR, 1981), 64-65.

38 The soldier was Abram Miropol'skii, who was drafted in 1941 and who received many medals for his courage in battle.

39 On the eve of the war, there were 10,500 Jews in Mariupol' (Altshuler, *Distribution of the Jewish Population*, 24).

40 L. Miropol'skii, "Kholokost v pamiati odnoi sem'i," *Shestye Zaporozhskie evreiskie chteniia* (Zaporozh'e, 2002), 74.

41 On the eve of the war, there were 8,000 Jews in Cherkassy (Altshuler, *Distribution of the Jewish Population*, 20).

42 Naum Dashevskii, *Vospominaniia bez vesti propavshego* (Moscow: Moskovskii rabochii, 1990), 217.

43 After his induction into the army, he served as a *politruk* in a company of riflemen and, in 1943, with the rank of Captain, he was deputy commander of a battalion that was responsible for the political sphere (F. D. Sverdlov, *V stroiu otvazhnykh: ocherki o evreiakh—geroiakh Sovetskogo Soiuza* [Moscow: A/O "Kniga i biznes", 1992], 285-86). See also Aron Abramovich, *V reshaiushchei voine: uchastie i rol' evreev SSSR v voine protiv natsizma*, vol. 2 (Tel Aviv: n.p., 1992), 170-71, 533.

44 On the eve of the war, there were one thousand Jews in all the villages in the Tyvrov district, except for the central village (Altshuler, *Distribution of the Jewish Population*, 48).

45 Sverdlov, *V stroiu otvazhnykh*, 285.

46 Iurii M. Liakhovitskii, *Poprannaia mezuza: kniga Drobitskovo Iara: svidetel'stva, fakty, dokumenty o natsistskom genotside evreiskogo naseleniia Khar'kova v period okkupatsii, 1941-1942* (Khar'kov: Osnova, 1991), 94-95.

47 Iosif Nudel'man, "Evrei na voine," in *Nam dorogi eti pozabyt' nel'zia: vospominaniia, stat'i, materialy iz semeinykh arkhivov uchastnikov Velikoi Otechestvennoi voiny 1941-1945 godov*, ed. V. D. Lesev (Jerusalem: n.p., 1995), 173.

48 On the eve of the war, there were over 25,000 Jews in Nikolaev (Altshuler, *Distribution of the Jewish Population*, 25).

49 For these letters, see Yad Vashem Archives, section 075, file 490.

50 Yad Vashem Archives, testimony no. 03/3686, 3.

51 For these letters, see Yad Vashem Archives, section 075, file 490.

52 Al'tman and Terushkin, *Sokhrani moi pis'ma*, 129.

53 See also Catherine Merridale, *Ivan's War: Life and Death in Red Army, 1939-1945* (New York: Metropolitan Books, 2006), 289.

54 For a collection of his poems, see Aleksandr Sobolev, *Bukhenval'dskii nabat: strokiarestanty* (Moscow: EKA, 1996).

55 Aleksandr Sobolev, *Efim Segal, kontuzhennyi serzhant* (Moscow: Izdatel'skii dom PIK, 1999), 194.

56 L. Dubossarskii, V. Gol'dman, A. Peisakhovich, eds. *Voiny-evrei vo Vtoroi Mirovoi i 50 let spustia* (Tel Aviv: Izd-vo zhurnala Alef, 1995), 196-201.

57 "Tzveyter plenum fun yidishen antifashistishn komitet in FSSR," *Eynikayt*, 3 March 1943.

58 *Stalingradskaia epopeia: vpervye publikuemye dokumenty, rassekrechennye FSB RF*, ed. Ia. F. Pogonii et al. (Moscow: Zvonnitsa-MG, 2000), 241.

59 Ben-Ami, *Vremia i pamiat'*, 131.

60 "A byl on lish' soldatom," 92.

61 For one such example, see: L. K. Brontman, "Iz dnevnikov voennykh let," *Arkhiv evreiskoi istorii*, vol. 2 (2005): 82-140.

Chapter 2

Il′ia Ehrenburg and the Holocaust in the Soviet Press

Joshua Rubenstein

The writer and journalist Il′ia Ehrenburg was the most significant voice in the Soviet press during World War II. Writing primarily for *Krasnaia zvezda* (*Red Star*), the newspaper distributed among Red Army troops, Ehrenburg became famous for his outspoken appeals to Soviet soldiers, insisting in article after article that they must hate the Germans in order to defeat them. His articles were so admired at the front that soldiers were instructed to cut them out and not use them for rolling cigarettes. Foreign Minister Viacheslav Molotov once told a visiting diplomat that Ehrenburg was worth a division, while Hitler, mindful of Ehrenburg's Jewish background and the impact of his articles, declared that he would hang Ehrenburg in Red Square were he to capture Moscow.

Ehrenburg was one of the few journalists to write about Nazi atrocities against the Jews in the Soviet press. Official Soviet attitudes about the Holocaust present a far more complicated picture than most people assume. Given Stalin's assault on Yiddish culture following World War II and the hostile actions of the Brezhnev regime toward Israel—including the Kremlin's concerted (and unsuccessful) attempt to quash the Jewish Emigration Movement—it is hardly surprising that even otherwise-informed Jewish observers accepted the widely held belief that the regime was studiously silent about German atrocities toward the Jews during World War II, including the terrifying, open-air massacres that took place throughout German-occupied Soviet territory. We now know that these massacres, including the use of mobile gas vans, resulted in the murder of over 2.5 million Jews, a startling percentage of the six million Jews who perished altogether. So how could the Kremlin ignore the mass murder of its Jewish citizens on its own territory by the regime's most dangerous enemy? In a word, it was not oblivious to these crimes.

It is undeniably true that the Soviet press did not cover the mass murder of its Jewish citizens with anywhere near the prominence it deserved. But it is a falsification of the historical record to claim that the press did not cover it at all. For example, in November 1941, when the regime marked the twenty-fourth anniversary of the Revolution, at a time when the Wehrmacht was threatening Moscow, Stalin delivered a defiant speech. Among German atrocities, Stalin explicitly accused them of "happily organizing medieval pogroms against the Jews, just as the tsarist regime had done before." Four days later, *Izvestiia* referred to a news source in New York in an article about the murder of fifty-two thousand Jewish men, women, and children in Kiev; this was the two-day massacre at Babii Iar. In December 1942, the Soviet press carried two prominent, front page denunciations of the massacres of Jews. On December 18, 1942, *Pravda* carried the full text of a joint declaration by eleven nations and the French National Committee condemning the persecution and murder of Jews in every territory occupied by the Germans, and declared that "such events can only reinforce the determination of freedom-loving peoples to overthrow Hitler's barbaric tyranny." On the next day, December 19, 1942, *Izvestiia* published an even more prominent article, under an impressive front-page headline: "On the Fulfillment of the Hitlerite Plan to Exterminate the Jewish Population of Europe." In three long columns, the article described the deportation and massacre of Jews throughout Eastern and Western Europe, including Scandinavia and the occupied Soviet territories. It declared without any equivocation that the plan was intended to rid Europe of all its Jews.

These official declarations—which, again, were few and far between—should not obscure what a handful of Soviet Jewish journalists managed to publish in the Soviet press. Two months after the German invasion, on August 24, the Kremlin arranged for a group of prominent Jewish cultural figures to participate in a public meeting and an international appeal over short-wave radio. The appeal was directed to Jewish communities in the West, primarily in England and America. Stalin understood that he required the support of the Western democracies to overcome the German onslaught, but after his two-year alliance with Hitler's Germany, he also understood that he had to repair relations with the West in order to secure desperately needed military assistance.

Several major figures gave talks that day, among them the Yiddish actor and theater director Solomon Mikhoels, the Yiddish poet Peretz Markish, and Il'ia Ehrenburg. They all highlighted the suffering of their fellow Jews in Poland and in newly occupied Soviet territory. All the speeches, of course, had been vetted by Soviet officials, and it is a mark of how far they were willing to compromise on what had been their policies toward the Jews that Mikhoels, Ehrenburg, and the others were able to appeal to their "brother and sister Jews" and invoke the image of a united Jewish people. Before that, Soviet propaganda had denied that there was any such thing as the Jewish people; it preferred to recognize the existence of separate Jewish tribes scattered in various countries around the world with little connection between them. In addition, the rally marked the first step toward the creation of the Jewish Anti-Fascist Committee (JAC), one of five anti-fascist committees that Stalin would soon establish to help improve relations with the West. Mikhoels, Markish, and Ehrenburg became leading members of the JAC. By 1943, when the Red Army began to drive the Wehrmacht out of Soviet territory, Ehrenburg used his connections with the JAC to organize two dozen Soviet writers and journalists to follow the Red Army into liberated territory, locate survivors of the Holocaust, and collect documents and testimonies about the massacres. It was his intention to publish the material in *The Black Book*, a volume that the regime eventually banned. It was finally published in 1979 by Yad Vashem in Jerusalem.

These articles make clear that Il'ia Ehrenburg may well have been the first person, outside of the German High Command, to grasp the full magnitude of the Holocaust. Under appalling conditions, constrained by wartime deprivations, Soviet censorship, and indifference to Jewish suffering, he did what he could to alert the Soviet public and the West.

His speech in Moscow on August 24 was carried in *Izvestiia* on August 26, 1941:

To the Jews

When I was a child, I witnessed a pogrom against the Jews. It was organized by tsarist police and a small group of vagabonds. But individual Russians hid Jews. I remember how my father brought home a letter by Lev Tolstoy that had been copied onto a slip of paper. Tolstoy lived next door to us. I often used to see him and knew he was a great writer. I was ten years old. My father read "I Cannot Be Silent" out loud; Tolstoy was outraged by pogroms against the Jews. My mother broke out in tears. The Russian people were not guilty of these pogroms. The Jews knew this. I never heard a malicious word from a Jew about the Russian people. And I will never hear one. Having gained their freedom, the Russian people have forgotten the persecution of the Jews as if it were a bad dream. A generation has grown up that does not know even the word "pogrom."

I grew up in a Russian city. My mother tongue is Russian. I am a Russian writer. Like all Russians, I am now defending my homeland. But the Hitlerites have reminded me of something else: my mother's name was Hannah. I am a Jew. I say this with pride. Hitler hates us more than anything. And this adorns us.

I saw Berlin last summer—it is a nest of criminals. I saw the German army in Paris—it is an army of rapists. All of humanity is now waging a struggle against Germany, not for territory but for the right to breathe! Is it necessary to speak about what these "Aryan" swine are doing with the Jews? They are killing children in front of their mothers. They are forcing old people in their agony to behave like buffoons. They are raping young women. They cut, torture, and burn. Belostok, Minsk, Berdichev, and Vinnitsa will remain terrible names. The fewer words the better: we do not need words, we need bullets. They are proud to be swine. They themselves say that Finnish cattle mean more to them than Heine's verses. They insulted the French philosopher Bergson before his death; for these savages, he was just a *Jude*. They ordered the books of the late Tuwim to be used in soldiers' latrines. *Jude*! Einstein? *Jude*! Chagall? *Jude*! Can we speak about culture when they rape ten-year-old girls and bury people alive in graves?

My country, the Russian people, the people of Pushkin and Tolstoy, are standing up to the challenge. I am now appealing to the Jews of America as a Russian writer and a Jew. There is no ocean to hide behind. Listen to the sound of weapons around Gomel! Listen to the cries of tormented Russian and Jewish women in Berdichev! Do not block up your ears or close your eyes! The voices of Leah from the Ukraine, Rachel from Minsk, Sarah from Belostok will intrude on your still-comfortable dreams—they are crying over their children who have been torn to pieces. Jews, wild animals are aiming at you! Our place is in the front line. We will not forgive the indifferent. We curse anyone who washes his hands. Help everyone who is fighting this rabid enemy. To the assistance of England! To the assistance of Soviet Russia! Let each and every one do as much as he can. Soon he will be asked: What did you do? He will have to answer to the living. He will have to answer to the dead. He will have to answer to himself.[1]

Ehrenburg found himself needing to counteract antisemitic attitudes among his fellow Soviet citizens and the frequently held assumption that "Ivan is at the Front while Abram is in Tashkent." On November 1, 1942, Ehrenburg published an article in *Krasnaia zvezda* in which he focused on Jewish heroes.

Jews

The Germans tortured young Jewish women and buried elderly Jews alive. Hitler wanted to make a target out of Jews. Jews showed him that a target shoots back. Jews had been scientists and workers, musicians and longshoremen, doctors and farmers. Jews became soldiers. They will not hand over to anyone their right for revenge.

Falkovich was over 40. He was a philologist and had spent his life at a desk. Germans lick their lips over such types: catch and hang them. Cut off from his unit, he pulled 18 soldiers together. They confronted an enemy company. Falkovich ordered: "Attack!" Eighteen brave souls captured 35 fritzes. The philologist killed eight Germans with his own hands.[2]

A year ago, the Germans approached Moscow. Hayim Dyskin is the son of Crimean farmers. He was studying at the Literary Institute. When the war broke out, Dyskin was 17 years old. He volunteered for the front. At Mozhaysk he saw German tanks. Dyskin was an artilleryman; he destroyed the lead tank at point-blank range. Several Germans jumped out. Dyskin ordered himself: "Fire at the Fascists!" Injured, he stayed with his weapon. He was wounded a second time. Bleeding profusely, he continued to beat back the attack by himself. Fourteen separate wounds on his body, a gold star on the chest of this hero, five disabled German tanks—this is the story of the 17-year-old Hayim.

Perhaps Germans think that Jews don't ski? This winter, Leyzer Papernik destroyed several dozen Germans in the village of Khludnevo. Seriously injured, he fell in the snow. The Germans hurriedly approached. Then Papernik lifted himself up and threw grenades at the Germans. Half-dead, he continued to fight against hundreds of Germans. With the final grenade, he blew himself up.

Perhaps the Germans think that Jews are not sailors? Israel Fisanovich is a Hero of the Soviet Union and captain of a Maliutka submarine; he showed the fritzes how a Jew can sink Aryan bandits. The Germans threw 329 bombs at the submarine, but the boat returned to its base. It sank four German transport ships. The fish rejoiced. But pure-bred German admirals were not too pleased.

Who in Leningrad does not know the heroic exploits of radioman Ruvim Sprintson? He broadcast into the air: "Fire into my position!" For three days, four radiomen were cut off from our troops: a Jew, two Russians, and a Ukrainian. Ruvim Sprintson carried out attacks, killing the enemy with his automatic weapon. The Germans came to understand: it is one thing to torment defenseless old women in Gomel; it is another thing to meet Ruvim Sprintson in battle.

Near Leningrad, Lev Shpayer burned a German tank and destroyed dozens of soldiers. The Germans thought they had the sacred right to disembowel unarmed Jewish women. With a Russian bayonet, Lev Shpayer pierced the greedy bellies of three predators. Shpayer fell in battle. Soldiers wrote a letter to his parents: "To the dear and beloved parents of Lev Shpayer: Your son was a hero at the front. He knew that behind him stood the pride of the Russian people—Leningrad. We will remember Lev—our heroic commander—to the Germans. And we will avenge him."

German tanks attacked at Stalingrad. David Kats was sitting in a trench. He threw a kerosene-filled bottle at the lead tank. The tank caught fire. A second tank wanted to turn. But Kats cried out "Stop this nonsense!" and threw a grenade under the tracks. The tank stopped, but a machine gun still fired away at our men. So Kats stuck his bayonet into the enemy muzzle. Injured, he continued to fight—he was defending Stalingrad after all. Only after he was wounded a second time did David Kats allow himself to be taken to a field hospital. How can we not recall the ancient legend of the giant Goliath and the young David with his sling?

There was a time when the Jews dreamed of the Promised Land. Now the Jew has a Promised Land: the front line. There he can take revenge on the Germans for the women, for the elderly, for the children.

The Jews have a great love for Russia. It is a love for its spirit and people, for great ideas and native cities, for a country that has become their savior, and for the soil where their ancestors are buried. "For the Motherland!" screamed the Moscow worker Laizer Papernik, throwing grenades at the Germans. He died with these words, a true son of Russia.

On April 29, 1944, Ehrenburg wrote about the Yiddish poet Abram Sutzkever. Little-known before the war, Sutzkever had been among the tens of thousands of Jews who were rounded up and kept in the Vilna Ghetto in 1941, very soon after the German occupation of Lithuania. Sutzkever led a group of Jews out of the ghetto, then joined a partisan unit; he also found and preserved precious literary manuscripts that had once been housed in a Vilna museum. In early 1944, Soviet officials brought Sutzkever to Moscow by air, where he befriended leaders of the Jewish Anti-Fascist Committee, including Solomon Mikhoels. Among all the people he met in Moscow he was closest to Ehrenburg, and it was Ehrenburg who paid tribute to him in a startling portrait that covered almost a full page in *Pravda*. Ehrenburg later arranged for Sutzkever to testify at the International Military Tribunal at Nuremberg in February 1946.

The Triumph of a Man

In quiet times the world seems gray to some: black and white, nobility and baseness are covered by the fog of everyday life. We live in terrible times: everything is revealed, everything is checked—on the field of battle, on the rack, at the edge of the grave. The Soviet people have displayed a grandeur of spirit during this time of testing. I want to tell the story of one man. Like many others, it testifies to the victory of one individual over the power of evil.

A few days ago, a fighter from a Lithuanian Jewish partisan unit came to Moscow—this was the Yiddish poet Sutzkever. He brought letters by Maxim Gorky and Romain Rolland—he saved these letters from the Germans. He saved the diary of a servant of Peter the Great, drawings by Repin, a painting by Levitan, a letter by Lev Tolstoy, and many other valuable Russian relics.

I had long heard of Sutzkever's poems. Both a wonderful Austrian novelist and the Polish poet Tuwim used to speak to me about them. This was a time when people could still speak about poetry. Now we are in different times, but first of all I will speak of something else—not about verses, but about weapons.

In June 1942, near the town of Novaia Vileika, a German ammunition train was blown up. Who laid the mines? Prisoners of the Vilnius ghetto. The doomed Jews were fighting. The German train was heading east; the Germans were preparing for another attack. Partisans from the Vilnius ghetto blew up the train. The poet Sutzkever was not thinking about verses at that time. He was thinking about weapons; he was obtaining machine guns.

There were eighty thousand Jews in Vilnius. The Germans did not want to kill them right away: they wanted to take pleasure from their prolonged agony. They set up two ghettos—two camps for the condemned. They stretched out the executions. They killed the doomed Jews for two years, one group after another.

A film actor named Kittel lived in Berlin before the war. He wanted to play villains, but even the less-than-gifted directors of UFA Studios considered Kittel too untalented. He found another calling: he became a famous hangman. He killed tens of thousands of inhabitants of Riga. Then he came on a tour of Vilnius. They entrusted him with the "liquidation of the ghetto."

The prisoners were lined up in the morning. They knew that if the order sent them "to the right," they would be sent to work. If the order sent them "to the left," it meant Ponary and death. Each morning they saw the same fork in the road and waited, to the right or to the left. For seven hundred days...

"Here are some presents for you," said Kittel. Sutzkever recognized his mother's dress. She had been shot the night before.

They burned people alive. Buried them in graves. Poked out their eyes and wrenched their arms.

On the first day of the war, the poet Sutzkever tried to make his way east. He had a child in his arms, someone else's child, a friend's child. Sutzkever could not abandon the child, and this small burden decided everything—the Germans captured Sutzkever. And Kittel himself killed Sutzkever's small son.

What went on in this world of death, where people awaited execution, where women gave birth knowing that they were giving birth to the condemned, where doctors treated the ill, understanding that execution awaited the ill and the cured and the doctors themselves?

In January 1942, a partisan unit was formed in the ghetto. A 40-year-old Vilnius worker named Wittenberg became its commander. The Germans learned that Wittenberg's spirit was not broken. They came looking for him, but he concealed himself in the underground. Then Kittel announced, "If Wittenberg does not surrender alive, then everyone will be killed tomorrow." Wittenberg knew that in any case the Germans would kill all the doomed Jews, but he wanted the partisans to have enough time to get out to the forest. He said, "It's too bad that I cannot shoot myself." Bidding his friends farewell he went out to give himself up to Kittel. The Germans tortured him, poking out his eyes. He kept silent. Sutzkever had accompanied him to the ghetto's gate; recalling Wittenberg, Sutzkever turned away from me to hide his face.

The partisans found type for an underground Polish newspaper. That was how prisoners of the ghetto helped their Lithuanian and Polish brothers. The ghetto was Soviet territory: the condemned listened secretly to the radio, printed communiqués from the *Sovinformburo*, and celebrated May 1, November 7, and February 23.

A German arsenal blew up in Burbishek. Two Jews from the ghetto perished. Kittel thought that it was an accident, but it was a military action. The two did not die in vain.

Tiktin was 16 years old. He penetrated a sealed wagon from which he took hand grenades. But he was discovered and wounded when he tried to escape. They let him recover before executing him. "Why did you take the grenades?" Kittel asked. Tiktin answered, "In order to throw them at you. You killed my father and mother."

One time they brought a group of Jews for execution. They threw themselves onto the Germans and strangled seven German soldiers with their bare hands.

Three hundred Jews in the ghetto obtained weapons. The Germans were blowing up houses with dynamite. The daring three hundred broke out of the ghetto and joined Lithuanian partisans. The poet Sutzkever was among them.

Those who were escaping the ghetto got out through the sewers. One went mad.

A Lithuanian peasant woman hid Sutzkever. A Lithuanian man had been hanged in that village. A sign on the gallows read, "He was hiding Jews." One German told this Lithuanian woman, "You know what is written there?" She responded, "Yes, I know." Then she saved the poet. The Soviet people know that friendship is not just a word.

"Rosenberg's headquarters" was located in Vilnius. This was an enterprise for plundering valuable books, paintings, and manuscripts. Doctor Miller directed this "headquarters." The Germans brought the Smolensk museum to Vilnius and handed it over to Miller. An institute with the finest collection of Jewish books and manuscripts in Europe was located in Vilnius. Sutzkever thought he himself would perish, but he wanted to preserve cultural monuments. He saved drawings by Repin, fifteenth- and sixteenth-century manuscripts, letters by Tolstoy, Gorky, and the Yiddish writer Sholem Aleichem.

I said that he was thinking of weapons, not verses. But a poet will always remain a poet. He obtained machine guns. He awaited execution. He saw Kittel. And he wrote poems. In the autumn of 1942, he wrote the long poem "Kol Nidre." Its subject recalls an ancient tragedy, but it was taken from the life of the ghetto. The Jews are awaiting execution in the courtyard of the Lukishki Prison. An old man is summoning death. The Germans had killed his wife, four sons, and grandsons. An injured man whose legs are broken is brought out. He wears a Red Army overcoat. That is the man's fifth son; they had not seen each other for twenty years. The father recognized his son. The son did not recognize his father. A German storm trooper arrives. He demands to be treated like a king. The wounded soldier throws a stone at the German. Then the father kills his son in order to save him from torture. This story might seem improbable. But anyone who saw Kittel knows that there was no limit to his baseness, and he who accompanied the worker Wittenberg to his death knows that there was no limit to selflessness.

The poet Sutzkever, together with other partisans, fought for the freedom of Soviet Lithuania. There were Lithuanians and Russians, Poles and Jews in his unit. They were not saved by words but by love for their Motherland. The poet Sutzkever carried an automatic weapon in his arms, new poems in his head, and Gorky's letters in his heart. Here they are, pages with faded ink. I recognize this well-known handwriting. Gorky wrote about life, about Russia's future, about human strength. This insurgent of the Vilnius ghetto, a poet and a soldier, saved his letters as a banner of humanity and culture.[3]

By the summer of 1944, Soviet troops liberated Majdanek and Treblinka in Poland. They were uncovering more evidence of German atrocities on an unimaginable scale. Ehrenburg continued to write. With the Soviet army approaching German territory, he focused once again on the fate of the Jews. His article "On the Eve," which appeared in *Pravda* on August 7, was as forthright as anyone could expect in the Soviet press:

On the Eve

While there were still street battles in Vilna, I spoke with captured German officers in a suburb. One was an Austrian military doctor. He had a quick and observant mind. "The Germans are still hoping," he told me. I asked, "What exactly are they hoping for? For Fau 1? [This is what they call 'airplane-munitions.'] For total mobilization?" "No," said the Austrian. "For your forgetfulness." A year ago they said, 'Russian power is not strong enough.' Now they say, 'Russian memory is not long enough.'"

As the Red Army approaches the German borders, I want to speak one more time about the ferocity and malice of the Hitlerites.

Some people, perhaps, reading about Germans surrendering to supply convoys, even to children, think, "They are seeing the light." Perhaps some Muscovites, looking at the despondent processions of German POWs, are wondering, "Is it possible that they did the hanging?" Perhaps news about the conspiracy by German generals is giving hope to a naïve reader: "A conscience is awakening in the Germans." No and no: They remain the same. They surrender because they are scared of dying. They do not pity children, they pity themselves. Just a day or sometimes an hour before surrendering, they are still murdering the innocent. It is not their conscience that is awakening, it is their fear.

On the order of the Germans, slaves are digging up corpses of the tormented and burning them: the criminals want to conceal the evidence. They calmly murdered for three years. In the fourth they got alarmed: they began to destroy the corpses. This is their "conscience." They are already preparing for the day when they will yell, as if on command, "It was not us who did the killing. It was Hitler." Why did some colonel plant a bomb near his Führer? The colonel understood: Hitler is evidence. Captured Oberleutnant Philips told me that the German officers are reading the bulletins of the Extraordinary Commission with apprehension: they look to see if their names are there. They understand that there will be a trial.

I was at Bolshoi Trostianets shortly after the Germans escaped. Half-charred corpses stacked like firewood were still smoldering. The children were carefully placed at the end of each row. This was the last batch. And they didn't have time to burn it. I saw around me dug up earth and a field of skulls. Beginning in the spring, the Germans were burning the corpses of those who had already been buried. And they could not finish the job. Bolshoi Trostyanets near Minsk was one of the factories of death. There they killed Soviet POWs, Belorussians, Jews from Minsk, Vienna, and Prague, killed using a "gevagen"—a mobile gas van. A German engineer improved these machines: he made it possible for the compartment filled with corpses to automatically tip to disgorge the asphyxiated victims. More than a hundred thousand innocent people perished in Bolshoi Trostianets.

There were more "factories of death" in Ponary near Vilna, in Belzhets near Rava Russkaia, in Novy Dvor, and in Sobibor. The trains with Jews arrived from France, Holland, and Belgium. They were told: "You will be working here." They were led to the barracks: "Take off all your clothes—disinfection, bath." They shaved off the women's hair and collected it in bags. Then they asphyxiated the doomed. Then through a tunnel leading from the "bath" the bodies were taken to the ovens. The Germans used to say: "The daily capacity was up to two thousand people."

In the "death factories" they killed Jews, they killed Soviet POWs, they killed Russians, Belorussians, and Poles. In Vilna whole neighborhoods "went to

Ponary." The executioners had a schedule: on some days they killed Jews, on other days Poles. There were "Russian days" too.

This is hard to imagine: millions of people, neat, quiet elderly women, mothers with nursing babies, beautiful young women and girls with braids, were murdered in the "death factories." Each and every one of them lived their own life....

A German clerk would note down: so many units destroyed. I cannot describe this terrible picture, for centuries people will come back to this trying to comprehend the full magnitude of the suffering.

I will write about Valia Komarova. She lived in Yalta. She was affectionate and given to laughter. The Germans killed and violated her: they cut off her left breast, the breast of a forteen-year-old girl. I will tell about a Belorussian girl, Marusia Ponomareva. She was seven. The Germans burned her. She screamed: "Mama!" Her mother could not hear her. She had been murdered the night before. But there is Mother Russia. She heard Marusia's screams and she will never, never forget them.

A doctor from Yalta, Druskin, treated children for fifty years. In a guidebook about the Crimea from 1899, you can read: "Dr. L. M. Druskin—Children's Diseases." The Germans killed the old man near Krasnaia Budnia. They buried hundreds of children alive with him. And next to the babies, in the same mass grave, lay the tortured bodies of sailors.

Here is the place where, until recently, the Russian village of Artiukhovo was. On the road from Dukhnovo to Idritsa. The village was burned, burned with all its inhabitants. Sergei Stepanovich Stepanov was 67. The Germans were hitting him with the butts of their rifles and yelling "Dance!" In front of Matrena Leonova, a German took her baby and threw it in the fire. The list of those burned alive is terrifying. It includes the old woman Vera Semenova and the little babies—Maria Kuzmina, ten months; Nikolai Ivanov, six months. Anyone who ever caressed the soft hair of a baby, anyone who has seen a mother's tears will never forget the ashes of Artiukhovo: these are people's ashes.

Ekaterinapol is a small town where Jews lived. They killed them all. No one is left except for a little girl named Sonia. She recounts the sorrow of these people. The old barber Azril Pritsman lived in Ekaterinapol. He was seventy-six. Five of his children were at the Front. The barber cried out to the Germans: "Shoot me. My children will avenge me." The cooper Glikov was eighty. Wounded, he raised himself from inside the pit and said: "Bastards, shoot. One bullet will not kill me." I do not know if the barber's sons are alive, but every tortured old man has sons:

the Soviet people. They are already in the Beskids, approaching Warsaw, on the Prussian border. The hangmen will pay.

The pilot Andrei Filipovich Kolomeets received a letter from his sister at home. Andrei Filipovich was surprised: "Why didn't father write?" Then the sister responded: "Andriusha, don't get angry with dad—he cannot write with his own hand because the Germans burned out his eyes. He did not want to work for them. They took him to the Gestapo, kept him there for two days, and when they let him go he had wounds instead of eyes." Pilot Kolomeets says: "I became more sharp-eyed from that day on. Now the Germans have nowhere to hide from me." Together with Lieutenant Kolomeets, our entire army is searching for hangmen. We see an old man with empty sockets instead of eyes and this image will stay with us until the end. Woe to the Germans!

Here is a letter from a fifteen-year-old boy named Senya Deresha: "Dear Uncle Misha! I am writing from my hometown Iziaslavl, which you would not recognize now. A pitiful half of the town remains. It would be better if it never existed. It would be better if I had never been born! Now I am not the Senya you used to know. I do not know who I am anymore. Out of eight thousand people that used to live in Iziaslavl, only I and our neighbor Kiva remain. Everyone is gone: my dear mother, my father, all our relatives. If I were to tell you everything that I lived through, I doubt you would understand. I looked death in the eye often, worked with partisans, only a German bullet stopped me for awhile. But I am okay now. My leg healed and I will be searching for the enemy to take my revenge. Uncle Misha, remember that this is our worst enemy, the fascist cannibals. Strike them, cut them into pieces. My letter turned out to be chaotic, like my chaotic life, but I am still alive for revenge. It is as if I returned from the next world, now I am beginning a new life—that of an orphan. Write me often. My address is the same, actually I will receive the letter wherever you send it. I am the only one here." He is alone in a dead city. He hears voices from under the ground. The silence of endless cemeteries lit by the cold moon—this silence invades our nights. It pulls us to the west. The boy Senia is marching. Uncle Misha is marching with his military decorations of Glory—our entire army is marching decorated with fire and blood.

I received a letter from a twelve-year-old boy. He writes: "They murdered the young right away, and forced the elderly and us children into the forest. There they surrounded us and started to shoot, they threw children into a pit. I ran away. A German ran after me. I climbed a tree and he couldn't find me. I saw how they killed everyone and for three days I could hear the sounds of blood crying out from the earth." What can I add? Words fail me: blood is crying out.

Our scouts found eighty people in the Prenetskii woods near Lvov. They lived in the forest for two years. A three-year-old girl did not know what a "house" was. She was very surprised when she saw a house. But even this girl waiting for our troops said: "Father Stalin will get here and we will go home." The doomed never lost hope. Many could not hope that they would survive, but they all knew that Russia would survive. The Belorussian peasant Shura Gorbunova screamed at the butchers: "It is easy to kill me, but you will never destroy my Motherland!" In Iarishev, in the Vinnitsa region, they took out the mathematics teacher Gita Iakovlevna together with her six-year-old son Leva to be executed. She cried out to other victims: "Our brothers are there at the Front. They will be back. Soviet power is there. It is immortal. Stalin is there. He will never forget." Then she screamed at the butchers in German: "Did you hear me? Stalin will not forget this." Yes, Stalin is not only our commander-in-chief, not only our inspiration: Stalin is our conscience. All of us are thinking about the man who in the fall of 1941 knew that the Red Army would be in Berlin, a man who suffered everything our people suffered, a man who knows the agony of every mother and the tears of every child; thinking about this great and simple man, we all understand that he will not forget this.

The newspaper *The Catholic Herald* shamelessly writes: "In this war, the Germans conducted themselves more properly than in the previous war." I do not know what these gentlemen mean by "proper": wells filled with children, or the gas chambers, or perhaps blinded old men? I would take them to Ganusievich, the dean of a Catholic cathedral, who told me: "I am an old man who has read many books about the nature of evil, but I could not imagine such bloodthirsty and heartless creatures walking on the face of the earth." Ganusievich saw a woman throwing a baby out of a burning building. A German picked the baby up and carefully, as if it were a smoldering log, threw it back into the fire. They took the old prelate Lubenets from the village of Kleban and tortured him to death. Two Catholics priests were tortured in Pershov. In Ponary, Gonsporovsky, the oldest priest in Vilnius perished. They collected all the parishioners inside an orthodox church in Dorii, then set the church on fire.

I know the Germans will say: "Isolated criminals carried out the killings. Drops in the ocean." But in front of me is a "Summary Report." It is signed by Captain Zauer. This is a report about the liquidation of the residents of Pinsk. Captain Zauer writes: "Fifteen thousand people were forcibly driven to the collection point. The sick and the children who had been left at home were executed on the spot. In this manner an additional twelve hundred people were executed in the ghetto. The units carrying out the combing of the ghetto had to use axes, pole-axes, and other tools because almost all the doors were locked shut. Even when there were no cellars, a large number of people hid under the floors. You need to use search dogs (in Pinsk the dog Asta performed remarkably)." We will remember all this in Berlin—not the dog—but Captain Zauer and many other Germans. We will remember "the factories of death." We will remember those who gave the orders and those who did the killing. Why is it that the heart of every Soviet citizen is racing with emotion when he hears these words on the radio: "The order of the Supreme Commander?" We are not only on the German border, we are on the eve of a trial.

Near Vilnius, I spoke to fighters who had just advanced 400 kilometers on foot in ten days. They were covered in dust, and this gray dust looked like gray hair. Their eyes were red with fatigue and their lips were dry. They said, "We are getting closer." They were inspired by the proximity of the German border. To some foreigners our advance may look like an easy walk. In fact this is a road covered in blood. Who will describe the heroism of the infantry which crossed the Pinsk swamps? People were carrying heavy weapons on their shoulders. In Vilnius, infantrymen, for five days and nights without a break, stormed the ancient walls. In western Belorussia, the general of a tank unit, together with his soldiers, carried logs of wood for crossing a river. A colonel was carrying a cannon. These people were drenched with sweat, sweat and blood.

One colonel told me, "There were fortifications in Brest. The Germans thought they were safe. We went around. In the forts, we beat them, stabbed them, and cut them. I literally walked on the corpses of these monsters. I remembered my murdered mother, brothers, sisters, children. We will soon be in Germany."

Once more, the Germans are foolishly deceiving themselves, counting on our forgetfulness. But if there could be a winter without a thaw, there could be hatred without relenting. Each soldier knows that we have to reach Berlin; otherwise our conscience will eat us alive. We could forgive for ourselves, but we cannot forgive on behalf of our children. We could try to forgive a bad person, but not the inventors of the mobile gas vans. It is not revenge that is leading us, but a longing for justice. We want to stamp out the serpent's nest. We want to make sure that the Germans will never fight again. Not only the followers of Hitler, but the rebellious generals of the Reichswehr, who hope to be able in 1964 to correct the mistakes of 1944. We want to march through Germany with a sword so that the Germans will forever forget their love of the sword. We want to go to them so that they will never again come to us. The shadows of the martyrs are always with us. They rise from their graves, they emerge from ravines, wells, and ditches; the elderly and the infants, Russians and Ukrainians, Belorussians and Jews, Poles and Lithuanians, they all wanted to live, they loved the sun and the flowers; slaughtered, they tell us, "Remember." I know that we will soon reach the Spree: I saw our army filled with wrath. I know that justice will prevail. And when life appears unbearable, for me or for any of us, I sustain myself with the beautiful words: "Stalin will not forget."

In December, the Red Army was about to invade East Prussia. Ehrenburg was not above calling for revenge even as he invoked the number six million to refer to Hitler's Jewish victims; this was likely one of the first times this iconic number appeared in a major newspaper. "To Remember" appeared in *Pravda* on December 17, 1944.

"To Remember"

"*Die Pommersche Zeitung*" writes, "Our struggle was honest from the very beginning; we did not cross our borders in blind madness intending to subjugate other nations. On the contrary, needing to leave our borders behind us, we went as the messengers for a new order and a new justice. Not one German ever dreamed of annihilating Englishmen or punishing Frenchmen or enslaving the Dutch or any other peoples in order to live by the blood and sweat of other nations. On the contrary, our victories emitted tranquility."

Poor dears, apparently they were forced to go to the Caucasus and to Egypt in order to emit tranquility, and now, when they are allowed to return to Cologne and to Eastern Prussia, they meekly say, "whoever we hurt, we don't hold it against them."

What were their intentions when they crossed their borders? This question can be answered by the maps they published between 1939 and 1942. This is an atlas of "blind madness:" "Greater Germany" included Lille and Kiev, Riga and Nancy.

They did not want to enslave other nations and live by others' blood and sweat? Didn't Grupenführer Gasse declare not long ago to the newspaper *Hamburger Fren den blatt*, "The former Russia will be colonized by Stormtroopers and their children"? And the *Danzigger Fortpost* was estimating, "Every German colonizer will be served by eight to ten families." Yes, at that time they were not overly modest. And the German firm Bremen was promising stockholders cotton from Turkmenistan. At that time they declared that "a nation of merchants, Englishmen do not deserve a place on Earth" (*Felkisher Beobachter*). At that time they were threatening, "Shooting hostages will show the French that nothing will stop us" (*Parizer Tzeitung*). Shipping off the Dutch to the Ukraine, they declared, "Only history books will remember Holland as a state" (*Antriff*).

Where did they "emit tranquility"? In the "desert zone" or perhaps stoking the ovens of Majdanek or Treblinka?

Isn't it too early for them to renounce themselves? They are still shooting and already starting to whimper. They are still tearing children's bodies apart and already starting to wash their bloodied hands.

We have a saying, "To remember is to live." Indeed, a man who loses his memory loses half his life and starts to fade away. But to remember means not only to live, it also means to save a life, to save future generations, to preserve the idea of what it means to be human.

There occur historical events which confound wise men. Hitler's Germany is not a sphinx. It is typhus-bearing lice. Now everyone understands what fascism is but not everyone wants to remember what they understood. To forget means to forgive. And to forgive the stokers of Majdanek means to bring up children for even more efficient future ovens. I am not a politician, but in my work I deal with human feelings because every writer is a psychologist. Every writer is also a moralist, even if he does not think about morality. As a writer I want to remind you about the spiritual sources of fascism.

For many years, the Nazis brainwashed German youth. What were they conveying to the little fascists? A feeling of superiority. Now the world knows what racial or national arrogance means. If every nation decided that they were first in the world and therefore had the right to order others about, we would see new Majdaneks in the twentieth century.

So where is the foundation of this German feeling of superiority? In the past, some will say. There is no doubt that in the past Germany had remarkable philosophers, musicians, poets, and scientists. No anti-fascist thinks about putting down Goethe or Beethoven, but you cannot live off the legacy of culture. Culture is a continuing process of creation. And in fascist Germany nothing is left from the glorious past. We laugh at the degenerate who tries to replace a lack of wisdom and knowledge with an impressive past. It is ridiculous and despicable for a nation to burn museums and libraries while at the same time pointing to Schiller and Kant.

Others would argue that Germans are proud of their present. What is there to be proud of? A money-grubbing Goering? A lascivious Goebbels? Ignorant and lewd ministers? A hardworking Himmler? Or are they perhaps boastful of their sophisticated technology, well-kept cities, and comfortable houses? But the fascists did not create any of this: Hitler only ravaged Germany. It is also good to recall that American technology is more highly advanced, that Dutch cities are cleaner, and that Swedish housing is more comfortable. Besides, technology alone cannot be the pride of a people unless the strength of a nation is connected to its higher aspirations. And in fascist Germany civilization serves only the lowest aspirations. So the gas chambers for the mass murder of children became a natural expression of German technology.

No, the feeling of superiority that the fascists instill in their children is based neither on the past nor on the present. German superiority is steeped in prejudice, in the belief in the magic properties of German blood, a conviction that everything German is better than anything non-German.

About thirty years ago I witnessed an amusing conversation; this was in Champagne, where a Russian brigade was stationed at that time. A soldier from Gascogne saw Russians cooking groats in a pot and said, "We only feed this to cattle." To which a Russian replied, "You eat frogs, and our cattle would never eat that." There is no arguing over taste. (Personally I like groats and frogs.) But the fascists drowned the whole world in blood to establish the superiority of German taste and German lack of taste. A young fascist is instilled with the opinion that blond Kathen is better than olive-skinned Jeannette, that beer is better than cider or kvass, that Berlin is more beautiful than Leningrad or London, that the person who says in place of *"Guten tag"* *"Zdravstvuite"* or *"Bonjour"* is inferior.

The origins of rivers of blood appear to be seemingly innocent swamps of human stupidity. Children sometimes make fun of things they are not familiar with; then mothers reproach them and the child, as he grows up, learns that the world does not end at the corner of his street. Each person and each nation loves what they grew up with. What Russian would be indifferent to a white birch tree? But we have never claimed and never will claim that a birch tree is more noble or more worthy than a cypress tree or a cedar tree. Your mother may be smarter than your neighbor, but you do not love her for that, you love her because she is your mother. Genuine patriotism is modest and has nothing to do with nationalism: patriotism is brotherhood; nationalism—carnage and death.

"*Man muss die Slaven an die Wand drucken.*" "We need to put the Slavs against the wall." The Germans were raised on this stupid and vile expression. They were never told that the Slavs gave the world Hus and Copernicus, Tolstoy and Chekhov, Chopin and Tchaikovsky, Mendeleev and Lobachevskii. They were repeatedly told: "Against the wall!" And their brutal disciples really did decide to put large, talented, vibrant nations against the wall. Why? Because Hans is wearing a green hat with a feather, because Willy adores Nine-Pin Bowling, because Franz whispers "*ketzken*" to his wife.

In the countries they captured, the Germans killed all the Jews: the elderly and nursing babies. Ask a captured German, why did your compatriots annihilate six million innocent people. And he will say, "They are Jews. They are black (or red-haired). They have different blood." This began with vulgar jokes, with name-calling by hoodlums, with graffiti, and all this led to Majdanek, Babii Iar, Treblinka, to ditches filled with children's corpses. If before Treblinka antisemitism could appear to be a common, ugly outburst, now it is a word soaked with blood; the Polish poet Julian Tuwim says, "Antisemitism is the international language of fascists."

The whole world now sees the consequences of racial and national arrogance. The ovens of Majdanek—where the Germans consumed people of thirty nationalities because they were Russians, French, Poles, or Jews—these frightening ovens did not emerge right away. They grew out of an upbringing based on the hatred of whole nations. People all over the world need to remember that nationalism is the road to Majdanek. If a nation builds its freedom on the oppression of another, if a state restricts the rights of citizens of a different color, if a society persecutes a man because the shape of his nose or the way he speaks differs from that of his neighbors, so that nation, that state, that society is in danger. We gave the world a vivid example of friendship among peoples. We see how these same ideas inspire the new Yugoslavia where people, who until recently hated each other, today feel as brothers. We believe that all nations, large and small, will declare any manifestations of racial or national intolerance as the most severe crime.

Fascism was born at the very bottom of human consciousness. It is not surprising, therefore, that some of the initial followers of fascism were people devoid of morals: murderers, pimps, resentful ne'er-do-wells, and bandits. It is not sufficient, though, to recognize the origins of fascism; we need to remember that many "respectable" people (or those regarded as such) were assisting these criminals. In recent years some have forgotten about the founder of fascism—the vainglorious and bloodthirsty Duce. Since Italy woke up to its new life, Mussolini became a common German parasite. But we need to recall his successes: recall in order to remember, and remember in order to live. For many years some democrats admired Mussolini as a wise statesman. And yet Mussolini began his career with pogroms: his Blackshirts burned houses, destroyed books, forced castor oil down the throats of teachers, students, and workers, and they murdered honest citizens. At the time, some "democrats" thought: better Italian castor oil than Russian books, in the same way that later, during the time of Munich, they reassured themselves: better Hitler than the triumph of freedom. Insane statesmen wanted the use of rabid wolves as if they were chained dogs. They figured that rabid wolves would bite only when ordered to. Europe and the world now see the moral of this amoral policy: ruined Warsaw, grieving Paris, wounded London—this is the price nations paid.

We must remember: fascism was born out of the greed and stupidity of some, and the perfidy and cowardice of others. If mankind wants to put an end to the bloody nightmare of these years, it must put an end to fascism. Half measures will not do here. If fascism is left somewhere to breed, then in ten or twenty years we will again see rivers of blood. A nail drives out a nail, but you cannot drive fascism out with fascism. You cannot liberate nations from one brand of fascism and deliver them into the hands of fascists of a different brand. Fascism—a terrifying cancerous tumor. It cannot be treated at mineral spas. It needs to be removed. I do not believe in good-hearted people who cry over executioners: these alleged do-gooders are preparing the deaths of innocent millions. The nations of Europe fought courageously against the invaders; and nations are not Moors who could leave after finishing their work. The French have a good saying: "in his house, the collier is a master." It is not only the French who understand this saying. The Red Army has demonstrated what it means to liberate: the Poles, Norwegians, Serbs, and Slovaks understand this. We do not install half-fascists in place of fascists: we liberate without quotation marks. We know that democracy is the daughter of a nation and not a glamorous lady whom you could only adore from a distance. But even then you need connections.

Nations who experienced the fascist tyranny will understand us without any lengthy explanation: this is a time of nations and not diplomats. The courageous people of France will understand us. Our allies will understand us. There was a time when the British believed in the magical properties of the English Channel. Now they understand that the Channel is not a barrier against fascism. For a long time, the British prohibited the entry of dogs into the country: this is how they try to protect their country from rabies. But rabid, two-legged creatures in contrast to four-legged ones possess different "Fau." And only the complete destruction of fascism—from Warsaw to La Linea—can protect England from a new disaster.

When *Die Pommersche Zeitung* dares to claim that the Germans left their borders as the most peaceful of missionaries, it means that the fascists now have only one hope: the loss of memory. After a severe injury, doctors sometimes diagnose a condition called amnesia. The injuries to the world are immense, but nations do not suffer from amnesia. They will remember everything in the days of judgment. Even after the victory, they will not forget these terrible years. We must remember: this is our obligation to the dead heroes and to the children.

These cruel visions must remain before our eyes: this is the price for saving our world. I know that it is easier to forget but we will not forget. We solemnly swear: remember, remember, remember!

Notes

[1] Unless otherwise noted, all translations are by Joshua Rubenstein.
[2] Eli Falkovich (1898-1979), a leading Soviet Yiddish linguist, was awarded the Order of Lenin in 1942.
[3] First published in English in *An Anthology of Jewish-Russian Literature: Two Centuries of Dual Identity in Prose and Poetry*, vol. 1, ed. Maxim D. Shrayer (New York: M. E. Sharpe, 2007), 535-38.

Chapter 3

Jews at War: Diaries from the Front[1]

Oleg Budnitskii
Translated by Dariia Kabanova

The title of this article refers to the relatively unknown bimonthly magazine of *Jews at War*, published for a short time in the beginning of World War I.[2] The journal narrated the military feats of Jewish soldiers in the Russian Army. Of course, according to state policy, there could be no Jewish officers in the Army at that time. The magazine grew out of the Jewish community's concerns over the fact that the military valor of Jews was underappreciated, or worse, unknown to the general public. A quarter of a century later, during World War II, the number of Jews who served in the Red Army was comparable to the number of Jews who used to serve in the Imperial Russian Army—more than four hundred thousand men. During World War II, there were thousands of officers among them, and nearly three hundred generals and admirals.[3] And, again, the Soviet Jewish community was concerned that the military feats of the Jewish soldiers on the fronts of Great Patriotic War remained virtually unknown. Il'ia Ehrenburg addressed this issue at the plenary session of the Jewish Anti-Fascist Committee in March 1943:

> In order for the Jewish soldiers and officers to continue performing their duty, it is our responsibility to speak about Jews fighting at the front. Not to brag, of course, but in the interests of our common cause—in order to eradicate Fascism as soon as we can. In order to do this, it is our responsibility to create a book, and, in it, to demonstrate convincingly the role of Jews in the war. Statistics alone would not be enough. We need real stories, we need vivid portraits. We need a collection about Jewish heroes who participate in the Great Patriotic War. We must tell the truth, the whole truth. And this truth will be enough.[4]

Without dwelling on what this "whole truth" meant for Ehrenburg, especially in the context of the war, it is worth noting that the lion's share of books and articles devoted to Jewish participation in the war deals with heroes and military valor. Thus, these publications are not much different from the rest of the post-war narratives that categorized wartime feats of arms according to the heroes' ethnicity.

War, however, cannot be reduced to military valor only. War is never only about killing and dying. Card-playing, drinking, singing, jealousy, love, and theft are also part of war. That is, war is life. The enormous literature about the war contains very little description of the everyday life of a "Private Ivan" (or Abram).[5]

Where would we need to look for information about the everyday life of a "Private Abram" (this hypothetical Abram could, of course, be a sergeant or a junior officer) at the front? Where do we turn to learn about his frame of mind, about his feelings? The answer seems to be clear: one must consult the personal sources like diaries, letters, and memoirs. Herein, however, lies the problem. Diaries were banned at the front; letters were censored.[6] Memories of the war were meticulously unified and leveled after 1945. The vast number of war memoirs (published in the famous "War Memoirs" series) were written by war commanders of various ranks. The texts were, of course, carefully edited and underwent scrupulous approval procedures; moreover, they were written, as a rule, not by the generals and marshals themselves, but by hack writers, who, in the majority of cases, lacked any talent whatsoever.

"War memoirs became something akin to the 'Mémoires d'Outre-Tombe,' composed by the Chateaubriand-aspiring generals," former machine-gun company commander Zinovii Chernilovskii wrote:

> while soldiers like Nekrasov or Bykov were focused on the artistic vision of the war.[7] Where, one might ask, is that company commander who would be brave enough to show the greatest of all wars from the point of view of the participant. To show it in a simple, everyday way, that is, not as a "man with a gun," but in a much simpler, straightforward way, in the spirit of a famous French saying, à la guerre comme à la guerre.[8]

This situation began to change in the years of *perestroika*; in post-Soviet Russia, a true "source revolution" occurred. The number of texts about the war grew exponentially, along with the degree of their sincerity. Dozens, if not hundreds, of memoirs were published. War history enthusiasts recorded thousands of veterans' stories. It turned out that many soldiers in this Great War kept diaries despite all kinds of bans. They also wrote memoirs about their war experience without much hope of ever publishing them. They wrote for their children and their grandchildren, "to make history." Sometimes, official lies about the war and the complicity of "officially appointed" veterans in these lies stimulated the creation of those memoirs.

Vasyl' Bykov described this phenomenon as follows:

> No country in the world has such remarkable veterans as our native and beloved USSR. Not only are they not promoting the truth and justice of the war, but on the contrary—they are most concerned with hiding the truth, most eager to replace it with mythologizing propaganda, in which they appear to be heroes and nothing else. They like this inflated role of theirs, and would not tolerate any attempt to challenge it.[9]

Characteristically, it was in 1996 that Bykov wrote this letter, addressed to N. N. Nikulin, the author of the fabulous *Memoirs of the War* (written in the mid-1970s and published in 2008). For Bykov, the USSR continued to exist as far as social attitudes towards the war were concerned.

Of course, one has to be very careful analyzing memoirs written forty or fifty years after the events took place. The same caution needs to be applied to oral histories and interviews. The problem is not just the weakness of human memory. The very people who write and narrate these stories have changed: they are different people and not who they were during the war. Personal experiences, the social environment, books read and films seen, decades of propaganda—all of this undoubtedly influences the content of written or spoken texts. Sometimes the veterans unconsciously insert certain stories from films they have seen into their own narratives; sometimes they polemicize with what they have read or seen. Without going into too much detail about source study here, I must note that, while it is possible to use these "new memoirs," it is hardly productive to give too much credence to them.

Among the authors of the "new memoirs" there are many Jews. The memoirs of Jewish veterans have been published not just in the countries of the former Soviet Union. Several individual memoirs and collections were published in Vancouver, Tel Aviv, Netanya, Detroit, Palo Alto, and other places where émigré veterans have settled. Hundreds of interviews with Jewish veterans have been recorded. The specific mission of the Blavatnik Archive Foundation in New York is to interview veterans who live in different countries of the world. At present, more than eight hundred interviews have been recorded. Many narratives by the Jewish veterans can be found on the website "Ia pomniu" ("I remember"), www.iremember.ru.

Yet, diaries remain the most valuable—and the rarest—of the "personal sources" about the war. Jews comprise a surprisingly large percentage of authors of the few diaries available to us now. Statistically, the reasons for this are quite clear. Data suggests that 430,000 to 450,000 Jews served in the Red Army and Navy during the war. Of these, 142,500 died in the war.[10] According to the 1939 census, Jews comprised 1.78% of the USSR's population. At the same time, they comprised 15.5% of Soviet citizens with post-secondary education (in absolute numbers [171,000], Jews with post-secondary education were second to only Russians [620,209], leaving behind Ukrainians [147,645]). As much as 26.5% of Jews had a secondary education.[11] The majority of Jewish soldiers in the Red Army, then, were educated people, more likely to keep a diary.

Diaries, as we remember, were banned on the front lines. The commissar of Chernilovskii's company, upon seeing a notebook in Chernilovskii's possession, confiscated and burned it: "Remember, commander, comrade Stalin's orders: everyone found to keep a diary will be executed ... I do not know whether such order truly existed, but I have not kept a diary since. Just like everyone else," Chernilovskii wrote more than half a century later.[12]

Yet, historians are lucky because orders were made to be broken in the USSR. While a formal order prohibiting keeping a diary does not seem to have been ever issued (at least, I was not able to identify it), keeping a diary was prohibited in the context of the general rules of secrecy; as it will become evident below, these rules were quite open to interpretation.

In this article, I will attempt to answer the question of who kept war diaries and why. I will also analyze several common themes in the diaries. It is impossible, of course, to give a comprehensive analysis of even a limited number of war diaries within a single article. This is why, along with several plots concerning the authors' combat experience, I will discuss the Soviet Jews' perception of Jewishness as it emerges from the war diaries. I will also analyze the attitude towards Jews in the Red Army, in the measure that it is reflected in the diaries of Jewish soldiers.

Private Mark Shumelishskii wrote on separate sheets of paper, sometimes omitting the date. He understood that recording his impressions (and especially his opinions) was dangerous. "Much of what I would like to record and then ponder later using these concrete examples, I cannot record … I cannot record everything. What has been written down can get into the hands of the enemy, and harm will be done." The problem was not that Shumelishskii was afraid that he would be reported to the authorities. He was afraid that the enemy could use some dissenting passages from the diary to their advantage. Criticism of the war, he thought, was for the future. "It is more like potential criticism."[13]

In contrast, Sergeant (later, Lieutenant) Vladimir Gel'fand openly kept a diary and sometimes read fragments of it to his comrades-in-arms. His immediate superior even advised him to use a lead pencil instead of ink to better preserve the writing.[14] In a separate instance, Gel'fand received instructions from his political instructor:

> My political instructor told me how to keep a diary. After he discovered, incidentally, the silly things I wrote in the diary, I now write just like he suggested. He says the diary should be only about what work the company does, about how the battles go, about our skillful commanders, about the political instructors' talks with the soldiers, about the Red Army men's reaction to these talks, etc. This is the way I will write from now on.[15]

In two days, an even more surprising entry appears in the diary:

> This night, the political instructor slept here by my side. Today, too. I am now at the mortar's firing position and not in the trench anymore. I am much more comfortable now. I am excited! If not for the political instructor, who would have coached me?[16]

Gel'fand's seemingly excessive enthusiasm for his writing coach has an explanation. The reason for the sharp contrast in content and tone of the diary is clarified by an entry Gel'fand made two weeks later: "For the first time I can write here openly again, because I got rid of the political instructor who instructed me how to write a diary and what to write in it!"[17] It need hardly be mentioned that Gel'fand returned to writing "silly things" (sometimes even without quotation marks), which are the most valuable part of this voluminous text.

Military interpreter Junior Lieutenant Irina Dunaevskaia was interrogated by the officers of military counterintelligence, SMERSH (an abbreviation of *Smert' Shpionam*, Death to Spies). Having ascertained, however, that her nearly stenographic notes contained no information about military units or about their location, they warned her, in language that left no doubt, about the necessity of keeping military secrets, but did not explicitly prohibit her from keeping a diary.[18]

Why did Red Army soldiers keep diaries? Many of the authors were not without literary aspirations, and possibly planned to use the diaries for their potential books: secondary school graduates Vladimir Gel'fand and Boris Komskii wrote poetry and dreamed of literary careers. "I will not ever cease the study of literature and literary work, this is my life," Gel'fand wrote on June 6, 1942.

Private David Kaufman was a student at the Moscow Institute of Philosophy, Literature and History (IFLI), training to become a professional author; he even published his first poem in a "thick journal." Later, Kaufman would go on to become a prominent poet. He published under his nom-de-plume, David Samoilov.

Mark Shumelishskii, an engineer, kept asking himself "again and again:"

> Why the hell am I always trying to keep this diary? I am obsessed with the idea of collecting enough material and, in time, writing a good, truthful book, which would reflect the true mindsets of certain groups of people on the home front at this important time. The book can be written many years later, of course, when everything can be assessed properly. But now, it is imperative that I write down as many minutiae as I can.[19]

Senior Lieutenant Boris Suris notes down the last names of the Germans, from the personnel list of one platoon that ended up in his hands: Nittel, Liebold, Wagner, Winkler, Wolf—so that "[I] wouldn't have to rack [my] brains over Kraut last names when I write my super novel.»[20] The Odessa native mocks his own literary ambitions, and writes the word "novel" (*roman*) with three *r*'s. Yet, Suris's ambitions were very real: later, the diary features several entries about stylistic peculiarities of J. B. Priestley, Dos Passos, and Hemingway, naturally his greatest favorite (Suris read them in translation). Suris, the future art scholar, did not end up writing a novel, but he did produce several short stories, published twenty years after his death, in the twenty-first century.

Of course it was not necessary to be a Jew to aspire to be a writer. Similar ambitions are exhibited in the voluminous diary by Sergeant Nikolai Inozemtsev, the future Soviet academician and economist and Leonid Brezhnev's speechwriter.[21] Writerly ambitions are also apparent in the diary by Private Vassily Tsymbal, a former instructor of literature at Yeisk Pedagogical College, whose pre-war literary exercises failed to gain approval of Maxim Gorky.[22]

Irina Dunaevskaia kept her diary since childhood (she destroyed it when she joined the People's Volunteer Corps in July 1941). She was sent back to Leningrad very soon, together with other women who joined the Volunteer Corps. She resumed her diary, which became a diary of the Leningrad Blockade. This diary, too, was destroyed in April 1942 when Dunaevskaia joined the regular army. In the army, however, she could not let go of her habit and continued to write down her impressions of her "works and days," of her emotions and surroundings.[23] She was not entirely devoid of literary ambitions either: "If I am mutilated, and not able to work, I will write a book about myself—about an ordinary girl who grew up in between the two wars and who fought in the Great Patriotic War. I know I can do it." The "girl," however, was far from being "ordinary": Dunaevskaia, a student of philology at Leningrad State University, read Chateaubriand before bedtime, vexed at the necessity of reading the French author in Russian, because "nowhere could [Chateaubriand] be found in French."[24]

Sergeant Pavel El'kinson, on the other hand, did not plan to write a novel. He began his diary for a very particular reason. On August 28, 1944, El'kinson wrote:

> Finally, the long-awaited day came: the Germans are expelled from our land at this sector of the front. Here it is, the river Prut, the border is right there. Only six days since we commenced our advance, and so much has been already done. Bessarabia is now completely cleared. A peace treaty with Romania is signed. Tomorrow, we cross the border. Could I have ever thought that I would have a chance to go abroad? It turns out that I have this chance. I very much want to remember all that I have seen, and to note it down. Because this is a once-in-a-lifetime thing.[25]

El'kinson, who served as a scout in an artillery unit, had a chance to "travel" quite a lot all over Europe: between August 1944 and May 1945, he went through Romania, Bulgaria, Yugoslavia, Hungary and Austria.

While working on this article, I consciously tried to limit the sources I used to diaries. Though not all of the sources conform to the "genre conventions" of a diary, all of them reflect the impressions of those who participated in the war and who wrote down their impressions at the time the events occurred, or several days afterwards. I also include a "diary *ex post*," by Sergeant Viktor Zalgaller, who after the war, went on to become a mathematician. In 1972, when leaving his wartime letters to his mother in the care of his grandson, Zalgaller wrote a commentary to the letters, often inserting the dates and restoring, from memory, the bits and pieces that were either censored by the military officials, or simply not written down because of Zalgaller's "inner censor." This "memoir-commentary," of course, was not meant to be published at that time. The author found a very precise title for his memoir: "The Everyday Life of War."[26]

How representative are these texts? Can one assess the war experience of hundreds of thousands of Jewish Red Army soldiers from only a small number of diaries? This is, again, an eternal question for a historian. How many sources have to be analyzed in order to be able to ascertain that something is typical, while something else is not? It is clear that these particular texts do not reflect the experience of *all* Jews who served in the Red Army. At the same time, there is no doubt, in my opinion, that these young men and women (who, as the fates decreed, became participants in the Great War and recorded their experiences right away) are sociologically representative of many of their peers. All of them, just like nearly half of the Soviet Jews immediately before the war, lived in large cities (Moscow, Leningrad, Kiev, Zaporozh'e, Dnepropetrovsk, and Odessa). All of them either graduated from high school, or were students, or had a college degree, which was also quite typical: in 1939, there were 98,216 Jewish post-secondary students in the USSR (11.1% of all such students). In Moscow, 17.1% of all post-secondary students were Jewish; in Leningrad, the number was 19%, in Kharkov—24.6%. 35.6% of all students were Jewish in Kiev, and 45.8% in Odessa.[27] While relatively typical, the war and life experience of every author of the diary was, of course, unique and interesting in and of itself.

All of them were hardcore Soviet patriots. The oldest of this cohort joined the People's Volunteer Corps, or joined the Army as volunteers. High school graduates, who also were eager to get into the battle as soon as they could, were normally drafted according to official schedules.

Viktor Zalgaller, a student of Leningrad University's Department of Mathematics, transferred to Leningrad Institute of Aviation in December 1940, responding to the Komsomol's call. The meaning of the "call" was evident: the war was imminent, and the Air Force needed specialists. However, Zalgaller did not get a chance to join the Air Force. Soon after the war began, he entered an artillery school, and on July 4, 1941, a day after Stalin's radio address to the nation, he joined the Volunteer Corps. He was not alone: four hundred people from the Institute of Aviation joined the Volunteer Corps at that time. The image that stuck in his memory was this: "We march in formation, in civilian clothes. The wives walk along the sidewalk. While marching, I eat fresh, tasty sour cream from a paper cone."[28]

In hindsight, the short-sightedness of Zalgaller's superiors (in allowing 400 future aviation specialists to go to the front as Privates) can hardly be overestimated, especially if one considers the monstrous casualties sustained in the war by Soviet aviation. Almost half of the losses were the so-called "non-combat casualties."[29] Of course, 400 men would have hardly changed the fate of Soviet aviation in any radical way, but there is no doubt they were not the only ones not used effectively. Zalgaller was offered a chance to study at an artillery school, but he considered accepting the offer an act of cowardice. This potential aviation specialist first served in the artillery, then became a signaler.

One of the most representative cases of true Soviet patriotism is the story of Mark Shumelishskii. In 1941, he turned 31. A "self-made man," in 1922, at the age of 12, he began to work, because his mother lost her income and his family was on the brink of starvation. He worked for more than 12 years at the State Bank: first as a messenger, then as a clerk, then as an accountant, and later as a senior accountant. He did not attend school and was largely an autodidact. In 1932, he began to take evening classes at the Moscow Bauman State Technical University, then became a full-time student and received his diploma in Mechanical Engineering in 1938. The same year, he began to work at the "Kompressor" factory in Moscow. During the first year of the war, he was a deputy shop superintendent in the department that produced chassis for the rocket launchers (the ones that would be soon known as the "Katyusha").[30]

This job was of crucial importance for the military, and thus he was exempt from the draft. Moreover, he had severe myopia. Yet, Shumelishskii was bursting to go to the front: he was a frequent visitor to his local Military Registration and Enlistment Office, where he insisted that he be drafted. One has to have in mind that this was not during the first days of war, when many naïve "enthusiasts" were afraid to be "late" for the war.

After another unsuccessful attempt to join the army, on October 11, 1941, Shumelishskii wrote: "In general, a person who wants to join the army when he has an opportunity to avoid it, is considered an idiot, even by the Military Registration Office officials."[31] In May 1942, Shumelishskii finally got what he wanted and joined the army as a volunteer. For Irina Dunaevskaia, who was quite critical of the Red Army policies, Communist ideals were, nonetheless, as indisputable as they were for Shumelishskii. She submitted her Party application just before the offensive that aimed to break the Leningrad Blockade.[32]

Was there a difference between "Abram's war" and "Ivan's war"? Not really. Death did not distinguish between a Hellene and an Israelite. That is, of course, if the Israelite did not become a prisoner of war. Life at war was always marked by death, and this death was as diverse as the soldiers themselves. Seldom was this death heroic: often, it was a dull, everyday kind of death; at times, it was stupid. And, death was always disgusting. To the contrary of what contemporary films about the war would have one believe, this death was far from being "aesthetic." Viktor Zalgaller's diary entry for July 14, 1941, makes this point clearly:

> The front. It smells nasty here. Flies swarm around. In the ground, I can see the nose and the lips of a carelessly buried corpse. The nose and the lips are black. It is hot. Artillery fire. Something flew from afar and is swinging from a tree branch. It is a piece of human intestine.[33]

Death could catch up with anyone anywhere: a group of officers from the infantry regiment (where Dunaevskaia served) was directly hit by a shell at their command post. Their mutilated corpses were brought, on a wood sledge, to the regiment's dressing station (as if they needed dressings):

> Somebody took [Major] Begul's felt boots in no time. [Senior Lieutenant] Vogel had his pants down—I could see his yellow body and sparse hairs on his lower abdomen. Horror! Someone tried to cover his nakedness with a sheepskin coat, but the flap was iced over

and would not lie flat. And the eyes of the dead man, black, unusually large, scary, were watching and not seeing us.[34]

It has to be noted that diaries were also kept by people not on the front lines, who had no immediate contact with the enemy. Boris Suris and Irina Dunaevskaia were military interpreters; Boris Tartakovskii was a political worker; Boris Komskii, too, went on to become a political worker. Mark Shumelishskii served as a technician in an artillery unit. Of course, these people also found themselves in unanticipated situations. Suris went on a reconnaissance mission with the scouts, aiming to capture a prisoner for interrogation, only to receive a missile wound. Tartakovskii had to fight at the front lines during the bloody battle of Kuban', when every man capable of holding a weapon was fighting. Dunaevskaia was wounded several times—luckily, never seriously.

All the more valuable, then, are the diary entries which pertain to the battles themselves. Among the diaries available to us, the texts by Boris Komskii and Pavel El'kinson stand out in this respect. These texts are lapidary, devoid of any stylistic extravagances, and they accurately reflect the atmosphere (I am compelled to say, the fever) of battle. The quotes from Komskii and El'kinson's concise diary entries feel documentary, authentic.

Boris Komskii began his war in July 1943. He, together with his classmates from the Orel Infantry School (which at that time was evacuated to Chimkent, in Central Asia), was never given either a chance to take his final examinations, or his officer rank. Instead, they were sent into the heart of the Battle of Kursk.[35] At first, Komskii was assigned to a mortar crew; then, after his mortar was destroyed by a German shell, he ended up in infantry. Komskii's concise entries, made from July to August 1943, at the height of one of the bloodiest battles in world history, are in essence a chronicle of the demise of his detachment and his regiment as a whole.

> July 22:
> We took a firing position in a deep hollow. Every unit fired at least a dozen mortar shells. The Germans keep us under artillery fire all the time. Sasha Ogloblin has a head wound. He went to the medical battalion. Yesterday, the commander of regiment headquarters was killed. This day, my mortar fired 45 shells. So far, this is a record. They just brought the body of a j[unior] l[ieutentan]t who burned alive when he got surrounded together with 12 wounded soldiers.

July 23:
A difficult day today. The Germans broke away, and it seems like they dug in and pulled the forces together. We covered around 15 kilometers. They are constantly slamming us with artillery and mortar fire. My company lost just three men during the march—one dead.

July 26:
We have an important railway station ahead of us, 12 kilometers from Orel. We must take it. The battalion is thinned out. Not more than two platoons are left. The battalion commander lost both legs and died. The headquarters commander is wounded. In the evening, the sergeants carried thermoses with lunch to the front lines. One of them played a harmonica, another one complained that they soon would have to carry dinner. Both were killed.[36]

The thinned-out regiment was consolidated to form one battalion. Yet, even this battalion did not last long:

August 3:
A hard day. Sergeant Tyrkalev was blown up by a mine. For two years he fought in this war. He supported my Party application, and yesterday wrote me a reference letter for my medal "For Courage." Three men are wounded. The battalion commander, Cap[tain] Fornel', while drunk, led the battalion under crazy fire, without any preparatory bombardment; only memories remained of the battalion, though this battalion was what was left of the whole regiment. Fornel' himself was killed.

On August 6, Komskii got lucky (as it will turn out)—he was wounded. Later, he wrote about the circumstances of this battle, in the vicinity of some village in the Orel region that was burned to the ground:

People become casualties one by one. Our troops have fallen behind, again. Oshkov crawled to join them, he promised to come back for us: just five people are left. My machine gun is a target for the German ones. They see us, and spray us with bullets when we dare to move. My second gunner, Grinshpun, has a serious leg wound. The "Vanyusha"[37] started "talking." There is nowhere to carry Grinshpun and nobody to do it. Oshkov is not back. I raised myself a little for a moment and saw our guys follow the hollow on the left, about 700 meters from my position. It was very hard to reach them—the rye field that could give us cover didn't go that far. Still, I ordered the two men who were left to crawl away and drag Grinshpun with them on canvas. I myself wanted to crawl towards our rear, and that's where my turn came: a shell splinter hit me in my right arm; the medic dressed the wound. I was very calm, even my heart did not pound too much, and I waited for all of this to end. I was not really worried about the wound, though I saw the splinter tear out a piece of my flesh together with my shirt. I crawled back through the rye field. He keeps pounding me with machine gun fire, I can't even get up to my knees. Somehow I got to the other side of the hill and was able to stand up. By the evening, I was at the aid station.

Komskii ended up in a hospital. It was there that he learned that all of his comrades-in-arms perished:

August 19:
A hard day. Godik Kravets came to visit me. He was also brought to this hospital. His leg was wounded by a shell splinter on August 9, three days after I was wounded. It was a fatal day for our company. At the whim of the battalion headquarters commander, who is a total idiot, they began to "better" our positions and caught the suppr[essive] fire of the German mortars. Yasha Maliiev, Islamov, Oshkov, Mikhailov and J[unior] Leut[enant] Kushnerev were killed. Only five men are left from the whole company, no one from our platoon. This news devastated me. My main cause of grief is Yasha Maliiev, a dear comrade, a great guy. In the evening, the divisions were led out to rest and regroup. So many men lost in vain, because of the commanders' sluggishness and stupidity.

The Battle of Kursk was, of course, a real meat-grinder. Yet, the Red Army continued to sustain heavy casualties even after this battle. The enemy kept fighting till the very end: some remarkably heavy battles occurred in Hungary. Pavel El'kinson wrote on November 11, 1944:

The battles are very violent. Every day is harder than the last one. The enemy does not surrender an inch of their soil without a fight. Almost every day we lose the best of our men. On the night of November 4, we were the first to enter the town of Tsegled. Here, our reconnaissance comm[ander] was killed. Such is human fate. Just one minute before, I stood next to him. I just moved away, and the shell exploded next to him.[38]

Death could have been waiting even when the enemy did not put up much resistance. Three men from El'kinson's unit died upon touching a hot wire that the enemy left along the bank of the Danube on November 23, 1944.

El'kinson's unit moved in the direction of Budapest. "Beautiful place, here. Like a resort. Many gardens, vineyards too. We drink wine and march forward," El'kinson wrote on November 24.

This idyll did not last long, however. Though Sergeant El'kinson, judging by his brief notes, was not disposed towards despondency or reflection, on the next day a distinct note of despair appears, for the first time, in his diary:

> Again, the heavy, violent battle is underway. Will it ever end? The damned Krauts don't want to retreat. All day, with no interruption, we are being bombarded. Not really a pleasant thing, this. By the end of the day, we were attacked by tank units. The weather is bad, foggy, so they were able to creep up to us at the distance of 350 meters—only then did we notice. It was hard to make them fall back. Again, one man was killed today, two were wounded. What nerve should one have to watch and experience this every day for three years without a break. I can hear it in my head, against my will: when is your turn?

The characters in our story, unlike Babel's alter-ego Liutov, did master "the simplest skill—the skill of killing a human being." At war, murder may seem not like murder at all, it becomes more akin to a job. Moreover, one has a choice to kill or be killed. And yet, reading the diaries and the memoirs one begins to feel, at times, that the soldiers are ill at ease performing this job. To be more precise, one feels that the soldiers cannot forget that the Germans are people, too, no matter how much both the war experience and propaganda claimed the contrary. One is reminded of Ehrenburg's adage: "We know now: Germans are not human beings."[39]

Sometimes, the diaries represent Germans as stick figures: "At the hill, two Germans with a mortar brazenly attempt to shoot us. But we shoot them down with a volley from our carbines" (Zalgaller, September 4, 1941). At other times, soldiers could see faces of those who they wounded or killed: this happened to Boris Komskii during a battle on August 5, 1943:

> We charged on. The Germans ran. Our platoon charged forward, ahead of the rest—there were eight people in the platoon. We went through the village. The Germans now retreat through a rye field. We run after them. I went down on one knee, shot my rifle. One Kraut fell down. I'm excited. I run forward. I see two of them falling behind. I order my men to surround them. One raised his hands, surrendering. I ran up to the second one, he turned out to be the man who I had shot. He has a head wound. He shoves a package of bandages into my hands. I didn't dress the wound. A burly Kraut with an order and a ribbon. I took his automatic rifle and searched him. Somebody shouts at me: "Take his watch—what are you waiting for!" And I'm thinking, really, what am I waiting for, and I take his watch.

Sergeant Komskii will make a good use of this watch, and not to keep track of time, either. Less than ten days after the battle described above, Komskii exchanged the watch for lard, canned meat and bread at hospital where he was a patient. "I feed myself," he wrote. The exchange points to the fact that the hospital personnel stole food and supplies from the wounded: it is hard to imagine that the senior hospital nurse (who took Komskii's watch) would have had a personal source of extra food in the middle of a destroyed Orel village.

According to Komskii, the wounded were not fed well, and the mess hall (where one could not sit down to eat) was "a terrible mess." The wounded had to sleep on the floor in a hut with broken windows; four people shared two mattresses that had to be padded with straw. "My soul burns—is this no way to treat wounded soldiers," Komskii wrote.[40] Without going into a detailed discussion of this topic here, it has to be noted that other servicemen's diaries are also peppered by multiple testimonies of theft and corruption in the army. While soldiers were appalled by theft and corruption, they also perceived it as an inevitable, even historically given, evil. In the words of one of David Kaufman's comrades-in-arms, the fact that the sergeant stole sugar was, of course, not too pleasant. Yet, "this is the original sin; nothing can be done about it."[41]

Let us return to the servicemen's attitudes towards their enemy, not to the Germans *en masse* but to the individual Germans, including those who had to be killed. Pavel El'kinson wrote down on November 11, 1944: "Bumped off another one today. This one is the fourth. No compassion whatsoever."[42] Boris Suris, on the other hand, felt compassion for a German who he interrogated in late January 1943, when the battles of Don were underway:

> He was a handsome, plump young guy of about twenty. He had fair hair and a pleasant baritone. He was seriously wounded in the chest; he sat stooping and coughed a lot. He told us that he was expelled from the Hitlerjugend organization: he and his friends tore down and burned a banner with a swastika, and they were sent to a concentration camp for three months. I had a lot of compassion for him, but nothing could be done: he was seriously wounded and we had no resources to take care of him. I took him to a gully not far from the quarters… Next morning I went to have a look at him: somebody has already taken his shoes off and cleaned out his pockets. He lay on his back on a little mound of dirt, his head thrown back, and he didn't look like himself. His hair fell back and froze into the snow, and the blood around his head was very bright red. For him, I had a lot of compassion, but nothing could be done.[43]

Perhaps it was under the strong impression of the shoeless, plundered corpse of a prisoner, who he himself had executed, that Suris ironically "amends Ehrenburg": "Kill the German and clean out his pockets!"[44]

Irina Dunaevskaia, who witnessed her immediate superior, Major Reznik, beating a German prisoner (Dunaevskaia was the interrogator), wrote: "Very disgusting." This particular beating does not seem to be a unique case; soon another entry appears in Dunaevskaia's diary: "Major Reznik's beatings of POWs are disgusting. I have no pity for the prisoners, but this is loathsome."[45] This was not just an emotional reaction to a beating of a disarmed enemy soldier: the spirit of internationalism, an integral part of the mindset of a Soviet intellectual, proved very enduring. While at the hospital, Dunaevskaia had an argument with the head doctor, Chechelashvili, who despised the "Krauts" "as such." Dunaevskaia tried to convince the doctor that, "their nationality does not matter as much as their notions and actions, imposed on them by their Führer after he did away with the dissidents!"[46]

Zalgaller, who shot the German mortar men in cold blood, heard a radio exchange between two Soviet tank crew members on July 20, 1942.

> The terrifying words remain in my memory:
> —Two of them are surrendering here.
> —We have no time. Run them over.
> And then I hear the driver breathing as he is murdering those people.

Zalgaller does not use the word "Germans" here. He writes "people."

The same Zalgaller, in a suburb of Danzig in 1945, saw a wounded German soldier at the crossroads: "There is no face, he breathes through foaming blood. It looks like there are people in the house nearby, they are just afraid to go outside. I tap on the door with my pistol grip and tell them to help the wounded."[47] What was that wounded German to Zalgaller? To Zalgaller who saw the corpses of those who perished from hunger in the blockaded Leningrad; to Zalgaller who saw people frying human meat cutlets in a pan and showing no remorse? Why did Sergeant El'kinson write that he had no compassion for the German he killed? Why would he even mention compassion at all, as if he had to feel it? After all, his family, with the exception of a brother (who was in the army and was seriously wounded during the first days of war) was executed by the Germans in Zaporozh'e. It seems that humanity did not leave those people easily, even when the conditions were inhuman.

Speaking about the Soviet Jews at war, it is impossible to ignore the question of what kind of Jews they were, just as it is impossible to ignore the issue of antisemitism, which flourished in the Soviet Union during the war years. The Soviet Jews—those who grew up during the years of Soviet rule—were Soviet people first and foremost. They might have been "the most Soviet" of all Soviet people. They were able to formulate the differences between themselves and other Jews in precise terms, after they finally met these formerly Western Jews who became Soviet citizens in 1939.

Boris Tartakovskii, struck by the crowds of evacuees in Stalingrad, wrote on October 31, 1941:

> Who of this mass of people, filling up the street, crowding near the store entrances, pushing and shoving to get a place in line to the soda fountain—who of them is an actual Stalingrad native? I saw women

wearing once-fashionable coats with wide shoulders, colorful dirty caps or headscarves, brown ski boots. Where have I seen them?

Tartakovskii saw them in the beginning of the same year 1941 in Lvov, where he was on university business, and repeated almost verbatim his previous observation about the evacuee women:

> February of this year. Cold, biting wind. The wind throws dry sleet into my face, blows little snow snakes along the streets of this strange city, the likes of which I have never seen. There is a little snow twister next to the Mickiewicz monument. The marble, mediaeval magnitude of Polish Catholic churches. The Gothic, fifteenth century. Narrow, four-story houses, three windows on the façade. Blackened statues of saints, cramped stone courtyards. Suddenly, just around the corner, a huge gray building, with a cupola and statues, reveals itself. The Diet of Galicia—"Lviv derzhavnyi universitet" [Ukrainian: Lvov State University.—translator's note.] And the Biblical-looking Jews, with their sidelocks and gray beards, and those women in fashionable coats with broad shoulders, wearing bright colorful headscarves, brown ski boots… Alienated and exhausted, they now stroll around the market of a huge city on the Volga. Why and how did they end here, so far from home? All the time, one can hear the sharp sounds of Jewish speech. Against one's will, one is reminded of Khurenito[48] and his opinions about the fate of the Jewish people. Indeed, fate of this unlucky, talented people, fate itself pushes to mysticism, to Zionism. Yet, the future of this people lies in assimilation. Having no land of one's own, it is impossible to attempt to preserve all the national habits, customs and prejudices. It is reactionary and utopian to try.[49]

Mark Shumelishskii, too, met Western Jews in some hamlet on the Volga. He calls them "the Jews from Lvov." It is possible that they were indeed from Lvov, yet it is far more likely that "Lvov" stood for Shumelishskii for something "Western." "The Jews from Lvov" worked as loggers. Several families lived in a barracks-type room:

> In the past they likely were petty merchants or owners of small craft shops. They are typical Polish Jews, yet untouched by the Soviet

culture's assimilating influence. They keep together, but do not seem to be living in accord with each other. Everyone looks for the best piece of pie. They deal in second-hand items. It is their main source of income. They work as loggers only because it is the only way to obtain rights and benefits. They have no other option. This entire house, swarming with its lively and loud population, produces a distinctly unpleasant impression. These people have not realized yet that Jews can and even need to be loggers.[50]

Yet, the young Soviet intellectuals failed to find kindred spirit not only in the "Western" Jews, but even in the Soviet Jews of the provincial mindset, in the "old-regime" Jews. Grigorii Pomerants, for example, confessed that he did not take to heart the information about the Nazi extermination of Jews. He was too "Russian" and too much of a big-city dweller for that:

The Russian army's "us" crept up in my first impression of the genocide. We talked of it as of someone else's grief. And this was how I took it in—as someone else's grief. I thought of the dead as of those "shtetl Jews," that is, Jews so unlike me. And I felt compassion for them, but this compassion was an alienated one.

Pomerants hoped that the majority of Jewish intellectuals had a chance to evacuate from big cities. And, he thought, at war, where millions of people perish, it is no use to sort the dead according to their ethnic origin.[51]

Yet, whether the Soviet internationalist Jews wanted it or not, in the Soviet Union not just the dead, but the living, too, were sorted according to their ethnic origin. The Jews felt it more acutely than the other peoples of the Soviet Union. The majority of Jewish veterans who reminisced about their combat experience spoke of battlefront camaraderie and believed that antisemitism flourished in the rear, not on the front. Even considering that the veterans tend to idealize the past as they juxtapose this glorious war past to the following years of pervasive state-level antisemitic policies (compared to which the antisemitic incidents at the front may seem insignificant), it is hard to imagine that *all* of the veterans tend to color the truth of war to such an extent. It is clear, on the other hand, that the antisemitic sentiment in the rear does not quite fit with the "brotherhood of the nations" on the front. The rear and the front were not separated from one another by an impenetrable wall; they were more like communicating vessels. From the rear, came reinforcements and letters; to the rear, went the wounded, who then went back to the front.

Many veterans tell other stories of the front-line inter-ethnic relations; those stories do not resemble at all the conventional narratives of war camaraderie and "the friendship of the peoples of USSR." In the words of infantry Private Viktor Granovskii, "if anyone in my company knew I was Jewish, I'd get a bullet in my back during the first engagement… I am not exaggerating… I would have been shot in the back."

Granovskii was lucky: a captain in the Military Registration Office in Gomel, processing his paperwork (at that moment, in 1943, Granovskii was just sixteen), entered his nationality as "Belorussian" instead of "Jew," and his patronymic as "Mikhailovich," not "Moiseievich". Thus, Granovskii became "Vitia, a Belorussian from Gomel"; he spoke Russian with a Belorussian accent, having studied in a school in Belorussia for six years. He wrote:

> I was amazed at how vehemently my fellow company men hated Jews. I get it, a good part of the soldiers were criminals, many others had to spend two or three years on the occupied territories, and maybe the German propaganda influenced them, but the rest of them, the "regular Soviet citizens," where did their hate come from? At the halts, in the dugouts, I heard only, "kikes did this, kikes did that," "we're fighting and these Jewish lice fatten themselves in the rear." It was painful for me to hear that, I was all shaking with indignation on the inside, but I kept silent.[52]

It is safe to assume that the degree of Jewish servicemen's assimilation into Soviet Russian culture played a large role in their experience, as did their ranks, positions and the people in their immediate milieu. According to the front diaries, Jewish soldiers' relationships with their comrades-at-arms differed from those of the Jewish commanders. Lieutenant Vladimir Gel'fand constantly lamented the insults and harassment he sustained as a Jew. He felt completely alone, and sometimes shared his feelings with his comrades, which only exacerbated the situation and sometimes even brought real suffering. On the other hand, Senior Lieutenant Boris Suris, who believes he has a "rotten" disposition, wonders: "I do not understand why I have so many friends, why everybody treats me well, why complete strangers say hello to me and ask me about how things are."[53] He never mentions any problems in connection with his Jewishness.

Sergeant Pavel El'kinson's diary does not feature the word "Jew" at all. More than sixty years after the war ended, El'kinson told the interviewer that during the war "there were no open manifestations of antisemitism." In his view:

> The people from Central Asia had it worse. Take nutrition, for example. They did not eat pork. It was a tragedy for them. They would go hungry, well, some of them would adjust to the diet in the end, but many would not… I do not know, maybe I was lucky, but I never felt I was treated badly in the army. Maybe it is because I never was in any position to feel it, I was a private all the way.[54]

El'kinson himself had no problems eating pork, just as other Soviet Jews. Lieutenant Boris Itenberg wrote to his wife that, to celebrate the Red Army Day, they were served "red wine and roasted *pork* [italics mine—OB] (which I'm very fond of)." And, a month later: "We are very well fed. Roasted *pork* with potatoes prevails, and I wouldn't want anything else."[55] David Kaufman entered a memory of a simple wartime pleasure into his diary: "We are staying the night … having gorged ourselves on *pork* and milk."[56] Kaufman's grandfather and especially his great-grandfather (who was very religious and even abandoned his family in order to go to Palestine before his death) would surely turn over in their graves if they knew how loosely their good-for-nothing progeny interpreted the tradition.

It has to be noted that no matter how soldiers treated the Jews,[57] their treatment of the people from Central Asia and Caucasus was much worse. Suris, who found himself in a hospital as a result of his wound, noted the persistent hatred and contempt exhibited towards "national minority soldiers, [called derisively] the '*ioldash*.'"[58]

Sergeant Boris Komskii encountered no ethnic conflicts either. His diary features interesting details. One bit is about the peasants' dark, mediaeval antisemitism: "the Germans cannot shut up about the Yido-Bolsheviks, and the women call the Germans 'the mute Yids,'" he writes in the town of Trubchevsk on October 11, 1943. The peasants' mediaeval consciousness is not a rhetorical figure here: the Russian word for "German" is *nemets*, meaning "the mute one." The word appears in Rus' in the Middle Ages upon the first encounter with the Germans, whose speech was incomprehensible to the Russians: thus, they became "mute" for all practical purposes. "Mute Yids" comes from the times of Muscovite Rus': it seems that some Soviet peasants failed to notice that the times had changed. It is characteristic that the Germans, who inflicted real suffering on the peasants, are conflated here with the Jews, who were never a staple of the Orel backwoods.

Another entry in Komskii's diary explicitly discusses the attitudes towards Jews in the army. Once, an aged soldier who recognized Komskii as a Jew told him that he conceals his nationality because of the "horrendous antisemitism" reigning supreme in the army. Komskii, who told the soldier that he was wrong to do this, wrote his story down:

> His name is Il'ia Cherepakha, he is from Belorussia. It was there that he first encountered the Germans. All of his family, 35 people, were killed. He himself was executed two times, but he stayed alive and had to crawl from under the corpses at night. His wife is a Ukrainian, she married a Vlasovite, she wandered around with this Vlasovite, and then she left for Germany. He was in the partisan detachment: "We drank their blood. I avenged my family in full." There was a lot of antisemitism among the partisans, too. A Jew who happened to be a commissioned officer still could not occupy a command position. Only when the front came nearer did the situation begin to change. He told me a lot of stories about his life as a partisan and about his life here, in the army, and I regretted that I said he was wrong [to conceal his Jewishness]. What moral right do I have to judge a person who has seen and experienced a thousand times more than I did? I cannot justify a person who abandoned his nationality. But man's dearest possession is life. It is given to him but once,[59] and he lost it twice already.[60]

Incidental entries in the soldiers' diaries convincingly demonstrate that antisemitism was not a thing of the past in the country of internationalists. It was evident from the first days of war at different levels, at first—primarily at the basic level of social organization.

In early September 1941, near Leningrad, Viktor Zalgaller realized that the lieutenant who led the group of soldiers (in an attempt to avoid being surrounded by the Germans) did not know his way. Zalgaller, who did, attempted to lead the group, and very soon heard one of the soldiers uttering: "Why would we follow a kike?" In the end, the group did follow Zalgaller, and managed to reach the Soviet positions. Another episode concerns Zalgaller's first acquaintance with Nikolai Tikhonov, who "answered my orders to move with 'I'm not going with a kike.' Then he became my best friend and [I even remember him saying to me], 'Viktor, we're not taking this scumbag with us.'"[61]

Irina Dunaevskaia, too, had encountered antisemitism. Once, she accidentally overheard a phone conversation of an officer who she refused to date, with another "military girl." The officer was mocking her burr, implying her nationality. No mistake could be made: the officer was using a well-known shibboleth, *kukuruza* (corn). Offended, Dunaevskaia slapped him. Another episode, when Dunaevskaia was already in Germany, was not as harmless: at the central square of the town of Puschendorf, Dunaevskaia wrote, a blind-drunk major, "looking at me with his mad white eyes, started shouting some nasty antisemitic words and raised his hand against me, trying to hit me in the face." Dunaevskaia, who recalls she could not think straight at the moment, pulled out her gun and shot. Luckily for her, the bullet went above the major (Dunaevskaia did not have many chances to shoot during the war), and a captain accompanying her quickly led her away from the scene of the incident.[62] The authors of the diaries, nevertheless, did not draw any far-reaching conclusions from such unpleasant incidents.

The Soviet government persistently battled antisemitism, especially in the late 1920s and early 1930s. In the war years, fighting antisemitism was out of the question: any such government effort would effectively support the basic thesis of the Nazi propaganda, which stated that the Soviet rule is the rule of Jews. This thesis, however, was taken in approvingly by a significant part of the Soviet population.

The war influenced the Soviet soldiers' and officers' perception of their own Jewishness in very different ways. There is no data to measure the growth or decline in the Jewish identity of Soviet servicemen during the war, of course. Yet, it is evident that for some, Jewish identity was perceived as a peculiarity inherited by birth, which may not have precisely hindered their existence but did not add much to it, either.

In January 1945, in Poland, Viktor Zalgaller's platoon had to sleep in the forest, on the fir twigs, at -13°F. Zalgaller went up to the river, where he discovered several dugouts built by another unit (there was no space for

Zalgaller's platoon) and a makeshift bathhouse. An old Jew was in charge of the bathhouse. Zalgaller recollects,

> He asked me, "Yid?"—"Yes." He started mumbling something in Yiddish. And I couldn't understand. "Never mind," he said, "You go to sleep, and I'll sing over you." And then I go to sleep on the damp plank bed ... For the first time in my life, my *odd* [italics mine—OB] national identity helped me.⁶³

Others, while remaining internationalists, may have first felt the sense of belonging to Jewry. Boris Tartakovskii wrote down, on May 10, 1944, his impressions of the last several days. The unit where he served was in Ukraine, liberating it from occupation. In Kamenets-Podolsk, the Old Town became a town of death:

> At one time, these districts were populated, for the most part, by Jews. The Germans first turned the Old Town into a real ghetto, and then destroyed all its inhabitants and the district itself. The steps ring hollow in the city squares overgrown by grass, the broken windows watch you silently, scraps of wallpaper can still be seen on the remnants of wrecked walls. Only seldom can one see a man pass by, or a stray dog run through. Silence.⁶⁴

The Jews who were assembled in the Zhmerinka ghetto (included in the Romanian Transnistria), were lucky: the Germans, who replaced the Romanians, did not have time to shoot them. In the morning when Tartakovskii came to Zhmerinka,

> the town was full of people who came back to life. For the first time in two-and-a-half years they could walk the streets with their head raised high, freely and independently, without the degrading yellow star on their chests. The pickets with barbed wire are demolished, the horrifying border is no more. It was a moving sight ... And for the first time in my life I regretted that I do not know the Jewish language.⁶⁵

Grigorii Pomerants was "moved" on the way back from Germany, at Majdanek, when he saw "children's shoes piled together": he "felt as if the dead were [his] own children, and for the first time [he] could relate to the words of Ivan Karamazov about little children who are completely innocent."[66] This response is very characteristic for a Russian-Jewish intellectual: the tragedy of the Jewish people allows him to "fully" comprehend an idea of a Russian writer, an idea that is one of the most humanistic in Russian literature, even though it belongs to a character in Dostoevsky's most antisemitic novel.

On the other hand, the tragedy of the Jewish people and their personal war experience did not seem to affect the identity and the course of life of these diarists in any great measure. All of them survived the war and had relatively successful careers. Boris Komskii became a war reporter; when he retired, he moved to Lvov. Until recently, he was an editor of a local Jewish newspaper. He still laments the "misfortune"—the fall of the Soviet Union. Pavel El'kinson became an engineer, and was a shop superintendent at a large factory in his native Zaporozh'e. He lived in Israel for several years, raising his granddaughter together with his wife. He then came back to Zaporozh'e—the climate of Israel proved too harsh for an aging man. The granddaughter, of course, stayed in Israel. Viktor Zalgaller became a scientist and obtained a doctorate in Physics and Mathematics. In 1990s, his "odd" national identity allowed him to immigrate to Israel. Irina Dunaevskaia received her degree in Hittitology and worked at the Leningrad branch of the Soviet Academy of Sciences Institute of Eastern Studies. She lives in St. Petersburg. Boris Suris graduated from the Academy of Arts in Leningrad and became an art scholar. Unfortunately, his war diary was not published until nearly twenty years after his death. Boris Tartakovskii worked at the holy of holies—the Institute of Marxism and Leninism, a department of the Central Committee of the Communist Party of the Soviet Union. His war diaries, too, were published posthumously.

A direct opposite was the course of life of Grigorii Pomerants, who spent three years in the labor camp in the later years of Stalin's rule and went on to become a famous scholar of culture and a dissident. Vladimir Gel'fand's career was not exceptional—he taught history and political science at a vocational school in Dnepropetrovsk. He died in 1983, and his voluminous diary was published by his heirs who moved to Germany. It is noteworthy that Gel'fand's diary was never published in Russian as a book.

All in all, even after the war, these diarists remained Soviet Jews (with the exception of the "antisoviet" Pomerants). More *Soviets* than Jews, that is.

Notes

1. The study was implemented in the framework of the Basic Research Program of the National Research University Higher School of Economics in 2012. This article was written, in part, during the time of the Ina Levine Invitational Fellowship at the U.S. Holocaust Memorial Museum in academic year 2009-2010. The author wishes to thank the staff of the Center for Advanced Holocaust Studies for their invaluable help.
2. *Evreii na voine: Dvukhnedel'nyi illustrirovannyi zhurnal* (Moscow, 1915).
3. A. L. Abramovich, *V reshaiushchei voine: Uchastie i rol' evreev SSSR v voine protiv natsizma* (St. Petersburg: DEAN, 1999); F. D. Sverdlov, *V stroiu otvazhnykh: ocherki o evreiakh—geroiakh Sovetskogo Soiuza* (Moscow: Kniga i biznes, 1992); F. D. Sverdlov, *Evreii—generaly vooruzhennykh sil SSSR* (Moscow, 1993); F. D. Sverdlov, *Voiny-evreii na frontakh Velikoi Otechestvennoi* (Moscow: Kholokost, 1999); F. D. Sverdlov, *Entsiklopediia evreiskogo geroizma* (Moscow: Dograf, 2002).
4. *Eynikayt* (1943), March 15. Cited from F. D. Sverdlov, *Entsiklopediia evreiskogo geroizma*, 10. For more on Ehrenburg, see Chapter 2 of the present volume.
5. For more on this topic, see Catherine Merridale, *Ivan's War: Life and Death in the Red Army, 1939-1945* (NY: Picador/Metropolitan Book, 2006).
6. For a discussion of available letters and diaries, see Chapter 1 of the present volume.
7. Viktor Nekrasov (1911-87) and Vasil' Bykov (1924-2003) became known as writers of realistic, "trench truth" prose about the war.
8. Z. M. Chernilovskii, *Zapiski komandira roty* (Moscow: Prospekt, 2002), 83.
9. "Vasyl' Bykov – N. N. Nikulinu, 25 March 1996," in N. N. Nikulin, *Vospominaniia o voine* (St. Petersburg: Izdatel'stvo Gos. Ermitazha, 2008), 236.
10. G. F. Krivosheiev, ed., *Rossiia i SSSR v voinakh XX veka. Poteri vooruzhennykh sil* (Moscow: Olma-Press, 2001), table 121. Also see Sverdlov, *Entsiklopediia evreiskogo geroizma*, 11-12. The total loss of the Jewish population (including those who resided in the territories annexed by the USSR in 1939-1940) was 2733 thousand people, or 55% of the total Jewish population of the Soviet Union in June 1941. This is more than 10% of all human losses in the Soviet Union during the Great Patriotic War. See M. Kupovetskii, "Liudskie poteri evreiskogo naseleniia v poslevoennykh granitsakh SSSR v period Velikoi Otechestvennoi voiny," in *Vestnik evreiskogo universiteta v Moskve* 2.9 (1995): 152, Table 9.
11. M. Altshuler, *Soviet Jewry on the Eve on the Holocaust: A Social and Demographic Profile* (Jerusalem: The Centre for Research of East European Jewry, 1998), 125; Yuri Slezkine, *Era Merkuriia: Evrei v sovremennom mire* (Moscow: Novoe Literaturnoe Obozrenie 2005), 288.
12. Chernilovskii, *Zapiski komandira roty*, 16.
13. M. G. Shumelishskii, *Dnevnik soldata* (Moskva: Kolos, 2000), 37.
14. V. N. Gel'fand, *Dnevniki 1941-1946*, entry on June 28, 1942. Online version at http://militera.lib.ru/db/gelfand_vn/05.html (accessed October 30, 2013).
15. Gel'fand, entry on September 10, 1942.
16. Gel'fand, entry on September 12, 1942.

17. Gel'fand, entry on September 27, 1942.
18. Irina DunaevskaiaDunaevskaia, *Ot Leningrada do Kenigsberga: Dnevnik voennoi perevodchitsy* (1942-1945) (Moscow: Rosspen, 2010), 8.
19. Shumelishskii, *Dnevnik soldata*, 19. Entry in March 1942.
20. Boris Suris, *Frontovoi dnevnik* (Moscow: Tsentrpoligraf, 2010), 85.
21. N. Inozemtsev, *Tsena pobedy v toi samoi voine: Frontovoi dnevnik* (Moscow: Nauka, 1995); *Frontovoi Dnevnik* (2nd edition) (Moscow: Nauka, 2005).
22. V. Tsymbal's detailed diary consists of twelve notebooks in his small handwriting and covers the years 1942-45. The diary is used courtesy of V. Tsymbal's son, Yevgenii, a film director.
23. Dunaevskaia, *Ot Leningrada do Kenigsberga*, 5-7.
24. Dunaevskaia, *Ot Leningrada do Kenigsberga*, 123, entry on January 1, 1943; ibid., 76, entry on October 30, 1942.
25. P. El'kinson. *Diary* (Blavatnik Archive, New York). I would like to take the opportunity to express my gratitude to the Blavatnik Archive and its Head, Iuliia Chervinskaia, for letting me use the scans of Pavel El'kinson and Boris Komskii's diaries. Both diaries will be published in full in Volume 6 of the *Archive of Jewish History*.
26. V. Zalgaller. "Byt voiny," in *Vestnik* (Baltimore) 11.270 (2001): May 22. Online version at http://www.vestnik.com/issues/2001/0522/win/zalgaller.htm (accessed October 30, 2013).
27. M. Altshuler, *Soviet Jewry on the Eve on the Holocaust*, 34-35, 120, 308.
28. Zalgaller, "Byt voiny."
29. More than 43 thousand planes were lost in the war as a direct result of combat operations; 45 thousand more were lost as a result of accidents (*Rossiia i SSSR v voinakh XX veka*, 479-80 [Table 186], and 482-83 [Table 187, 188]).
30. Shumelishskii, *Dnevnik soldata*, 5.
31. Ibd., 16.
32. Dunaevskaia, *Ot Leningrada do Kenigsberga*, 129, entry on January 8, 1943.
33. Zalgaller, "Byt voiny."
34. Dunaevskaia, *Ot Leningrada do Kenigsberga*, 166, entry on February 22, 1943.
35. Interview given by Boris Komskii to Leonid Reines, Lvov, June 27, 2009. The text of the interview courtesy of the Blavatnik Archive.
36. Here and later, Boris Komskii's diary is cited from a scan courtesy of the Blavatnik Archive.
37. "Vanyusha" is a colloquial name given by the Red Army soldiers to the German rocker mortar *Nebelwerfer*.
38. Here and later Pavel El'kinson's diary is cited from a scan courtesy of the Blavatnik Archive.
39. Il'a Erenburg, "Ubei," in *Krasnaia zvezda*, July 24, 1942.
40. Komskii, entries on August 9 and 10, 1943.
41. David Samoilov, *Podennye zapisi* (Moscow: Vremya, 2002), Vol. 1, 164. Entry on June 16, 1943.

42 El'kinson.
43 Suris, *Frontovoi dnevnik*, 80, entry on January 22, 1943.
44 Ibid.
45 Dunaevskaia, *Ot Leningrada do Kenigsberga*, 281-82, 283. Entries on January 14 и 15-23, 1944.
46 Ibid., 193, entry on April 20, 1943.
47 Zalgaller, "Byt voiny."
48 The reference is to a character in Il'ia Ehrenburg's 1922 novel, *The Extraordinary Adventures of Julio Jurenito and his Disciples.*
49 B. G. Tartakovskii, *Iz dnevnikov voennykh let* (Moscow: AIRO-XX, 2005), 32-33.
50 Shumelishskii, *Dnevnik soldata*, 37.
51 G. Pomerants, *Zapiski gadkogo utenka* (Moscow: Rosspen, 2003), 86.
52 http://www.iremember.ru/content/view/735/2/lang,ru/ (May 16, 2010).
53 Suris, *Frontovoi dnevnik*, 136.
54 Interview given to Leonid Reines, Zaporozh'e, June 13, 2009.
55 B. S. Itenberg, letters to his wife from February 26 and March 16, 1945 (B. S. Itenberg's personal archive).
56 David Samoilov, *Podennye zapisi*, Vol. 1, 208 (February 4, 1945).
57 On Soviet Jewish intellectuals' national identity, as well as on Red Army's attitudes towards Jews, see: Oleg Budnitskii, "The Intelligentsia Meets the Enemy: Educated Soviet Officers in Defeated Germany, 1945," *Kritika* 10.3 (Summer 2009): 647-56.
58 Suris, *Frontovoi dnevnik*, 128. Entry on June 16, 1943. For more on the non-Russians in the Red Army, see: Leo J. Daugherty III, "The Reluctant Warriors: The Non-Russian Nationalities in Service of the Red Army During the Great Patriotic War 1941-1945," *The Journal of Slavic Military Studies* 6.3 (September 1993): 426-45.
59 Translator's note: Komskii quotes from Nikolai Ostrovskii's 1932 novel, *How the Steel Was Tempered*, a Soviet classic.
60 Komskii, entries on January 7, 1945, Novo-Malinowo, Poland.
61 Zalgaller, "Byt voiny."
62 Dunaevskaia, *Ot Leningrada do Kenigsberga*, 328, 370-371. Entries on July 29, 1944, and February 1, 1945.
63 Zalgaller, "Byt voiny."
64 Tartakovskii, *Iz dnevnikov voennykh let*, 176.
65 Ibid., 171.
66 Pomerants, *Zapiski gadkogo utenka*, 158.

Chapter 4

Jews as Cossacks:
A Symbiosis in Literature and Life
Gennady Estraikh

In the compartmentalized Soviet world of letters, Yiddish literati were the principal holders of the "license" for portraying Jews. Therefore, translations of their works also prevailed among Russian books on Jewish aspects of the war. Such writers as Ikhil Falikman and Mikhail Lev focused on writing novels of wartime Jewish experiences and the Sovetskii Pisatel' (Soviet Writer) publishing house, the main Soviet producer of belles-letters, kept releasing Yiddish and Russian versions of their books.[1] Motifs of wartime friendship between Jews and non-Jews dominated the literary and journalistic production authored by Yiddish writers, such as Falikman and Lev, who in the 1940s belonged to the milieu of the Jewish Anti-Fascist Committee, were destined to survive the Stalinist suppression, and regrouped around the Moscow literary journal *Sovetish heymland* (*Soviet Homeland*), established in 1961.[2]

Trying to keep their balance walking along the peoples' friendship tightrope, writers populated their works with "good" and "bad" fictional embodiments of various ethnic groups. The lack of the "balanced approach" ingredient in the recipe for a socialist realist work might be construed as nationalism. Writers were reminded about the need for balance, for instance, in Nikita Khrushchev's speech of March 8, 1963 to the leading Soviet cultural figures. In his critique of Evgenii Evtushenko's poem "Babii Iar," the Soviet leader argued that the poet failed to "show political maturity" and represented "things as if only Jews [had been] the victims of the fascist atrocities." Setting an example of an ideologically correct approach, Khrushchev recalled a certain Kogan, a former Kiev functionary of the Young Communist League, who was among the German POWs captured during the Stalingrad battle.

An interpreter with the Field Marshal von Paulus's staff, Kogan exemplified a Jewish traitor.³ In this climate, writers tended to show in their works both Jewish and non-Jewish Nazi collaborators. Thus, a balanced set of villains and heroes was one of the factors that made possible the publication of Anatolii Rybakov's Russian novel *Heavy Sand*; its Yiddish translation promptly appeared in *Sovetish heymland* (issues 4, 5 and 6, 1979).⁴ In his novel *The Time*, Aron Vergelis, editor of *Sovetish heymland*, went so far as to describe a partnership among a Zionist agent, a Russian Nazi collaborationist, and the most publicized adventurer of Nazi Germany, Otto Skorzeny.⁵

Jewish heroism, too, had to be balanced against non-Jewish heroism. In the late 1940s and early 1950s, leading Yiddish writers were accused, and some of them executed, for "spreading the notion" that the Jewish people "displayed supposedly exceptional heroism in the struggle against fascism."⁶ Soviet Yiddish writers and editors would not forget this lesson, though their positive characters, most notably Red Army soldiers and officers, always, even before the repression, appeared as convinced internationalists. This chapter focuses on the "friendship of Jews and Cossacks" as one of the directions of prewar propaganda campaigns and a recurring trope in writings devoted to the Great Patriotic War.

* * *

Traditionally, Jews considered any representatives of the Don, Kuban, or other communities of warriors-cum-farmers—who were predominantly Russian, but before the revolution belonged to a special social estate, enjoyed vast autonomy, and served in separate cavalry detachments of the army—as enemies. On numerous occasions the tsarist government used Cossack units as a repressive force. In the Jewish press and other contemporary reports, particularly during the First World War, they usually appeared as bloodthirsty, wild beings, who found pleasure in violence against Jews. "When the Russian army passed through many towns and villages, especially when there were Cossacks, bloody pogroms took place."⁷ During the Civil War, Cossacks also acted as perpetrators of anti-Jewish pogroms, which essentially continued the same wave of mass violence.⁸

Soviet Yiddish writers presented a different pattern of Cossack-Jewish relations. Thus, for Zalman Lifshits, the protagonist of Khaim Melamud's novel *In the Beginning of Summer*, a seminal event took place five years before the war, during a competition between collective farmers from the Jewish colony (village) Novozlatopol (*Nayzlatopol* in Yiddish), in southeastern Ukraine, with their counterparts from the Don Cossack *stanitsa* (village) Tsimlianskaia. Zalman, a young chairman of a Jewish collective farm, was born and grew up in the Jewish colony, established in the 1840s as part of the tsarist government's efforts to cultivate among Jews a "useful" segment of the population. The years of military service in the Red Army made Zalman an experienced cavalryman. In Tsimlianskaia, however, people did not know about his atypically Jewish background, and Zalman's riding skills astonished the Don Cossacks. As a sign of their appreciation (and good sportsmanship), they decided to include him on the list of local Cossacks, and to present him with a Cossack uniform and a sword. That episode determined Zalman's fate during the war. When, in the summer of 1941, following the beginning of the German-Soviet (or "Great Patriotic") War, Zalman was drafted into the Red Army, he wound up in a Cossack unit.

It was not easy to be the only Jewish soldier among hereditary warriors recruited from Cossack *stanitsas*. Andrei, a soldier from the same squadron, singled out Zalman for his Jewish name and for having questionable Cossack credentials. Zalman, however, tolerated Andrei's jokes, realizing that these quips entertained other soldiers in the difficult days of retreat. Still, he was surprised when Andrei chose him as a partner in a reconnaissance assignment—to get to a forest situated a couple kilometers from the frontline trenches, hide there, and monitor the situation on a highway. It was an ill-fated expedition: the highway was full of German tanks, cars, and motorcycles; both soldiers found themselves surrounded by the enemy troops and understood that they would be taken as POWs. Andrei, who heard Zalman speaking Yiddish while sleeping, warned him to be careful and suggested that he use a non-Jewish name. Thus, Zalman became Zakir, a Tartar. Andrei approved this choice—first, Zalman "looked like a Tartar"; second, even Grigorii Melekhov, the protagonist of Mikhail Sholokhov's novel *And Quiet Flows the Don*, had Tartar blood. Ultimately, the uniform saved Zalman, because not one of the Nazis and their collaborators expected to find a Jew among the captured Cossacks.

Following some period of incarceration in a camp, Andrei and Zalman seized the moment to escape when their group of POWs was marching westward, dispatched to Germany as slave labor. Freedom came with a price: Zalman fell into a pit and broke a leg. Andrei did not leave Zalman behind;

he put him back on his feet by boiling for him a healing mixture of pine tar, needles of spruce, bark of birch, and oak leaves. Eventually, the two friends joined a Czech partisan group, and thus ended the Cossack-Jewish storyline, which appears as flashbacks in the main narrative, whose two-dimensional characters ("good" Jews and non-Jews and "bad" Jews and non-Jews) interact mainly in the summer of 1945, after Zalman's demobilization.

The Cossack-Jewish trope appears also in the writings of Shmuel Gordon (1909-1998), a writer of the same generation as Khaim Melamud (1907-1993).[9] In one of Gordon's stories, several Jewish collective farmers from Crimea survived the German occupation, hiding in a Kuban Cossack *stanitsa*.[10] Like Melamud's Zalman Lifshits, the central character of Gordon's other story entitled "A Fruit from the Tree of Life," the Jewish collective farmer Shiye-Mikhl Royz, became a heroic soldier in a Cossack division.[11] In the style of Sholem Aleichem's Tevye the dairyman, Shiye-Mikhl the cavalry man tended to talk to himself about urgent problems of his life:

> The Germans have concocted about us, Jews, more calumnies than the number of stars in the sky. One of the calumnies is that we, Jews, are cowards. I myself have seen so many surrendered Germans with raised hands and with faces pale as death. I asked a few of them: tell me, feed my curiosity, did you have the occasion to see an armed Jew with raised hands? Did you? They answered that no, they didn't. Can you see now who the cowards are—Germans or Jews?[12]

* * *

It is no coincidence that both Melamud and Gordon decided to portray their soldiers of the Cossack divisions as dwellers in Jewish villages. Partly, it had to do with their own involvement in the lives of the five Jewish national districts, which before the war existed in the European part of the Soviet Union. Melamud used to live in Novozlatopol, the administrative center of one of the districts, where he served as editor of the local Yiddish newspaper and wrote his early literary works. Although Gordon was a Moscow dweller, he visited Jewish villages many times, particularly in Crimea, and developed a name for himself as a writer on Jewish colonization. More important was the role of the Jewish peasants in the Soviet and (partly) non-Soviet model of contemporary Jewish life. To many enthusiasts of Jewish nation-building through agricultural colonization, the Soviet Union was a happy place, particularly as the design of Soviet Jewish territorial units began to come into view. According to Boruch Glazman, the American Yiddish prose writer, the Soviet Jewish agricultural colonization "is a great joy for all of us, because here also our life is being normalized, because a peasant class is being created among Jews—and not only in the Soviet Union but among the whole Jewish people; a peasant class that must bring new freshness and new content in our lives."[13]

"Normalization" meant making Jews "productive," economically independent, and physically strong. Jews, particularly of older generations, often considered Sovietization as compliance with *goyish*—rather than simply radically new—moral principles. As I contended elsewhere, this perception was natural for people who lived in a binary world where "Jewish" meant *comme il faut*, "correct," whereas *goyish* was a generic term for deviation from the norms accepted in Jewish society.[14] Cossackness represented the ultimate *goyishness*, combining its positive and negative stereotypes. In the poem "Buy cigarettes!" (an allusion to Herman Yablokoff's popular song "Papirosn"), by the American Yiddish poet Malka Lee, a young Jewish female street vendor is sexually attracted to a Cossack whose "lion's eyes" undressed her while she was patting his horse like her "grandfather's *tephillin*."[15] Significantly, Cossacks were antipodes of the stereotypically feeble dwellers of the shtetl, which had been written off by modernizers of various hues as a bastion of backwardness and a dead weight on the modern economy. The historian Yisroel Bartal describes the influence of the Cossack model upon the outlook and behavioral patterns of Zionists who moved to Palestine in the beginnings of the twentieth century.[16]

The appeal of Cossackness to Jewish communists found its best-known expression in Isaac Babel's literary portrayals of the Civil War. Babel adopted the Cossack hero, although the "historical Cossacks were enemies of his people."[17] During the Civil War, some Jews joined the Chervone (Red) Cossacks military units, formed in Ukraine to fight on the side of the Bolsheviks. Several Jewish "Red Cossacks," such as Dmitrii Shmidt (David Gutman), Semen Turovskii, Mikhail Zyuk (Nekhamkin), and Il'ia Dubinskii became senior commanding officers of the Soviet cavalry corps.[18] The Cossack model again played a role in the 1920s and 1930s, during the Soviet Jewish colonization drive, when thousands of shtetl dwellers resettled to Crimea, southeastern areas of Ukraine, and, from 1928, to

Birobidzhan. The migrants had to be brave and strong "like Cossacks" in order to overcome the momentous difficulties of rebuilding their lives in the new, often hostile environment. Their trailblazing endeavors also had to become an important factor in fighting antisemitism. Special excursions to the colonies would be organized in order to convince non-Jewish citizens that the Jewish population had thousands of real toilers, similar to all other hardworking peasants.[19]

The Cossack topic found its place also in literary portrayals of Jewish life in Birobidzhan. Viktor Fink, who in the early 1930s wrote the Russian play *Novaia rodina* (New homeland), included in its *dramatis personae* positive and negative characters representing three groups of the Birobidzhan population—Jews, Cossacks, and Koreans—and reinforced the positive characters' brotherhood through mixed marriages, such as Jewish-Cossack and Jewish-Korean. Emanuil Kazakevich, whose 1932 poetic collection *Birebidzhanboy* (Birobidzhan construction) marked the beginning of Yiddish *belles-lettres* publishing in that part of the world, portrayed the celebrations of May 7, 1934—when the Far Eastern territory was granted the status of the Jewish Autonomous Region—as an interethnic event, which was welcomed also by the local Amur Cossacks.[20] To all appearances, some local Cossacks did hope that the Jewish resettlement would facilitate the rebuilding of their habitat, devastated by the Civil War.[21]

* * *

Khaim Melamud did not invent the Cossack-Jewish competition. Indeed, in 1936 a group of Jewish collective farmers had won the contest in Tsimlianskaia, and their success was immortalized in numerous articles and stories, while the German Jewish writer Lion Feuchtwanger, who visited the Soviet Union in 1937, "was told of big, friendly contests between non-Jewish and Jewish settlements in the Ukraine, in the Crimea, and in the region of the Don. Don Cossacks told me that it was not the fact that the Jews had beaten them in agricultural competition which had overcome their former mistrust, but that the Jews had proved themselves to be the better riders."[22]

On April 27, 1936, six representatives of the Novozlatopol district arrived at the old *stanitsa* of Tsimlianskaia, today the town of Tsimliansk, about 300 kilometers from Rostov-on-Don. The place was best known for its wine, mentioned in Alexander Pushkin's poetic novel *Eugene Onegin*. During the

Civil War, Tsimlianskaia was one of the centers of Cossack resistance to the Soviet regime. In 1919, when the Bolsheviks conducted the "decossackization," or, the campaign of merciless suppression of resistance in that area, the Soviet tribunal established in Tsimlianskaia oversaw the execution of hundreds of people.[23]

The reasons for sending the Jewish delegation to Tsimlianskaia went well beyond routine propaganda exercises orchestrated countrywide on the eve of the May Day proletarian holiday. First, the competition and the press campaign around the visit had to demonstrate the momentous achievements of Jewish collective farmers, and that by this time they had nothing in common with the "parasitic" shtetl dwellers, who attracted ridicule and violence. To a considerable degree, the Soviet regime further developed the tsarist government's strategy of (to use the term made current by Benjamin Nathans) "selective integration," or, the process of gradual dispersing of certain, most notably "productive," categories of Jews into the broader society.[24] In 1926, a strategic program had divided the Jewish population into two groups: proletarians and other productive cohorts who should take a short cut to socialism and all but certain assimilation, and "non-productive elements" who were encouraged to settle in rural areas, where their route to integration would involve the stage of consolidation into a socialist Jewish nation of toilers.[25] A decade later, Soviet ideologists sought to show the accomplishments of their social engineering.

Second, Cossack readiness to forge a friendship with Jews had to indicate their radical transformation, proof that years of efforts to win them over had achieved success. The timing of sending the Jewish delegation was carefully chosen by the propaganda apparatus: on April 20, 1936, a week before the Jewish delegation's arrival in Tsimlianskaia, a decree issued by the Soviet government hailed the socialist transformation of the Cossacks and, essentially, absolved them of their sins of fighting against the Red Army during the Civil War. According to the decree, Cossacks were no longer debarred from being drafted into the Red Army. Moreover, that year five existing cavalry divisions of the Red Army were converted into Cossack ones.[26]

Shmuel Godiner, a leading Yiddish prose writer in the pre-war Soviet Union (killed in action in 1941), paid much attention to the competition, authoring two documentary stories—with strong elements of "mythic realism"—about the Cossack-Jewish fraternization in the spring of 1936.[27] The first of the two pamphlets came out in Russian in July 1936, hot on the heels of the events, whereas the second story, published in Yiddish in 1939, was more fictionalized. In the spirit of the new relations between Germany and the Soviet Union, the 1939 story did not contain anti-fascist rhetoric, whereas the 1936 version condemned the "ugly snout of Germany's chauvinist fascism;"[28] an old Cossack was happy to see that Jews could be fine swordsmen and, mentioning the fascists, suggested that "we'll together chop off [their] heads."[29]

The winner of the competition, Matvei (Motl) Berdyshev, became the prototype for Melamud's Zalman Lifshits. Like Lifshits, Berdyshev chaired one of the Jewish collective farms. Godiner's chronicle does not mention that any Jewish rider had been included on the list of local Cossacks, but it contains a story of a Cossack uniform given as a present. It was a gift to the whole delegation, though, rather than solely to Berdyshev. On March 4, 1936, a special badge, the "Voroshilov Rider," was established for those civilians who achieved good results in military training as cavalrymen and women. (Marshal Kliment Voroshilov, People's Commissar for Defense, was extolled by Leyb Kvitko in his children's poem *Letter to Voroshilov*, whose Russian translation from the Yiddish, by Samuel Marshak, came out in August 1937 with a printrun of one million copies.) According to Godiner, Berdyshev promised the Cossacks to commit himself to forming and training in Novozlatopol a detachment of Voroshilov riders.

In his last, autobiographical novel, *My 1930s Years*, Melamud once again returned to the events of Jewish and Cossack delegations:

> Two national groups, whose reciprocal hatred had a centuries-old history. Jewish children would be scared by Cossacks, and Cossack children were frightened by Jews. The only difference was that Jews were victims of pogroms, while Cossacks were the perpetrators. And suddenly the history brought them together in a completely different way and revealed to each other their real face. Initially, not everything went smoothly in their encounter. I remember how in some Jewish villages people ran away, catching sight of a group of Cossacks dressed in blue riding pants with a red stripe down the side. I also remember how in Tsimlianskaia, when a delegation of our district visited it, one old Cossack, Kirei Ivanovich, said: "Until I see it with my own eyes, I'll never believe that Jews cultivate land, plant wine grapes, and raise stock."[30]

Next year, Kirei Ivanovich, and several other Cossacks, visited the Jewish district. By the end of the visit he was so overwhelmed by what he had seen that he told during the farewell dinner:

> "I want to ask you to forgive me. My whole life I hated Jews. So, when my son married a Jewish woman in Rostov, I damned him. Now I am telling all of you that I am revoking my condemnation."
>
> Then the milkmaid Rosa Lurye […] stood up, approached the old Cossack and told him:
>
> "Speaking of that… My daughter married a Cossack in Rostov. Perhaps, he is your son. It means that we are family now. Let's give each other a hug!"[31]

There is no way to tell if Melamud's memoirs describe real events of the 1930s or (most probably) represent a literary remake of the final scenes—the wedding of Roza (a Jewish re-settler) and Kornei (an Amur Cossack)—in the 1936 Soviet talkie *Seekers of Happiness*, set in Birobidzhan.[32]

* * *

The Red Army did not have Ukrainian Cossack units, but the historical importance of Ukrainian Cossackdom was recognized by introducing, in October 1943, the Order of Bohdan (or "Bogdan") Khmelnytskyi, the only Soviet military order named after a non-Russian historical personality. At the same time, the town of Pereiaslav, where in 1654 the so-called Pereiaslav Council of the Russian Tsar Aleksei Mikhailovich and the Ukrainian Cossacks led by Khmelnytskyi had laid the foundation for Ukraine's integration into the Russian state, was renamed in Pereiaslav-Khmelnytskyi.[33] (Incidentally, Pereiaslav is also known as the birthplace of Sholem Aleichem.) A legendary figure in Ukrainian history, *Hetman* (Commander) Khmelnytskyi has quite a different reputation in Jewish history: generations after generations of Jews condemned him as a monstrous personality, responsible for the annihilation of whole Jewish communities, most notably in 1648 and 1649. Any mention of Khmelnytskyi would be accompanied by the curse "may his name be blotted out" ("ימח שמו וזכרו": *yemakh shmoy vezikhroy*).

In January 1940, a remarkable academic event took place in Moscow, at the History Institute. The Odessa scholar Saul Borovoi had successfully defended his doctoral dissertation on Jewish history in Ukraine. One of the chapters concentrated on the Khmelnytskyi Uprising. Borovoi argued that it was wrong to follow the tradition of presenting the Jewish population as victims of the Ukrainian Cossacks and peasants. Rather, the Jews were part of the general military conflict, supporting predominantly the Polish colonizers, and, as such, were a fair game of the Ukrainian militants. This interpretation of one of the bloodiest pages in modern Jewish history provoked outrage among Yiddish literati, notably the literary historian Isaac Nusinov and the poets Peretz Markish and Shmuel Halkin, who could not accept that—in Halkin's words—the "murderer" Khmelnytskyi was hailed as the leader of the Ukrainian national-liberation movement.[34]

In fact, Borovoi's dissertation was a footnote in Khmelnytskyi's Soviet re-mythologization in the late 1930s and early 1940s, with a play and a film script by the Ukrainian writer Aleksandr Korneichuk at the center of the process under Stalin's personal control.[35] There is little doubt that Stalin, Korneichuk, and the majority of other politicians and intellectuals involved in the canonization of the legendary Ukrainian figure, did not pursue any anti-Jewish agenda. Rather, in the fall of 1943, when the Red Army was liberating Ukraine, the government sought to send an encouraging message to the second-largest ethnic group of the Soviet population.

In the meantime, the 1943 decision to aggrandize Khmelnytskyi resonated in Jewish circles all over the world. The pro-Soviet press cultivated the image of Cossacks as liberators from the Nazis. For instance, Zishe Weinper, a left-wing American Yiddish poet and activist, had developed this theme in his poem "When a Cossack Rider Came to the Dniepr River."[36] Granted, similar topics had also inspired left-wing literati, including the Canadian poet Sholem Shtern, before October 1943.[37] Meanwhile, the New York-based *Forverts*, which was the biggest Yiddish daily, contended that the Soviet government's decree was a step similar to renaming a town after Hitler. Mendel Osherowitch, a *Forverts* journalist (he also played a leading role in the American Federation of Ukrainian Jews), quoted various sources estimating the number of Jews murdered by Khmelnytskyi's Cossacks at between 100,000 and 650,000.[38] The Israeli historian Shaul Stampfer, who has analyzed the scale of anti-Jewish violence in seventeenth-century Eastern Europe, comes to the conclusion that the chronicles gave very inflated numbers of victims and that "the impression of destruction was greater than the destruction itself."[39] Indeed, the "impression" was very strong, and the

London newspaper *Jewish Chronicle* commented on the Soviet government's decision:

> This man Chmielnitski [sic] was a Cossack Hetman in the seventeenth century and under his direction 300,000 or more Ukrainian Jews were massacred by the Cossacks. Naturally this elevation to the status of a patriot or a hero whose deeds are presumably to be regarded as an inspiring example to all Russians was not a little painful to Jews. It is not surprising, therefore, that the two distinguished representatives of the Jewish Anti-Fascist Committee in Russia—Professor Mikhoels and Lt.-Col Fefer—who are now in London, should have been asked to explain.[40]

The director of the Moscow Yiddish theater, Solomon Mikhoels, and the Yiddish poet Itsik Fefer were winding up their tour of the United States, Canada, Mexico, and Great Britain. On the longest, American leg of the Soviet Jewish representatives' trip, the Cossack topic had already been mentioned in one of Fefer's speeches. The poet, who was referred to as a lieutenant-colonel of the Red Army (during the war many writers had military ranks as political instructors), told a joke that should show the American Jews that their Soviet counterparts had become stronger than the Cossacks, once the most terrifying enemy of Russian Jews:

> I was told that a tourist from Argentina came to Birobidjan [sic] once and he stopped to talk with a Jewish settler there.
> "How are things going," he asked.
> "Very well," answered the Jew from Birobidjan.
> "Who are your neighbors," the Argentinean wanted to know.
> "Cossacks."
> "Cossacks?"
> "Sure," said the Jew from Birobidjan, "but we leave them in peace."[41]

The *Jewish Chronicle*, however, expected a serious explanation. "Their [Mikhoels and Fefer's] reply that what Chmielnitski [sic] did was to lead a rising of subjugated Ukrainian masses against their Polish oppressors and those whom they believed to be associated with them can scarcely be regarded as very satisfactory." The newspaper also expressed the hope that Soviet Jewish combatants would not "through an act of sheer forgetfulness, be insulted by decoration with the order of Bogdan Chmielnitski [*sic*]."⁴² Nonetheless, a number of Jews were "insulted" by this award and, apart from a couple of unverified cases when Jewish combatants rejected the order,⁴³ they, products of Soviet upbringing, either did not know about Khmelnytskyi's historical record or saw the calumnious event as ancient history, with no direct relevance to their world.

Coincidentally, or most probably intentionally, among the first officers honored by the distinction was the Lieutenant Colonel Iosif Kaplun.⁴⁴ Among the Jews decorated by the Order of Bohdan Khmelnytskyi were also the Heroes of the Soviet Union Army General Iakov Kreizer, Colonel General Leontii Kotliar, and Lieutenant General Matvei Vainrub. The poet Boris Slutskii, whose war-time memoirs provide an insight into the interethnic relations in the army, argued that by 1943 soldiers of various nationalities had got used to each other and that their relations became much friendlier than in the earlier stages of the war. He also wrote about Jewish officers who did their utmost to show that Jews were not cowards. One of the bravest officers was a young man, not physically very strong, a philology student at the Kiev University before the war. He volunteered for a reconnaissance detachment, and in the short interval of six months was decorated by four orders, including the Order of Bohdan Khmelnytskyi. Significantly, in Slutskii's memoirs the award is not mentioned as an affront to Jewish combatants.⁴⁵

It is no coincidence that Natan Rybak (1913-78), a Ukrainian writer of Jewish origin and a Soviet person of the same generation as Slutskii (1913-86), portrayed Khmelnytskyi as a heroic figure in his 1947-53 novel *Pereiaslav Council*. In general, the absence of the seventeenth-century massacres in the Jews' historical imagination can be seen as a litmus test for Sovietization. In 1943, Lazar Fagelman, a heavyweight among the *Forverts* writers (in 1962-68 he would edit the paper), wrote about the abyss that had divided the Soviet Jewish and the American Jewish worlds: "Now we have to understand that Soviet Jews differ from us: their habits, values, and manners are different; their vision of life is different; they have a different attitude to people, to the world and to all political, economic, and moral problems."⁴⁶

* * *

I have not come across any statistics of Jewish participation in the Red Army cavalry detachments, though it is known that Jewish cavalrymen fought in various regiments and divisions, including Cossack ones. Thus, Efim Podoksik served as a private, sergeant, and sergeant major in a Cossack detachment. According to him, he never had problems with being a Jew among non-Jewish cavalrymen. When Mikhail Sholokhov visited his regiment, Podoksik's commanders were happy to show him off to the venerable novelist.[47]

Indeed, a Jewish cavalryman belonged to a rather exotic category of soldiers serving in Cossack units. In fact, I remember very well Matvei Berdyshev, whose wife happened to be one of my mother's sisters. To the best of my knowledge, during the war he was a Red Army officer, a captain, but had nothing to do with Cossacks. Thus, the wartime travails of Zalman were a product of the creative imagination of Khaim Melamud, an old friend of Berdyshev. In general, an ethnic breakdown of the Red Army's Cossack units, if such statistics could be found, would certainly reveal low numbers of Jewish cavalrymen, because such units had been formed in the areas populated by Cossacks.[48] Jews, on the other hand, predominantly lived in urban areas of Ukraine, Belarus, and Russia and, apart from some enthusiasts (for instance, successful "Voroshilov Riders"), had little to do with riding. No doubt, this is one of the reasons why the realists (even socialist ones) Melamud and Gordon described their fictitious Jewish Cossacks as village dwellers.

The situation was somewhat different with officers of Cossack detachments. Career officers as well as mobilized doctors, political instructors (often teachers in their prewar life), and other categories of reserve officers certainly included some number of Jews. It is illuminating, for instance, that among the officers of the 5th Don Cossack Corps was Vladimir Piatnitskii, whose father Osip (Iosif) Piatnitskii, a leading Bolshevik, had vanished during the Stalinist purges. Vladimir Piatnitskii describes how his father's friends, who survived the Stalinist purges and the war, were shocked to see him in a Cossack uniform and reminded him that his father hated Cossacks, particularly the Don ones.[49]

The topics of Jews' participation in the Red Army and their heroism dominated the communications and correspondence written by the literati of the Jewish Anti-Fascist Committee.[50] However, stories about Jewish cavalrymen can be counted on the fingers of one hand. For instance, the novelist Hershl Polyanker wrote a documentary story about Avrom Revutski, whom the writer met in one of the regiments fighting in the north Caucuses. In June 1941, Avrom finished secondary school and several days later volunteered to a cavalry unit of the Red Army. Although Avrom had previously never sat astride a horse, he soon became a confident rider and a valiant soldier. By the end of the short story, he appears as a seasoned warrior, instructing new recruits before their baptism of fire.[51]

Yet, among the stories that appeared in the newspaper *Eynikayt* (*Unity*) of the Jewish Anti-Fascist Committee, more attention was paid to Jewish commanding officers of cavalry regiments and divisions. The journalist Moyni Shulman introduced to readers Colonel Khaim (Efim) Popov, commander of a Kuban Guards Regiment. Granted, the colonel's Jewishness is clear only from his name; otherwise it does not play any role in Shulman's text.[52] More pronounced is the Jewishness of the commander of a cavalry division, and later of a cavalry corps, General Vladimir Tsetlin. Shmuel Persov, the author of the documentary story "The Glorious Cavalry Man," mentioned that Tsetlin grew up in Odessa, in a proletarian Jewish family, and that he spoke Yiddish.[53]

Biographies of Jewish cavalry generals and colonels often reveal their participation in the First World War and the Civil War, and then a military career in the Red Army. For instance, Vladimir Tsetlin was a soldier in the tsarist army, in the division under the command of General Anton Denikin. During the Civil War, Tsetlin, an officer in the brigade of the Red Army commander Grigory Kotovskii, fought against Denikin's White Guard troops. In the 1930s, he was lucky to be spared during the Stalinist repressions, when tens of thousands of officers and generals, including Jewish ones, were executed or sent to Siberian labor camps.

The ethnicity of the legendary general Lev Dovator, commander of a guard cavalry corps, remains up for debate. The majority of scholars and journalists maintain that Dovator was Jewish, though his Russian biographers and Aron Abramovich, the Israeli authority in the field of Jewish participation in the Red Army, contended that the general was born into a family of Belorussian peasants.[54] Even if Dovator had nothing to do with Jews, his Jewish legend began to circulate soon after (or even before) his heroic death in December 1941. In the beginning of 1942, Solomon Mikhoels announced that his Yiddish theater, evacuated from Moscow to Tashkent, would stage a play devoted to Dovator, "the Soviet Jewish general who led the Cossack attack on the Nazis."[55] A volume released in February 1943 by the Soviet embassy in the United States carried the following quote of Mikhoels: "The popular Jewish playwright, David Bergelson, is writing a play for us about the talented Jewish cavalry general, Lev Dovator, who covered his name with glory in the present war."[56] In reality, Bergelson, mainly a novelist, eventually wrote a play set in medieval Italy.[57]

A Red Army commanding officer, an uncle of the protagonist, appears in Anatoly Rybakov's 1979 novel *Heavy Sand*: "Uncle Misha was mad about horses. He would give his soul for the chance to gallop a horse with a Cossack saddle, or a cavalry saddle or bareback." Rybakov painted this character from life. During the First World War, his sixteen-year-old uncle Misha run away from the shtetl to join a cavalry squadron and then became a Red Army commander. In his analysis of Rybakov's novel, Gary Rosenshield comes to the conclusion, "The uncle achieves what the narrator of Babel's Cossack stories can only dream of: the ability to ride a horse like a Cossack, a guarantee of never being mistaken for a Jew."[58] It echoes the remark made by one of Isaac Babel's characters: "A Jew who mounts a horse ceases to be a Jew and becomes a Russian."[59]

My own experience of growing up with an uncle (also an Uncle Misha, or Meir), who was a career officer and by the end of the war led a regiment in the elite Kantemirov Guards Division, and of meeting many other career officers of that generation, did not leave me with an impression that any of them sought to hide their Jewishness. Uncle Meir was a diehard Communist and a bitter anti-Zionist, but he spoke Yiddish at home and, generally, remained a proud Jew. No doubt, such people did not mount a horse or (more typically) become members of tank or gun crews in order to be Russians—never mind that the Soviet bureaucratic system made it next to impossible to change the nationality in their documents. In any case, their motivations were, as a rule, similar to the motivations of their Russian, Ukrainian and other Soviet peers, namely to become a Red Army officer, a status that was very high in Soviet society. As for cavalry or Cossack soldiers and officers, their heroic image was particularly attractive, both for Jews and non-Jews.

In other words, it is important not to confuse two essentially different agendas: first, that of Soviet Jews, who intentionally or unwittingly found themselves in the Red Army; second, that of Soviet Jewish—most notably Yiddish—writers who portrayed the events of the Great Patriotic War. While personal agendas might have specifically Jewish elements, such as setting an example of Jewish bravery or using the military career as a route to complete assimilation, Soviet Jewish writers "combine[d] writing about the Holocaust in the strict sense of the word with writing about resistance"[60] and sought to emphasize heroism in their Jewish characters. Cavalrymen appear in their oeuvre as one of the ultimate symbols of Jewish heroic resistance.

In the story "Flora," written by Der Nister in 1946, the protagonists, heroic Jewish partisans Berl and Flora, dance "in the Cossack manner" at the reception given by "a Jewish social organization" (presumably, the Jewish Anti-Fascist Committee) on May 9, 1945:

> In a non-Jewish way, he gave her a lift with his right hand, on the right side of her back, going in a trot and a circle around her. She smiled, yielded, and danced with him.
>
> Then, he exchanged the right hand for the left. Holding the left side of her back, he performed the same as before—this time with bended knees, crouched at half his height and dancing as if seated.[61]

Thus, a Cossack dance became a dance of victorious Soviet Jews, whose symbiosis with hereditary Russian warriors did not denationalize them (significantly, Berl and Flora celebrated the victory at a Jewish organization), but allowed them to achieve an extraordinary level of heroism. Socialist realist writers continued to extol this symbiosis in the remaining years of the Soviet Union's existence.

Notes

[1] See, for instance, the Russian books by Ikhil Falikman: *Obrechennye berut oruzhie* (1959); *Chernyi veter* (1968 and 1974); *Ogon' i pepel* (1977); by Mikhail Lev: *Partizanskie tropy* (1958); *Sud posle prigovora* (1982); *Esli by ne moi druz'ia...* (1968, 1976, and 1986); *Izbrannoe* (1983); *Dlinnye teni* (1989).

[2] For the periods of the Jewish Antifascist Committee and the *Sovetish Heymland*, see Shimon Redlich, *Propaganda and Nationalism in Wartime Russia: The Jewish Antifascist Committee in the USSR, 1941-1948* (Boulder, CO: East European Quarterly, 1988); Joshua Rubenstein and Vladimir P. Naumov, eds., *Stalin's Secret Pogrom: The Postwar Inquisition of the Jewish Anti-Fascist Committee* (New Haven and London: Yale University Press, 2001); Gennady Estraikh, *Yiddish in the Cold War* (Oxford: Legenda, 2008).

[3] Priscilla Johnson and Leopold Labedz, *Khrushchev and the Arts: The Politics of Soviet Culture, 1962–1964* (Cambridge, MA: MIT Press, 1965), 181–83.

[4] The novel first appeared in the Moscow Russian literary monthly magazine *Oktiabr'* 7-9 (1978).

[5] Gennady Estraikh, "Literary Images of the 'Birobidzhan Generation,'" *Slavic Almanac* 11.1 (2005): 91.

6   Rubenstein and Naumov, eds., *Stalin's Secret Pogrom*, 487.

7   S. Ansky, *The Enemy at His Pleasure: A Journey Through the Jewish Pale of Settlement During World War I*, ed. and trans. Joachim Neugroschel (New York: Metropolitan Books, 2003), 6. See also Gennady Estraikh, "Viewing World War I from across the Ocean: The New York Yiddish Daily 'Forverts' on the Plight of East European Jews," *Jews and Slavs* 23 (2013): 371-84.

8   Oleg V. Budnitskii, *Rossiiskie evrei mezhdu krasnymi i belymi, 1917-1920* (Moscow: Rosspen, 2005), 286.

9   For Melamud and Gordon, see, e.g., Mikhail Krutikov, "Soviet Yiddish Literature of the 1960s-80s and its Russian Translations," in *Yiddish in the Contemporary World*, ed. Gennady Estraikh and Mikhail Krutikov (Oxford: Legenda, 1999), 80-82; Gennady Estraikh, "Shmuel Godiner: A Yiddish Writer in 'the Ocean of Russian Literature,'" in *The Yiddish Presence in European Literature: Inspiration and Interaction*, ed. Joseph Sherman and Ritchie Robertson (Oxford: Legenda, 2005), 134-51.

10 Shmuel Gordon, *Vechnaia mera* (Moscow: Sovetskii Pisatel', 1981), 189.

11 Shmuel Gordon, *Milkhome-tsayt* (Moscow: Emes, 1946), 7-12.

12 Gordon, *Milkhome-tsayt*, 8.

13 See Gennady Estraikh, "From 'Green Fields' to 'Red Fields': Peretz Hirschbein's Soviet Sojourn, 1928-1929," *Jews in Russia and Eastern Europe* 56 (2006): 61.

14 Gennady Estraikh, "Pig-breeding, *Shiksas*, and Other *Goyish* Themes in Soviet Yiddish Literature and Life," *Symposium* 57.3 (2003): 164.

15 Malka Lee, *Lider* (New York: Yidishe Kultur Gezelshaft, 1932), 98.

16 Israel Bartal, "Kazak i beduin: novyi mir natsional'nykh obrazov," *Vestnik Evreiskogo universiteta* 6.24 (2001): 263-78.

17 Judith Deutsh Kornblatt, *The Cossack Hero in Russian Literature: A Study in Cultural Mythology* (Madison: University of Wisconsin Press, 1992), 120.

18 Il'ia Dubinskii, *Trubachi trubiat trevogu* (Moscow: Voenizdat, 1962); Abraham Pribluda, "Yidishe komandirn tsvishn di sovetishe kozakn," *Morgn-Frayhayt*, September 26, 1973: 19; October 7, 1973: 5; October 9, 1973: 3; November 4, 1973: 3. (Dr. Simon A. Prussin kindly sent me copies of these newspaper articles).

19 Estraikh, "From 'Green Fields' to 'Red Fields,'" 68.

20 See Estraikh, "Literary Images of the 'Birobidzhan Generation,'" 83.

21 Felix Rynsky, "Jews and Cossacks in the Jewish Autonomous Region," *Refuge* 12.4 (1992): 21.

22 Lion Feuchtwanger, *Moscow, 1937: My Visit Described for My Friends* (New York: The Viking Press, 1937), 89.

23 Peter Holquist, "'Conduct Merciless Mass Terror': Decossackization on the Don, 1919," *Cahiers du Monde russe* 38.1-2 (1997): 127-62.

24 Benjamin Nathans, *Beyond the Pale: The Jewish Encounter with Late Imperial Russia* (Berkeley and Los Angeles: University of California Press, 2002), 78, 311.

25 Gennady Estraikh, "The Soviet Shtetl in the 1920s," *Polin: Studies in Polish Jewry* 17 (2004): 203.

26 Albert Seaton, *The Horsemen of the Steppes: The Story of the Cossacks* (New York: Barnes & Noble, 1996), 234.

27 See the two pamphlet editions: Samuil [Shmuel] Godiner and D. Lipshits, *Vstrecha v Tsymle: Dogovor druzhby kolkhoznikov kazakov i evreev* (Moscow: Der Emes, 1936); Shmuel Godiner, *Der yontev fun frayntshaft* (Moscow: Der Emes, 1939).

28 Godiner, *Der yontev fun frayntshaft*, 5.

29 Ibid., 26.

30 Khaim Melamud, "Mayne draysiker yorn," *Sovetish Heymland* 1 (1991): 61.

31 Ibid.

32 See Grigorii Kobets and Iogann Zel'tser, "Iskateli schast'ia: kinostsenarii," *God za godom* 4 (1988): 236-38.

33 Serhy Yekelchyk, *Stalin's Empire of Memory: Russian-Ukrainian Relations in the Soviet Historical Imagination* (Toronto: University of Toronto Press, 2004), 35-37.

34 Saul Borovoi, *Vospominaniia* (Moscow and Jerusalem: Gesharim, 1993), 200-16.

35 Vasilii Tokarev, "Vozvrashchenie na p'edestal: istoricheskii kommentarii k fil'mu 'Bogdan Khmel'nitskii' (1941)," *Istoriohrafichni doslidzhennia v Ukraïni* 18 (2008): 427-55.

36 Zishe Weinper, "Ven kozak oyfn ferd iz gekumen tsum Dnyepr," *Morgn-Frayhayt*, November 6, 1943, 3, 1.

37 See Gennady Estraikh, "Yidn un kozakn," *Forverts*, May 18, 2007, 11.

38 Mendel Osherowitch, "A shtot in Ukrayne oyfn nomen fun pogromshtik Bogdan Khmelnitski," *Forverts*, October 23, 1943, 2, 5; October 25, 1943, 2, 6.

39 Shaul Stampfer, "What Actually Happened to the Jews of Ukraine in 1648?" *Jewish History* 17.2 (2003): 222.

40 "A Cossack 'Hero,'" *Jewish Chronicle* (London), November 5, 1943, 10. See also "The Chmielnitski Order," published in the same issue, 6.

41 Solomon Mikhoels, *Birobidjan and the Jews in the Post War World* (New York: Ambijan, 1943), 18.

42 "A Cossack 'Hero.'"

43 See, e.g., Iakov Eidel'man, *Nezakonchennye dialogi* (Moscow and Jerusalem: Gesharim, 2000), 19.

44 See, e.g., Semen Averbukh, *Nasytilis' my prezreniem...* (Kiev: Glavnaia spetsial-izirovannaia redaktsiia literatury na iazykakh natsional'nykh men'shinstv, 2000), 442.

45 Boris Slutskii, *O druz'iakh i o sebe* (Moscow: Vagrius, 2005), 120-22.

46 Lazar Fagelman, "Di sovetishe yidn un di amerikaner yidn," *Forverts*, July 12, 1943, 4.

47 Efim Podoksik, "Gde nashi korni?" *Korni* 12 (1999): 107-12.

48 See, e.g., G. M. Kurkov, "Kubanskie kazaki na frontakh Velikoi Otechestvennoi," *Voenno-istoricheskii zhurnal* 4 (2006): 13-17.

49 Vladimir Piatnitskii, *Kazaki v Velikoi Otechestvennoi Voine 1941-1945 gg.* (Moscow: Iauza/Eksmo, 2007), 6-9.

50 Dov-Ber Kerler, "*Eynikayt* during the War," in *Why Didn't They Shout?: American and International Journalism during the Holocaust*, ed. Robert Moses Shapiro (New York: Yeshiva University Press, 2003), 225.

51 Hershl Polyanker, "Der rayter Avrom Revutski," *Eynikayt*, October 15, 1942, 2.

52 Moyni Shulman, "Der kazakisher polkovnik Khaim Popov," *Eynikayt*, October 19, 1944, 3.

53 Shmuel Persov, "Der rumfuler kavalerist," *Eynikayt*, May 31, 1945, 3.

54 Aron Abramovich, *V reshaiushchei voine: uchastie i rol' evreev SSSR v voine protiv natsizma* (St. Petersburg: DEAN, 1999), 31. See also, e.g., Reuben Ainsztein, "The War Record of Soviet Jewry," *Jewish Social Studies* 28.1 (1966): 10.

55 "Soviet Jews Honour General Dovator: Hero Who Beat Nazi Blitz," *Jewish Chronicle* (London), April 24, 1942, 1.

56 *Soviet Art in Wartime: Information Bulletin. Special Supplement* (Washington, DC: Embassy of the USSR, 1943), 48.

57 Jeffrey Veidlinger, "'Du lebst, mayn folk': Bergelson's Play *Prints Ruveni* in Historical Context," in *David Bergelson: From Modernism to Socialist Realism*, ed. Joseph Sherman and Gennady Estraikh (Oxford: Legenda, 2007), 269-84.

58 Gary Rosenshield, "Socialist Realism and the Holocaust: Jewish Life and Death in Anatoly Rybakov's Heavy Sand," *PMLA: Publications of the Modern Language Association of America* 111.2 (March 1996): 245; Anatolii Rybakov, *Roman—vospominanie* (Moscow: Vagrius: 2005), 13-16.

59 Richard William Hallett, *Isaac Babel* (New York: Ungar, 1973), 37.

60 Lukasz Hirszowicz, "The Holocaust in the Soviet Mirror," in *The Holocaust in the Soviet Union: Studies and Sources on the Destruction of the Jews in the Nazi-Occupied Territories of the USSR, 1941-1945*, ed. Lucjan Dobroszycki and Jeffrey S. Gurock (Armonk, NY: M. E. Sharpe, 1993), 52.

61 Der Nister, *Regrowth: Seven Tales of Jewish Life Before, During, and After Nazi Occupation*, translated from Yiddish by Erik Butler (Evanston: Northwestern University Press, 2011), 148, 153.

Chapter 5

How the Jewish Intelligentsia Created the Jewishness of the Jewish Hero: The Soviet Yiddish Press[1]

Arkadi Zeltser

In June 1943, *Eynikayt*, the Yiddish newspaper of the Jewish Anti-Fascist Committee (JAC), referred to Major Tsezar Kunnikov, a fallen commander of a marine unit, as a "Jewish hero" (*yidish held*).[2] The appearance of this term was not a case of negligence on the part of an editor or censor. It was the expression of the views of the Soviet Jewish intelligentsia and in full accord with the practices allowed by the Soviet regime. The preceding years had already seen articles that dealt with various aspects of the ethnic identity of Jews in the Red Army during the Second World War.[3] In this context it remained to be seen how the ethnically oriented Soviet Jewish intelligentsia would relate to Jewish heroes.

Soviet propaganda devoted considerable efforts to securing maximum support for the war against Germany, both among the Soviet population and abroad. For this purpose, two basic means were employed: 1) inculcating hatred toward the enemy by spreading information about Nazi cruelty and thus creating a negative image of the enemy, and 2) creating a positive image of the Soviet hero fighting for his people, his country, and all of humanity (providing a positive model to identify with). In the spring of 1942, the Soviet Information Bureau (*Sovinformbiuro*) established five anti-fascist committees—a pan-Slavic one to attract Slavs, and ones aimed at women, scientists, youth, and Jews[4]—in order to try to gain public support abroad for the war effort. The main tool of their influence-seeking was propaganda texts sent to foreign telegraph agencies, newspaper offices, as well as anti-fascist radio broadcasts and periodical publications based in the Soviet Union itself. Among the latter was the JAC's Yiddish-language *Eynikayt*, which began to appear in June 1942.⁵ According to JAC statements, the newspaper was mainly targeted at the "mass Jewish reader brought up and reeducated by the Soviet regime," as well as readers from the territories annexed to the USSR, "who had not attended the Soviet school of life."⁶ During the war a maximum of three thousand copies of the ten thousand copies printed were sent abroad, while the remaining seven thousand were distributed in various cities of the USSR, including two thousand that were sold in stores rather than by subscription.⁷

The very appearance of information in Yiddish in the newspaper spurred ethnic identification among the heroes and readers of the articles and encouraged interest in Jewish topics. As members of the Lithuanian Division of the Red Army cited by JAC activists in regard to the *Eynikayt*, "It contains what a Jew cannot find in any other newspaper."⁸ There was certainly no other publication in the USSR in which the 18-year-old Hero of the Soviet Union Chaim (Efim) Diskin, who came from the Crimean Jewish settlement of Kadima and was a student of the Moscow Institute of Philosophy, Literature, and History before the war, could write what he did in November 1942: "I am proud to know that I am a son of the great Jewish people [*groysn yidishn folk*] that has given to the world such great people as Marx and Heine, Sholem Aleichem and Einstein, Sverdlov and Kaganovich, Spinoza and Peretz.... Our people are mighty and talented and the fascist monsters will never destroy us or force us to our knees."⁹

Many writers in *Eynikayt*—especially Shakhno Epshteyn,¹⁰ the Soviet Yiddish journalist who was *Eynikayt*'s editor from 1942 to 1945 and also senior secretary of the JAC, and Itsik Fefer,¹¹ his assistant at the newspaper, the Yiddish poet and journalist—were well aware of the propagandistic goals they were appointed to pursue, and in many ways they fulfilled this propagandistic task. Nevertheless, within the framework of Soviet political censorship (and self-censorship), the Soviet Jewish Yiddish-language intelligentsia, which was largely composed of veteran Soviet Yiddish littérateurs (poets Peretz Markish, Leyb Kvitko, and Shmuel Halkin, and the prose writers David Bergelson, Shmuel Persov, et al.), attempted to express their own ideas in the JAC newspaper and convey their concern about the fate of their fellow Jews to their usual readers both in the Soviet Union and abroad.¹² Due to the efforts of its writers and editors, for the entirety of its existence *Eynikayt* was both Soviet and Jewish, not simply Soviet, as was intended by the segment of the Party bureaucracy that criticized the JAC for failing to publish more non-Jewish material in its newspaper.¹³

The concerns of the Yiddish intelligentsia about the reputation of the Jews during the war was nowhere as strongly expressed as in *Eynikayt's* articles about Jewish heroism. In this context four questions arise: 1) Were there any new approaches in the treatment of the topic of heroism during the war as opposed to the prewar period? 2) How did the ethnic component in the treatment of heroism change during the war? 3) Did the Soviet Jewish intelligentsia deal with the topic of heroism in the Yiddish press in strict conformity with the norms set by the Soviet authorities, or did they attempt to express their own views about Jewish national problems? And 4) how did the Yiddish-language intelligentsia create the Jewishness of Jewish heroes?

Patriotic Narratives

The image of the Jewish hero was in many ways formed in correspondence with the reigning ideas of the heroic in the Soviet Union in general. In the second half of the 1930s, due to changes in both domestic and foreign policy in the USSR, propaganda espousing world revolution was replaced with that which espoused the cultivation of Soviet patriotism in various ethnic versions. Previous revolutionary heroes (like the Decembrists, Emel'ian Pugachev, and Stepan Razin) who in the 1920s had been hailed by the Mikhail Pokrovskii school of history, were replaced by the tsars and military leaders of ancient Rus', Muskovii, and the Russian Empire (like Aleksandr Nevskii, Ivan the Terrible, Kuzma Minin and Dmitrii Pozharskii, and Peter the Great).[14] At the same time, during these years a balance was preserved between the new forms of etatism and Marxism-Leninism, between appealing to traditional ethnic heroes of the past and the idea of class struggle. In this situation, when a new emphasis was being placed on the history of the Russian people, it also became legitimate to appeal to the remote past of other ethnic groups.[15]

In the 1920s, Hirsh Lekert, a worker from Vilna who was executed for attempting to assassinate Governor-General Victor von Wahl in revenge for the humiliation of Jewish workers who had been arrested, was the symbol of Jewish heroism. During this decade, Soviet streets, enterprises, schools, and Jewish agricultural cooperatives were named after Lekert. Plays and even a film portrayed his life. The need at that time for an ethnically Jewish revolutionary hero was perceived to be so great (as was the case for other ethnic groups as well) that Soviet ideologists even ignored the fact that Lekert had been a member of the Bund (an early rival of the Bolsheviks) and that

Bolshevik historiography condemned the kind of individual terrorist acts resorted to by Lekert. In the first half of the 1930s, the official attitude toward the Jewish Lekert changed, as it did toward revolutionary heroes of other ethnic groups.[16]

In 1937, Lazar Kaganovich, the Secretary of the Communist Party Committee of Moscow and a member of Stalin's inner circle, attended a performance at the Moscow State Yiddish Theater of the play "Boytre the Thief" by the Yiddish poet and dramatist Moyshe Kulbak. Kaganovich demanded that the theater's director change the repertoire by abandoning the depiction of shtetl Jews and turn instead to heroic images of the Jewish past, like the Maccabees, the leaders of the Jewish revolt in 160 BCE who rededicated the Temple; Bar Kochba, the leader of the Jews' revolt against Rome in 132 CE; or the creators of the Jewish present in Birobidzhan. The interference of such a high-ranking functionary provided legitimacy for turning to the heroic theme of historic Judea.[17] Earlier under the Soviets such subject matter was problematic, since the images of the Maccabees and Bar Kochba had been popular in Zionist discourse.[18] Kaganovich's dictum relieved the Jewish intelligentsia of the threat that they would be accused of being Jewish nationalists by other writers or by Party supervisors from the Propaganda Division of the Party's Central Committee.

In accordance with this new approach, Shmuel Halkin's adaptation of Goldfaden's play *Bar Kochba*, which was published in Moscow in 1939, was staged by the Moscow and Birobodzhan State Yiddish Theaters in the same year. In this play, Halkin, a prominent Yiddish poet and playwright who was well-known for his interest in the Jewish national past, completely fit his heroes into the transitional canon of that time. On the one hand, his heroes were national: the last words of *Bar Kochba*'s beloved Pnina, killed by the Romans, are: "My last breath is for you, my people."[19] On the other hand, the play corresponds to the Soviet approach to class: both Bar Kochba and Rabbi Akiva, the spiritual leader of the revolt against Rome, come from the lower classes (peasants), while *Bar Kochba*'s main Jewish antagonist in the play, the pro-Roman Menashe, is a rich merchant. At this time, Soviet Jewish scholars also turned to ancient Jewish history, integrating into their research both class and ethnic approaches.[20]

In the historical discourse of the early war years, when the patriotism of the Soviet peoples (first of all that of the Russians) was increasing, the previous emphasis on class struggle was completely replaced by a stress on ethnicity.

Already in the radio speech delivered by Viacheslav Molotov on June 22, 1941, following the invasion of the Soviet Union by German troops, one could note the reference to the historical tradition of the Russians repelling aggression. The current war was declared to be a patriotic one, using the term "*otechestvennaia*" ("for the fatherland"), which had been used for the Patriotic War of 1812 against Napoleon. In Stalin's speech delivered in Red Square on November 7, 1941, the Soviet leader evoked the images of the "great [Russian] ancestors" who should be emulated that day: Aleksandr Nevskii, Dmitrii Donskoi, Minin, Pozharskii, Aleksandr Suvorov, and Mikhail Kutuzov. In the effort to stir the public's patriotism, there were also increasing references to names that incarnated the pride of "the great Russian nation" (Stalin's term) in the field of culture, such as Pushkin, Tolstoy, Gorky, Chekhov, Tchaikovsky, and Glinka.[21] This trend of extolling intellectual as well as military heroes of the past provided a model for other peoples, including the Jews. As a consequence, in order to evoke national pride, publications began to hail Jewish literary and philosophical figures whose works were particularly significant for Jewish culture (like Yehuda Halevi, Maimonides, Sholem Aleichem, and I. L. Peretz), Jews who made major contributions to universal knowledge (e.g. Marx, Spinoza, and Einstein), and famous Jewish Bolsheviks (like Iakov Sverdlov, Moisei Uritskii, and Lazar Kaganovich). This process of reviving ethnic heroes of the past and referring to non-Russian Bolshevik leaders, which was taking place among various Soviet nationalities, most likely increased ethnic pride among these peoples during the war years.[22]

The rejection of the basic Bolshevik postulate of the primacy of class was expressed in the rehabilitation of the term "*narod*" (people). In the 1920s, deviation from Lenin's principle that every nation consists of two nations—the exploiters and the exploited—was viewed as nationalism, and the term "*narod*" was symptomatic of this political error. However, starting in 1937–1938 "the great Russian people" ("*velikii russkii narod*") became a positive term in the Soviet political lexicon. At this time there emerged an official Soviet hierarchy of peoples, topped by the Russians, "the first among equals," followed next by the Ukrainians and Belorussians, and then by the other titular nations (ones that were the majority in their own union-level republic of the USSR). At the bottom of the hierarchy were the remaining ethnic groups.[23]

Another development of the war years was an alteration of the regime's attitude toward religion: in order to mobilize the population for the struggle against an external enemy, the Soviet leadership compromised on its atheistic ideological principles. Despite a general distrust of the clergy, who were on the whole loyal to the regime during the war, the authorities decided to demonstrate tolerance regarding religion to allow their subjects to resort to ethno-religious symbols and rhetoric in order to foster Soviet patriotism.[24] In the Jewish context, in the spring of 1942, in an interview with the Hebrew-language newspaper in Palestine *Haàretz,* Itsik Fefer not only mentioned the Prophet Isaiah but called him a poet and a genius. In April 1944, the third rally of representatives of the Jewish people organized by the JAC inserted into a letter of greeting to Stalin the following quote in Hebrew, together with its Russian translation, taken from "ancient Jewish agada" in order to emphasize Jewish military tradition: "The Torah descended from Heaven and it had a sword in it."[25]

A synthesis of ethnocentrism and etatism formed the basis for Soviet patriotic propaganda in the years 1941-1942.[26] Nevertheless, as David Brandenberger noted, "growing Russo-centrism during the first years of the war should be considered more of a tendency than an articulate central line."[27] In such frameworks, despite their general control over them, the Soviet creative intelligentsia retained some flexibility of action in regard to interpretation of historical events.[28] Sometimes, an ethnic intelligentsia initiated steps in this area. Such initiative was demonstrated by members of the Ukrainian intelligentsia who were close to Khrushchev, the First Secretary of the Communist Party in Ukraine at that time, when they suggested the introduction of a military decoration named after Bohdan Khmelnytskyi. This step was approved by Moscow.[29] At *Eynikayt,* Epshteyn and Fefer, who were close to the Soviet authorities, established maximum boundaries for what was permitted in regard to referring to Jewish heroism. In other words, it was those people who had considerable experience in Soviet ideological activity who introduced a degree of flexibility that was compatible with the policy set from above.

In addition to general problems related to ethnic themes, there were aspects of life at this time that affected Jews specifically. A major one was the increasing antisemitism (partly "inspired" by Nazi propaganda) among part of the Soviet bureaucracy and among the Soviet population. The Soviet authorities had to decide how to react to this antisemitism, on the one hand, and how Soviet policy toward its own Jews might affect the attitude of the influential Jewish lobby in America and Great Britain toward the USSR.[30]

A noticeable increase in Russo-centric attitudes among the mid-level Soviet bureaucracy affected all non-Russian ethnic groups. This new approach, formed between the summer of 1943 and March 1944, stressed the uniqueness of the development of the Russian people and culture, as well as the positive (heroic) aspects of the Russian past and present, while condemning the nationalism of ethnic minorities unless they recognized the positive role of Russia/the USSR in their fate.[31] Along with the further strengthening of the Russians' position, epitomized by the famous toast Stalin gave on May 24, 1945 to "the great Russian people," the Soviet bureaucracy returned to an emphasis on the principle of class struggle, including the Bolshevik thesis of the existence within each nation two opposing nations. (Stalin had already referred to the Soviet-German War as a class war).[32]

The authorities' advocacy of Russian nationalism was sometimes, paradoxically, accompanied by criticism of "great power" Russian nationalistic errors. This was especially the case when it was useful for government officials, as a rule in the speeches of Party apparatchiks that were closed to the public.[33] A clear example of such criticism was the negative reaction of Party functionaries to the remarks of the historian Aleksei Iakovlev, a corresponding member of the Academy of Sciences of the USSR, at a meeting of the People's Commissariat (Ministry) of Education in January 1944. He had said: "We very much respect the nationalities that have entered our Union, we relate to them with love. But it was the Russian people who made Russian history.... We, Russians, want histories of the Russian people, histories of Russian institutions, in Russian conditions."[34]

However, despite occasional criticism, such neo-nationalistic ideas were also, apparently, popular among many Party functionaries in regard to their contemporary situation. The spring of 1943 witnessed the further advancement of Russians, Ukrainians, and Belorussians to socially significant positions.[35]

Within the framework of the existing ethnic hierarchy (with the Russians, of course, being the "elder brothers"), the hardening of the attitude toward the "middle brothers" (the non-Russian titular nations—for example, in the campaign against Ukrainian film director Aleksandr Dovzhenko at the beginning of 1944[36]) had a serious impact on what was permitted to the "younger brother" nations, as well as the Jews. However, in contrast to the Ukrainians, Kazakhs, Bashkirs, and Tatars, there was no question of Jewish rivalry with Russians in terms of the territorial expansion of the Russian

Empire and hence the evaluation of the various ethnic heroes who had fought against Russians. For this reason, the tightening of general ideological control in 1944-1945 mainly affected the Jews in regard to the topic of Jewish heroism and its sources in the present rather than in the past.

Soviet Policy and the Theme of Jewish Heroism

According to data from the JAC, of 4,463 articles sent abroad in 1942-1943, 34.3 percent were devoted to Jews in combat and another 8 percent to Jews fighting with the partisans, which was more than the those about Nazi atrocities committed against the Jews (23.9 percent).[37] Evidently, a similar situation existed in regard to material published in *Eynikayt*: the degree of attention to the topic of Jews engaged in combat that were sent abroad was the same as that in material published in the USSR. The main propagandistic methods in both foreign-published and domestic materials were also similar.

The aim of the Jewish intelligentsia to show Jewish heroism involved not only transplanting to the Jewish field propaganda devices that were generally employed during the war years, but also including a specific apologetics for Jewish courage and heroism.[38] To a certain extent, the discussion of such issues was facilitated by the fact that the authorities allowed the establishment of frameworks for the collection of this type of information. At the first plenum of the JAC in May 1942, the decision was made to establish, along with a committee to collect materials about Nazi atrocities, a commission to collect material about Jews at war—in other words, about Jewish heroism.[39] At the same time, supervision on the part of Party organs and censorship within the official frameworks did not allow the intelligentsia to express their concerns in print about the negative approach in the USSR in regard to Jews, and also limited opportunities for pride in the valorous behavior of Jews as representatives of their specific ethnic group.

Consequently, the Jewish intelligentsia, who considered it their duty to respond to these issues that were so sensitive for Jews, sometimes tried to use "code words" that were understandable to people familiar with Jewish culture, though they were not always expressed in an unambiguous manner. One of the most sensitive issues was that of inter-ethnic relations.

In the typical ethnic stereotype current among broad segments of the non-Jewish population in the USSR, the Jews were seen as merchants, not warriors. The accusation that Jews were draft-dodgers, which had been heard in the prewar period, became much more widespread during the war, and not only among the masses but also among parts of the high-ranking Soviet intelligentsia.[40] This naturally aroused Jewish concern. However, the Soviet ban on mentioning inter-ethnic conflict, which had been in effect since the mid-1930s, became stricter during the war. In harmony with a required idealized picture of the situation in the country, the head of the *Sovinformburo*, Secretary of the Central Committee of the Communist Party Aleksandr Shcherbakov, stated that only positive information should be conveyed about the Soviet Union: "Why should we reveal to those abroad that we have traitors, that they are killing Jews, Russians, and Ukrainians. It is not appropriate for us to send those kinds of articles abroad." (The occasion for these remarks was an article sent abroad by the JAC about the murder of Jews by a Belorussian Nazi-collaborator.[41]) The trend toward a uniformly positive presentation of reality (in Il'ia Ehrenburg's pungent phrase, "in the style of [triumphant] salutes"[42]) became particularly pronounced in 1944.

Under these conditions, it was not possible to level direct accusations of antisemitism, including denying that Jews were not fighting at the front. At the second plenum of the JAC in February 1943, Ehrenburg reacted to the widespread view of the lack of Jewish participation in combat by proposing the issuing of a special publication devoted to the topic of Jews in the Red Army. However, when references to this antisemitic canard were printed in *Eynikayt*, objections were raised by the bureaucrats in charge of supervising the JAC; the supervisors expressed the view that too much attention was being paid to Jewish heroism. The critics of the "exaggeration" of Jewish heroism included Jews who were working in the general Communist propaganda apparatus, who were extremely sensitive to the current Party line. One of these was Bedřich Geminder (known in the Party as Fridrich), Director of the Press Department of the executive committee of the Communist International, a former Zionist and political emigrant from Czechoslovakia who lived in the USSR from 1938, who referred to this view among the Jewish intelligentsia as "inadmissible conceit and arrogance."[43]

Subsequently, at the third JAC plenum, in April 1944, in response to the new winds from the Soviet leadership, Epshteyn referred to antisemitism only indirectly (as the "revival of the remnants of the somber past, which have not yet been uprooted") and simultaneously criticized the "whiners" among the Jews as bearers of "unhealthy, narrow nationalistic attitudes."[44] This was a return to the tactic of "fighting on two fronts," which was common in the 1920s and 1930s. It involved condemning nationalists among one's own people in order to avoid being tagged as a "nationalist" oneself.

In view of the way that nationalism was then being targeted, in May 1944 Ehrenburg responded as follows in a private letter to a Jewish woman who had complained about the newspapers' intentional disregard of the heroism of Jews and their failure to indicate the ethnic origin of Jewish heroes: "You must have developed this view because you have fallen in with very backward people who are lacking in culture."[45]

However, there was a way that Jews could criticize antisemitism in the USSR—by criticizing Nazi antisemitism. Thus, remarks condemning German antisemitism, which were quite common in JAC's *Eynikayt*, served as an unimpeachable journalistic way by which antisemitism could be broadly and seriously criticized without the risk of being branded as a nationalist. In this vein, in 1944, Itsik Fefer dared to hint that there were some Soviet citizens who, like the Nazis, were denying Jewish heroism: "The Jews are cowards— shout the fascists *and their hangers on, their choirboys, and those who run after them*" (or, in the juicy, untranslatable original Yiddish: "*nokhtantser, nokhzinger, un nokhloyfer*").[46] The following citation from A. Shefer[47] can be seen as a logical response of Jews to all antisemitic (not only German) denigrations of Jews: "… [W]ay back in hoary antiquity, when the ancestors of today's German fascists wandered in animal skins through the wild forests of Europe, the Jewish people was already one of the bearers of world civilization. Already then it had a great culture and its banners reflected the glory of outstanding military battles."[48] Shefer's remarks were not published as written. However, even in the much milder version that was published in September 1942,[49] one could detect the desire of the Soviet Yiddish intelligentsia to defend Jewish dignity. This perception of a commonality between the Nazis and Soviet antisemites was in the minds of Soviet Jews also during the early postwar period.[50]

During the war itself, *Eynikayt* devoted much attention to the topic of the revolts in the ghettos of Warsaw, Białystok, and other places, and the participation of Jews in the partisan movement, in order to emphasize courage as a Jewish ethnic characteristic.[51] Ehrenburg formulated this idea in general terms in an article devoted to the anniversary of the Warsaw ghetto uprising: "They salvaged nothing except honor—their own and that of their people."[52] Other Soviet Jewish writers attempted to show "both themselves and the whole world" that we are "as good as others" (literally "no worse than others")[53] and that Jewish fighters "do not give cause either to their parents or to the Jewish people to be ashamed of them."[54]

From the very first years of the war, Soviet authorities were very wary about the glorification of Jewish heroism itself, regardless of the general Soviet patriotic context. Thus, in May 1942, when preparations were being made for the second rally of representatives of the Jewish people, a phrase was removed from the text of Aron Kushnirov, the Yiddish poet who was in active service at the time. Kushnirov mentioned that he "experienced the feeling of national pride for the respect that [his friend battalion commissar Leibovich] had won for himself by his daring and bravery in battle."[55] In the summer of the same year, the censor likewise removed from the journal *Inostrannaia literatura* (*Foreign literature*) the German-language article "The Attempt to Destroy the Jewish People," written by Klara Blum. She had wanted to include the idea of a particular Jewish heroism that was, apparently, common among Jews at that time:

> Jews, together with Russians, Tatars, and Armenians, who are defending their Soviet homeland, in this just war alongside their brave countrymen, are playing not an equal but a particularly outstanding role. The proportion of Jews serving in the Red Army who are engaging in heroic acts ... significantly exceeds the proportion of Jews in the total population of the USSR.[56]

In order to avoid being accused of overemphasizing Jewish heroism during the course of the war, the JAC and its newspaper provided information about Jews awarded commendation for heroism in absolute numbers rather than in terms of proportional indicators. The latter would have made clear the disproportionately heroic role of Jews.[57] Only half a year after *Eynikayt* published absolute figures about the ethnic background of Soviet heroes did Epshteyn (on November 8, 1944) write in the same newspaper that, while the Jews held seventh place in the USSR in terms of population, they were fourth in terms of military honors.[58] *Eynikayt* paid particular attention to awards given to Jews of the highest honor, that of Hero of the Soviet Union, and also awards to officers and generals of the newly introduced Soviet battle commendations named after top Russian military figures of the past like Suvorov, Kutuzov, and Ushakov.[59] This information was intended to make clear that patriotism and military prowess were no less characteristic of the

Jews than their Russian counterparts. Toward the end of the war, Solomon Mikhoels touted the twice-honored Hero of the Soviet Union Colonel David Dragunskii as the most outstanding Jewish warrior in the Red Army.[60]

Despite the similarity of its approach to that of Soviet patriotic propaganda, the Jewish treatment of heroism had certain unique features. For example, the latter lacked the kind of "mobilization" rhetoric addressed to Russians and Ukrainians that encouraged them to fight to liberate their native territories. In contrast, for Jews during the war years, the slogan "*undzer land*" ("our land") meant the USSR. However, the phrase "*undzer folk*" ("our people") was ambiguous, as it could refer either to the Jewish people or the Soviet people.

From its inception, *Eynikayt* stressed that Jews were fighting both for the whole Soviet homeland and for themselves, in a war of revenge for what the Nazis had been doing to their people—as David Bergelson put it, "*Far zayn foterland un zany yidishn folk*."[61] During the initial period the newspaper sometimes stressed the idea of a specific "Jewish war" even beyond this context. In an article of June 28, 1942, Peretz Markish noted that "a depressingly terrible picture of innocent Jewish bloodshed stands before the eyes of every Jewish Red Army man; he cannot take his eyes off it; it demands: revenge!"[62] However, even in such cases emphasis was placed on the joint heroic efforts of all Soviet peoples in the fight against Nazism.

However, it should be noted that, particularly during the late stages of the war, the idea of a special war of the Jews against the Nazis contradicted the views of contemporary Soviet bureaucrats regarding patriotism. In order to subordinate the idea of a particular Jewish war into the framework approved by the authorities, at the third rally of representatives of Soviet Jewry in April 1944, Epshteyn stated that the stimulus for the Jewish fighter was not the idea of "an eye for an eye, a tooth for a tooth" (i.e. revenge only for what had been done to the Jews), but the desire to take revenge for all Soviet civilian victims.[63]

The Jewish Heroic Tradition

As with any ethnic nationalism during the war, Soviet Jewish nationalism required its own variant of a mythologized, centuries-long heroic tradition that could be linked with the contemporary situation. The need to oppose antisemitism and to reject the view that Jews were incapable of engaging in combat added motivation to this search for historical continuity. In a 1942 article titled *"Undzer shtolts"* ("Our pride") Shakhno Epshteyn wrote that "the Hitlers of various times shouted that the Jewish people are ... cowards," although in the course of world history, by virtue of their heroism, Jews have shown that this is "an unfounded libel."[64] This reinforced the need to create their conception of the continuity of Jewish heroism and military valor, and stressed specific Jewish national components.

Two articles in *Eynikayt* by A. Shefer under the general title "*Di shlakhtn traditsye funem yidishn folk*" ("The military traditions of the Jewish people"), about military heroics by Jews in ancient times, the Middle Ages, and in modern times were completely devoted to this aim.[65] Shefer's basic point was that throughout Jewish history, "heroism and courage were typical characteristics" of the Jews. His argument about a heroic tradition recalled the philosophy of Diaspora nationalism that stressed the continuity of Jewish history. Shefer saw this heroic tradition as beginning with Deborah the judge, whom he referred to as the "Joan of Arc of the Jewish people," and continuing on to include Jews who fought in American and European wars of independence in the eighteenth and nineteenth centuries. His heroes included Samson, the Maccabees, Bar Kochba, and other ancient warriors, some of whom had become symbols of Jewish nationalism and were popularized in Zionist discourse. Among Shefer's modern heroes were Jews who fought in European armies against Napoleon, whom—due to his invasion of Russia—the discourse of Soviet propaganda viewed as a precursor of Hitler.

In an effort to demonstrate the East European roots of Jewish heroism and its continuity, Yiddish critics and literary scholars Yehezkel Dobrushin and Nokhem Oyslender analyzed the image of the Jewish fighter in the work of Sholem Aleichem. Among the works by this leading Yiddish writer that recall the heroism of Jewish soldiers, these literary critics referred to a series of stories from 1915 that were collected under the title "*Mayses fun toyzent eyn nakht*" (Stories of a Thousand and One Nights). The young hero, Shmuel Moyshe, volunteers for combat during the First World War. He was motivated by Russian patriotism, which had been quite negatively evaluated in the early Soviet period but was highly appreciated in the new wartime conditions. In the literary work the Jewish hero is awarded three medals, including the St. George Cross, for valor. Dobrushin and Oyslender stressed that all the stories are permeated with hatred for the German enemy, claiming that Sholem Aleichem's protagonist is a "clearly expressed positive model," who, armed with that hatred, proceeds from one battle to the next.[66] Oyslender and Dobrushin, however, did not mention that Sholem Aleichem indicates that Shmuel Moyshe had volunteered for military service not only for patriotic reasons but also out of the desire to show that Jewish public activity was not restricted to selling fish.[67] These stereotypes might well have reminded Oyslender and Dobrushin of anti-Jewish prejudices in their own time.

Various Jewish heroes of the past, both historical and literary, were viewed as leading to the figure of the Yiddish poet Osher Shvartsman, who fought in World War I and was killed in combat in the ranks of the Red Army in 1919. This image was also important, since it related to heroism in the Soviet period itself. (According to Meir Wiener, Shvartsman was "the creator of the lofty tradition of Soviet patriotism."[68])

During the war, the term "*Shvartsman-traditsie*," i.e. the heroic tradition exemplified by Shvartsman, was coined to connect Jewish heroism of the past to that of the present. In December 1944, to commemorate the twenty-fifth anniversary of Shvartsman's death, a World War I-era photograph of him was first published, showing him in the uniform of the dragoons, with two St. George Crosses on his chest.[69] Shvartsman became a model for members of the Soviet Yiddish intelligentsia, especially for those who fought on the front lines in the Second World War (prose-writer Shmuel Godiner, Kushnirov, poet and short-story writer Shmuel Rosin, and others). Rosin wrote: "Like you, Osher, I must fight with verse and sword."[70] Another Yiddish poet, Motl Golbshteyn, stressed his identification with his idol: "And if I have to fall from a bullet that landed in my heart, on a deserted road, in a green field, then [may it be] like you, my dear Osher Shvartsman, as a warrior, a poet, and a hero."[71]

Depending on the different cultural milieus in which they were raised, Jews hailed different Jewish heroes. Itsik Fefer, a former prominent member of a proletarian group in Soviet Yiddish literature, whose background included a rich Yiddish cultural environment and who during the war clearly emphasized Jewish themes and, sometimes, even clearly went beyond the boundaries of the officially sanctioned ethnic discourse, focusing on Jewish heroes who were a part of that traditional Jewish orientation. In various war writings that were devoted to Jewish heroism, including his famous poem "*Ikh bin a yid*" ("I am a Jew"), Fefer referred to Bar Kochba and Rabbi Akiva, the Maccabees, and to Jews in Madrid who were burned in the fires of the Inquisition. Although he did not explicitly use the term "*kiddush haShem*," one does encounter in Fefer's texts the idea of martyrdom for Jewish religious values: "Our ancestors often gave their lives for their people, for their ideals. They fell not as slaves but as heroes." Furthermore, Fefer does use the Yiddish term "*kdoyshim*," meaning "holy martyrs," in referring to the mass murders of Jews. Jewish readers could easily recognize this term as a sign that the victims were killed not simply as Soviet citizens, as official Soviet propaganda proposed, but for being Jews. In addition, when Fefer contrasts activity in the humanities and in military affairs, he cites examples not only from Russian history (for example, Tchaikovsky vs. Suvorov) but also from Jewish history (Yehuda Halevi and Bar Kochba).[72]

Allusions to Jewish historical symbols were addressed not only to the Yiddish intelligentsia. For example, when representatives of the Jewish religious community of Kuibyshev sent a telegram to Stalin (in January 1943) about their contribution of ten thousand rubles to the Soviet war effort, they proposed creating a tank column named after Bar Kochba, "the immortal hero of the struggle for the liberation of our people."[73]

However, these images, including Bar Kochba and the Maccabees, were basically alien to those Jews, like Ehrenburg, who had grown up outside a Jewish environment. For them, Jewish heroes of the distant past were limited to those from the Bible, like King David. At the same time, such Biblical heroes were also used in the general (i.e. non-Jewish, Soviet) propaganda, including by heads of the Russian Orthodox Church.[74]

Of course, emphasis on exclusively ethnic heroes was not solely a Jewish phenomenon. For example, the Ukrainian intelligentsia focused on their historical anti-German tradition, preferring to recall Danila Galitskii (of Galich), a thirteenth-century prince of Galicia-Volyn, rather than heroes of Kievan Rus', whom they would have to share with the Russians.[75]

During the last period of the war, the expansion of Russo-centric attitudes among the Soviet bureaucracy and of control over ethnic topics negatively affected the attempt of the Jewish intelligentsia to create a clearly manifest, uninterrupted centuries-long historical continuity, although the drawing of analogies with specific Jewish heroes of the past was, as before, allowed.

Soviet Jewish Heroes

Eynikayt tried to link the Jewish fighting tradition of the past with the heroism of Soviet Jews. In the newspaper, Fefer compared a contemporary Jew, Shloyme Gorelik, with a historical prototype: "Thus there fell in battle a Soviet

Bar Kochba."⁷⁶ An article by D. Leitses, sent abroad under the title "A Soviet Jewish Samson," used the image of Samson to describe the death at Stalingrad of Eli Shnaider, who used his last grenade to blow himself up along with the German soldiers who surrounded him.⁷⁷

Most of *Eynikayt*'s materials hailing Jewish heroism related to examples of individual Jewish soldiers, officers, partisans, and ghetto fighters. In order to stress the connection of the hero with his Jewishness, the newspaper used the hero's original Jewish name rather than his Russian one (Yankev instead of Iakov, Chaim instead of Efim, Shloyme instead of Solomon, etc.). Often the connection of the hero to his Jewish origin was indicated by familial continuity: the hero might refer to ancestors who were soldiers under Tsar Nicholas I and about whose heroism he had heard from family members.⁷⁸ In other cases, the connection was a spiritual rather than a physical one. In an article about two different persons with the same family name, Shoykhet—a simple religious Jew and a young Soviet lieutenant—David Bergelson, in his usual manner, encouraged the reader to draw his own conclusions, in this case about Jewish continuity: "They are very different, these Jews—the pre-revolutionary Moyshe-Leyb Shoykhet and Lieutenant Shoykhet. They did not know each other, but there was something profound that Lieutenant Shoykhet inherited from the Jew Moyshe-Leyb Shoykhet."⁷⁹

Shmuel Persov's article about General Iakov Kreizer, who was a member of the Jewish Anti-fascist Committee, conveyed the General's Jewish origin by referring to a German leaflet that called upon Russian soldiers to avoid fighting under the leadership of the Jew *Yankel* Kreizer. Kreizer kept a copy of the leaflet in the pocket of his uniform. He reported that his parents had called him Yankel and said that he was proud of this name. However, when the article was published, its original title "The Jew Yankel Kreizer" was replaced by the more ethnically neutral "Hero of the Soviet Union Yankev Kreizer."⁸⁰ *Eynikayt* also reported that in one of the questionnaires that he filled out during the war years, when he already had a command position in army artillery, General Izrail Beskin listed Yiddish as his native language.⁸¹

Most often, the link of the Jewish hero to a Jewish environment was conveyed by information about his family origin and childhood. On a number of occasions, an article presented a hero's biography based on a long-lasting pre-war propagandistic model that emphasized the contrast between the poverty-stricken and humiliating life of Russian Jews before the Revolution and the vast opportunities provided to them in the Soviet period.⁸²

This emphasized the theme of Soviet patriotism, which had featured more prominently toward the end of the war. Almost all of Persov's articles were constructed in that way. An article about General Mikhail Cherniavskii illustrates the way he connected the present to the past: "In Kiev his father, Leyb Cherniavskii, crushed [*kvetsht* in Yiddish] raisins to make raisin wine for *kidesh* and *havdole*. His son exchanged his father's profession for another one: with his tanks he crushed [*kvetsht*] the German fascist hordes."[83]

Many articles highlighted the skill and intelligence displayed by Jews in combat and related how proud their non-Jewish colleagues were of them. Praise for talented and courageous Jews was often linked to their characteristics as members of the intelligentsia. Heroes were portrayed as interested in poetry and music and possessing creative talents regardless of whether they were professional soldiers or professional linguists. Thus, *Eynikayt* readers learned that Isaak Kabo, the well-known commander of a submarine in the Baltic Fleet,[84] had played the violin from childhood and intended to become an architect. However, he refocused his energies and entered a military academy. Leyb Kvitko described this combination of military valor and love for the violin, which in the Russian Jewish tradition came to be considered a "Jewish" instrument, is this way: "*S'iz Itskhok Kabo der fidl-shpiler, der fidl shpiler—torpeder-tsiler, undzer shtolts un khies*" ("That is Itshok Kabo, a violinist who knows how to aim torpedoes, our pride and our vital strength").[85]

Another means of demonstrating Jewish heroism was by providing examples of how Jews fought courageously in all branches of the Soviet armed forces, on land and sea, in the air and underwater, with the partisans and in the ghetto.[86] In fact, Jews were even pointed out in places one would hardly expect them, in forces that were quite unusual for World War II. A striking example of this was the account of the exploits of Khaim (Efim) Popov, who was a commander of a Kuban Cossack cavalry division, known in the Jewish milieu for its hostility to and condescension toward Jews.[87]

More often, though, the presence of Jews was noted in quite up-to-date forces. This corresponded to the expectations of many of *Eynikayt*'s readers to see the contemporary Jew as fully modern and successful in social terms, especially in contrast to Jews of previous times. Fefer wrote about Israel Fisanovich, a member of the Jewish Anti-Fascist Committee and a famous submarine commander in the Northern Fleet, as follows: "His grandfather, a *melamed* from Konstantingrad, might well have said, 'underwater my Isrolik is like the prophet Jonah in the belly of the fish.'"[88]

In writing about Fisanovich, Fefer included another important innovation in the depiction of the Jewish hero. Before the war the image of a hero had to have the physical features of a "muscular Soviet Jew." During the war years this characteristic was no longer obligatory. The main criterion was personal courage—the idea (stressed in the mainstream Soviet press) was that in such a terrible war anyone, including members of the intelligentsia, a woman, or a child, might become a hero. This idea was confirmed by references to official decorations for bravery that were awarded to such people. An illustration of this idea is the way Fefer describes Fisanovich's physical appearance before continuing with the signs of his military prowess: "Short, frail, with an elongated face, he stands before you in a dark blue uniform, with gold braid on his sleeves, and two Orders of the Red Banner, an Order of Lenin, and a Gold Star on his chest." A similar description was penned about a heroic airman by the young Yiddish prose-writer Hershl Polyanker: "Six combat medals adorn the chest of a short Jewish lad with two bright, almost childlike eyes."[89]

It was demonstrated that not only could Jewish men be heroes, but also Jewish women. Often the Jewish heroine was a medical instructor or a physician, almost always serving in the armed forces as a volunteer. In regard to one Jewish heroine, the prose writer Faivel Sito wrote that before the war, Ida Epshteyn focused on her undramatic medical specialization as an oculist whose main tool was a rubber pipette. However, when war came, the reader was told how this unassuming woman volunteered for front-line duty and, exchanging her rubber pipette for a scalpel, became a surgeon in a front-line hospital.[90] The heroine's link to the Jewish people was often indicated by references to relatives who had been murdered by the fascists. This was especially the case in regard to Jewish women fighting in the ranks of the partisans; for these heroines the desire to take revenge had become their life goal and, hence, the motivation for their heroism.[91]

A similar approach was taken in the depiction of heroism on the part of Jewish children in the partisan ranks. Among the heroes in the ranks of the partisans were Simka, a 10-year-old girl who succeeded in smuggling one hundred Jews out of the Minsk ghetto, and 13-year-old Yankel Bobitskii, the member of a partisan unit that blew up trains. This lad was awarded three military decorations.[92]

As in the non-Jewish Soviet press, examples of children's heroism were exploited to encourage self-sacrifice on the part of adults. However, the Jewish variant of this theme also reflected the indestructible desire that *Eynikayt* writers saw in such children (as well as in Jewish adults who had survived in Nazi-occupied territories) to remain alive and to take revenge on the Nazis for their murdered families and the destruction of their *shtetl* homes.[93]

Conclusion

Many articles in *Eynikayt*, like the articles sent abroad by the JAC, were permeated with the theme of Jewish heroism and stressed the specific ethnicity of Soviet heroes of Jewish origin. The authors of these articles evidently believed that such an approached corresponded to the wishes of Soviet Jews.

Several factors affected the way that Jewish heroism was portrayed, especially during the two last years of the war. These included: the increase of Russo-centrism and antisemitism among Soviet bureaucrats, their patronizing attitude toward the Jews as one of the "little brothers" of the Russian people, and officials' fear that Nazi propaganda regarding alleged Soviet special treatment of the Jews would undermine Soviet patriotism. Although references in *Eynikayt* to the Jewish heroes of the past were still permissible, the depiction of an uninterrupted tradition of Jewish heroism became less pronounced as limitations on ethnic distinctions were imposed in regard to history as well.

In the post-war years, the topic of Jews in the war was viewed by the authorities as "out of date" and thus basically disappeared from the pages of *Eynikayt* (with the exception of publications devoted to particular events, like Victory Day [May 9] or the fifth anniversary of the revolt in the Warsaw Ghetto). However, the publication between 1946 and 1948 of books about the heroism of Jews in the army, in ghetto uprisings, and among the partisans testified to the fact that the need among the Jewish intelligentsia to extol Jewish heroism remained strong.[94] Even Fefer, much of whose writing during the first years after the war was in an aggressively Soviet style, saw in the deeds of those Jews who revolted in the Warsaw Ghetto a guarantee of the future proud existence of the Jews. He wrote: "The events that took place five years ago in Warsaw still await the artist who will commemorate them. The farther we get from those historic days the more pain we feel and, also, the more pride in our brothers who, once again, have shown the world that our people are still alive and will continue to live."[95] However, before being published in *Eynikayt,* these words conveying the feeling of many members of the Yiddish intelligentsia were censored to reduce their Jewish national content.

The theme of Jewish heroism and the idea of the unity of the Jewish people could no longer be used to oppose to Nazi antisemitic propaganda and to mobilize Jews in the USSR and abroad to support the fight of the Soviet Union against its enemy. The Soviet authorities already had other aims.

Notes

1. I thank my friend and colleague Dr. Yisrael Elliot Cohen for his help in preparing this article.
2. "Idn—heldn fun Sovetn-Farband," *Eynikayt*, June 25, 1943.
3. Zvi Y. Gitelman, "Internationalism, Patriotism and Disillusion," in *The Holocaust in the Soviet Union, Symposium presentations* (Washington, D.C.: Center for Advanced Holocaust Studies, United States Holocaust Memorial Museum, 2005), 95–125; Mordechai Altshuler, "Hamifgash lohamim yehudim batsava haadom leshoah," *Dapim leheker hashoah* 23 (2009): 9–27.
4. On the activity of Anti-Fascist Committees, see N. K. Petrova, *Antifashistskie komitety v SSSR, 1941–1945* (Moscow: Institut Rossiiskoi istorii, 1999). On the JAC, see Shimon Redlich, *War, Holocaust and Stalinism: A Documented Study of the Jewish Anti-Fascist Committee in the USSR* (Luxembourg: Harwood Academic Publishers, 1995); Gennadii Kostyrchenko, *Stalin protiv "kosmopolitov": Vlast' i evreiskaia intelligentsiia v SSSR* (Moscow: Rosspen, 2009); Ilya Altman, "The History and Fate of The Black and The Unknown Black Book," in *The Unknown Black Book: The Holocaust in the German-Occupied Soviet Territories*, ed. Joshua Rubenstein and Ilya Altman (Bloomington and Indianapolis: Indiana University Press, 2008), xix–xxxix.
5. On *Eynikayt*, see Avraham Grinbaum, "Todaa leumit yehudit bepublitsistika hasovietit betkufat ha'eynikayt,' *Dapim leheker tkufat hashoah* 1 (1979): 213–21; Dov Ber Kerler, "The Soviet Yiddish Press: Eynikayt During the War, 1942–1945," in *Why Didn't the Press Shout? American and International Journalism during the Holocaust*, ed. Robert Moses Shapiro (Jersey City, NJ: Yeshiva University Press, 2003), 221–49.
6. "Spravka o deiatel'nosti evreiskogo antifashistskogo komiteta v SSSR za period s 1 iunia 1945 goda do 27 iunia 1946 goda," Gosudarstvennyi arkhiv Rossiiskoi Federatsii (GARF) f. 8114, op. 1, d. 919, l. 69–70. The documents from the JAC collection that are cited were examined were copies at the Yad Vashem Archives in Jerusalem.
7. GARF f. 8114, op. 1, d. 1062, l. 8–12.
8. "Plenum Evreiskogo antifashistskogo komiteta: Otchet o rabote evreiskogo antifashistskogo komiteta" (GARF f. 8114, op. 1, d. 1064, l. 70). It is difficult to assess the influence of *Eynikayt* on Soviet Jews, either in the rear or at the front since the extent of its distribution in terms of readership at that time is not clear. The responses of Jews at the front to material in *Eynikayt* that were cited by the JAC ("Eynikayt na fronte" [GARF f. 8114, op. 1, d. 919, l. 72–74]; "Otchet o rabote evreiskogo antifashistskogo komiteta" [GARF f. 8114, op. 1, d. 1064, l. 68]) reflect other matters, i.e., the need of members of the Committee to justify the significance of the newspaper rather than the actual degree of its influence. It is clear that the thousands of its essays' subjects and their relatives and friends, both at the front and in the rear, knew about such

publications. In any case, the subject of the present article is those who wrote for the newspaper.

9   "A briv funem held fun Sovetn farband Khaim Diskin," *Eynikayt*, December 5, 1942, 2. On Chaim Diskin, see the article by Rakhmiel Fish, "Held fun ratn-farband Khaim Diskin," *Eynikayt*, August 25, 1942, 3, and the book by Moshe Khashtshevatski, *Khaim Diskin: Der held fun sovetn-farband* (Moscow: Der emes, 1943).

10 On Shakhne Epshteyn, see Gennady Estraikh, *In Harness: Yiddish Writers' Romance with Communism* (New York: Syracuse University Press, 2005), 71.

11 On Itsik Fefer, see Gennady Estraikh, "Itsik Fefer: A Yiddish Wunderkind of the Bolshevik Revolution," *Shofar* 20.3 (2002): 14–31.

12 It is those members of the Soviet creative intelligentsia, and not Party functionaries, who were the initiators of the Moscow renewal of the Yiddish newspaper in July 1941. They appealed for its reestablishment on the grounds that it would significantly contribute to the "mobilization" of Soviet Jews in the fight against Nazism (Redlich, *War, Holocaust and Stalinism*, 186). On general tendencies in Soviet Yiddish literature during the war and the first post-war years, see Ch. Shmeruk, "Yiddish Literature in the USSR," in *The Jews in Soviet Russia since 1917*, ed. Lionel Kochan (Oxford: Oxford University Press, 1978), 271–76.

13 Redlich, *War, Holocaust and Stalinism*, 287–89, 291.

14 On details of this campaign, see David Brandenberger and Kevin M. F. Platt, eds., *Epic Revisionism: Russian History and Literature at Stalinist Propaganda* (Madison: The University of Wisconsin Press, 2006).

15 On Soviet propaganda in regard to the Ukrainians, see Serhy Yekelchuk, "Stalinist Patriotism as Imperial Discourse: Reconciling the Ukrainian and Russian 'Heroic Pasts,' 1939–45," *Kritika* 3.1 (Winter 2002): 57–61.

16 Arkadii Zel'tser, *Evrei sovetskoi provintsii: Vitebsk i mestechki 1917–1941* (Rosspen: Moscow, 2006), 180–81; The removal of Lekert's name was not connected to his affiliations with the Bund. The Communist fight against the historical role of the Bund, especially in Belorussia, was strong in the 1920s when he was recognized as a hero. Lekert's name continued to appear in Belorussia until 1937, when a middle-ranking functionary wrote a letter to the Party leadership pointing out the Bundist Lekert's shortcomings and, hence, the inappropriateness of naming places and institutions in Belorussia after him. Lekert's name was removed from Soviet geography in Crimea only in 1945, when there was a massive renaming of places, especially those with Tatar names (Ibid.; Nikolai F. Bugai, *Deportatsiia narodov Kryma* [Insan: Moscow, 2002], 125).

17 Jeffrey Veidlinger, *The Moscow State Yiddish Theater: Jewish Culture on the Soviet Stage* (Bloomington: Indiana University Press, 2000), 159–60.

18 On Zionist heroes, see Yael Zerubavel, *Recovered Roots: Collective Memory and the Making of Israeli National Tradition* (Chicago: University of Chicago Press, 1995).

19 Shmuel Halkin, *Bar Kokhba* (Moscow: Der emes, 1939), 100. For more details about the production of the Moscow GOSET, see Veidlinger, *The Moscow State Yiddish Theater*, 168–73. In March 1942 the Belorussian GOSET began working while under evacuation in Novosibirsk with a production of "Bar Kochba."

20 Alfred Abraham Greenbaum, *Jewish Scholarship and Scholarly Institutions in Soviet Russia 1918-1953* (Jerusalem: Centre for Research and Documentation of East European Jewry, 1978), 121-23.

21 I. Stalin, *O Velikoi Otechestvennoi voine Sovetskogo Soiuza* (Moscow: 1943), 67, 95.

22 On the influence of nationalist propaganda on the Russian population, see David Brandenberger, *National Bolshevism: Stalinist Mass Culture and the Formation of Modern Russian National Identity, 1931-1956* (Cambridge, MA and London: Harvard University Press, 2002), 160-80. There was, apparently, a basis for the charge of increased nationalism against the ethnic intelligentsias of Ukraine and Kazakhstan. See. L. Gatagova, L. Kosheleva, L. Rogovaia, and J. Kadio, eds., *TsK VKP(b) i natsionlal'nyi vopros,* vol. 2: 1933-1945 (Moscow: Rosspen, 2009), 827, 858-59, 878-82.

23 Terry Martin, *The Affirmative Action Empire: Nations and Nationalism in the Soviet Union, 1923-1939* (Ithaca and London: Cornell University Press), 451-61; Yekelchuk, "Stalinist Patriotism as Imperial Discourse," 61-63.

24 Aleksandr Livshin and Igor Orlov, eds., *Sovetskaia propaganda v gody Velikoi Otechestvennoi voiny* (Moscow: Rosspen, 2007), 541-46; Mordechai Altshuler, *Yehadut bemakhbesh hasovieti: Bein dat vezehut yehudit bevrit hamoatsot 1941-1964* (Jerusalem: Merkaz Zalman Shazar, 2007), 23-42.

25 Shmuel Valkovits, "Alilot hagvura shel hayehudim berusiya," *Ha'aretz,* May 24, 1942; *Evreiskii narod v bor'be protiv fashizma* (Moscow: Ogiz, 1945), 4.

26 On Soviet patriotic propaganda during the war, see, for example, Jeffrey Brooks, *Thank You Comrade Stalin: Soviet Public Culture from Revolution to Cold War* (Princeton: Princeton University Press, 2000), 164-94.

27 David Brandenberger, *National Bolshevism,* 120.

28 For example, there is consideration of different attitudes toward the image of Ivan the Terrible on the part of Party functionaries, historians, and figures in the arts in the article by Kevin M. F. Platt and David Brandenberger, "Terribly Romantic, Terribly Progressive, or Terribly Tragic: Rehabilitating Ivan IV under I.V. Stalin," *The Russian Review* 58 (October 1999): 635-54.

29 Yekelchuk, "Stalinist Patriotism as Imperial Discourse," 68-71.

30 Il'ia Altman, *Zhertvy nenavisti* (Moscow: Fond Kovcheg, 2002), 388, 392-93, 399, 411-13; David Brandenberger, *National Bolshevism,* 117; Kostyrchenko, *Stalin protiv "kosmopolitov,"* 94-107. The Germans kept track of the promotion of Jews in the Soviet military, their attainment of the rank of general, and Soviet press accounts of Jewish heroism in battle. Nazi propaganda presented such material as proof of Bolshevik favoritism regarding the Jews (GARF f. 8114, op. 1, d. 1942, l. 197-98).

31 Irina Il'ina, "Novye dokumenty o soveshchanii istorikov v TsK VKP(b) (1944)," *Voprosy istorii,* no. 1, (1991): 188-205; Iurii Amiantov and Zoia Tikhonova, "Stenogramma soveshchaniia istorikov v 1944 g.," *Voprosy istorii,* nos. 2-7, 1996; Livshin and Orlov, eds., *Sovetskaia propaganda,* 494-535.

32 *Pravda,* November 7, 1944.

33 Irina Il'ina, "Novye dokumenty o soveshchanii istorikov v TsK VKP(b)," 202.

34 Ibid.

35 Kostyrchenko, *Stalin protiv "kosmopolitov,"* 97, 102; Il'ia Erenburg, *Liudi, gody, zhizn'*, vol. 2 (Moscow: Tekst, 2005), 390.
36 Valerii Fomin, ed., *Kino na voine: Dokumenty i svidetel'stva* (Moscow: Materik, 2005), 382, 391.
37 "Otchet o deiatel'nosti Evreiskogo Antifashistskogo komiteta SSSR" (GARF f. 8114, op. 1, d. 1063, l. 52–54).
38 An example of such an apology for Jewish heroism is the article by Itsik Fefer, "Azoy shlogn zikh yidn," *Eynikayt*, October 5, 1944, 2.
39 "Plenum Evreiskogo antifashistskogo komiteta: Otchet o rabote Evreiskogo Antifashistskogo komiteta" (GARF f. 8114, op. 1, d. 1064, l. 1).
40 Arkadii Zel'tser, *Evrei sovetskoi provintsii*, 210–11. Such views were expressed especially by Mikhail Sholokhov (Notes of Boris Frezinskii to the publication Il'ia Erenburg, *Liudi, gody, zhizn'*, vol. 3 [Moscow: Tekst, 2005], 495). Erik van Ree examines such currents in Stalin's own outlook in his article "Heroes and Merchants: Stalin's Understanding of National Character," *Kritika* 8.1 (Winter 2007): 41–65. The view of "the inherent lack of capability" of certain peoples (Uzbeks, Georgians, Azeris, etc.), for military service was widespread in the army and, possibly, also among broad segments of the population (*TsK VKP[b] i natsionlal'nyi vopros.* vol. 2, 757, 762).
41 *Antifashistskie komitety v SSSR*, 207.
42 Andrei Artizov and Oleg Naumov, eds., *Vlast' i khudozhestvennaia intelligentsiia: Dokumenty 1917–1953* (Moscow: Mezhdunarodnyi Fond "Demokratiia," 1999), 529.
43 Redlich, *War, Holocaust and Stalinism*, 211–12, 214, 287–89; *Eynikayt*, March 15, 1943.
44 *Evreiskii narod v bor'be protiv fashizma*, 71.
45 Il'ia Ehrenburg, *Na tsokole istorii... Pis'ma 1931–1967* (Moscow: Agraf, 2004), 329.
46 Iitsik Fefer, "Felker-brider," *Eynikayt*, March 2, 1944, 3.
47 There are some indications that Itzik Fefer wrote using the pen name A. Shefer. See Avraham Grinbaum, "Todaa leumit yehudit bepublitsistika hasovietit betkufat ha'eynikayt," 217, and GARF f. 8114, op. 1, d. 854, 218.
48 A. Shefer, "Vozrozhdenie voennykh traditsii evreiskogo naroda v Otechestvennoi voine" (GARF f. 8114, op. 1, d. 82, l. 544).
49 The newspaper's variant said, "... in those distant times when the ancestors of today's German fascists first began to appear on the historical scene, the Jewish people already had a glorious past rich in immortal military heroism" (A. Shefer, "Di shlakhtn traditsie funem yidishn folk," *Eynikayt*, September 5, 1942, 2).
50 Amir Weiner, *Making Sense of War: The Second World War and the Fate of the Bolshevik Revolution* (Princeton: Princeton University Press, 2001), 191–94.
51 A number of articles in *Eynikayt* by Ber Mark were devoted to the uprisings in some of the ghettos. See *Eynikayt*, May 15, 1943, 4; July 17, 1943, 2; June 1, 1944, 2.
52 Il'ia Erenburg, "Godovshchina vosstaniia v Varshavskom getto" (GARF f. 8114, op. 1, d. 88, l. 18).
53 V. Fink, "Vstrecha s polkovnikom Dragunskim" (GARF f. 8114, op. 1, d. 160, l. 291).
54 P. Lerner, "Shestero synovei" (GARF f. 8114, op. 1, d. 179, l. 331).

55 "Rech' evreiskogo sovetskogo poeta A. Kushnirova" (GARF f. 8114, op. 1, d. 1125, l. 5).
56 Livshin and Orlov, eds., *Sovetskaia propaganda*, 663.
57 "Yidn heldn fun sovetn-farband," *Eynikayt*, June 25, 1943, 7; Itsik Fefer, "Felker-brider." According to data for October 5, 1942, Jews accounted for 2.8 percent of those honored for heroism, and for January 1, 1944—for 2.1 percent, while the 1939 Soviet census had indicated that Jews comprised 1.8 percent of the Soviet population (*Evreiskii narod v bor'be protiv fashizma*, 67; L. Zinger, *Dos banayte folk* [Moscow: Ogiz, 1941], 35).
58 Shakhne Epshteyn, "Dos vidergeburt fun a folk," *Eynikayt*, November 8, 1944, 4; Fefer, "Felker-brider." This may have been a reaction to Stalin's remark, on November 6, 1944, at a meeting of the Moscow soviet, that "Soviet patriotism does not divide but, on the contrary, unifies all the nationalities and peoples of our country into a single fraternal family" (*Pravda*, November 7, 1944).
59 "Undzer heldn," *Eynikayt*, February 27, 1943, 8.
60 Sh. Persov, "A bagegenish mitn tsvey mol held fun sovetn-farband Dovid Dragunski," *Eynikayt*, December 1, 1945, 2. See also V. Fink, "Vstrecha s polkovnikom Dragunskim."
61 David Bergelson, "Der yunger sovetisher yid," *Eynikayt*, November 7, 1942, 6. On Bergelson's journalistic writing during the war, see David Shneer, "From Mourning to Vengeance: Bergelson's Holocaust Journalism (1941–1945)," in *David Bergelson: From Modernism to Socialist Realism*, ed. Joseph Sherman and Gennady Estraikh (London: Legenda, 2007), 248–67.
62 Peretz Markish, "Heroik un patriotizm fun yidishe roytarmeyer," *Eynikayt*, June 28, 1942, 3.
63 *Evreiskii narod v bor'be protiv fashizma*, 60.
64 Shakhne Epshteyn, "Undzer shtolts," *Eynikayt*, June 28, 1942, 2.
65 A. Shefer, "Di shlakhtn traditsie funem yidishn folk," *Eynikayt*, September 5, 1942, 2; January 7, 1943, 3.
66 Y. Dobrushin and N. Oyslender, "Der yidisher shlakhtman bai Sholem Aleykhemen," *Eynikayt*, February 10, 1944, 3.
67 Sholem Aleykhem, *Ale verk fun Sholem Aleykhem* (Vilna, Warsaw: Vilner farlag fun B. Kletskin, 1925), vol. 3, 216–17.
68 M. Notovich, "Mit biks in hant, mit vorem blut in hartsn" (GARF f. 8114, op. 1, d. 262, l. 44).
69 Shakhne Epshteyn, "Osher Shvartsman, groyser dikhter, heldishe shlakhtman," *Eynikayt*, December 14, 1944, 3–4. M. Notovich, "Tray der Shvartsman-traditsye," *Eynikayt*, October 28, 1943, 4. The collection of Shvartsman's poems "Ale lider" was republished in Moscow in 1944.
70 M. Notovich, "Mit biks in hant, mit vorem blut in hartsn."
71 M. Golbshteyn, "Osher Shvartsman," *Eynikayt*, October 6, 1942, 3.
72 The short version of "Ikh bin a yid" was published in *Eynikayt* in December 27, 1942, 3. For the full version, see Chone Shmeruk, *A shpigl oyfn a shteyn* (Jerusalem: Magnes Press, 1964), 694–97. Itsik Fefer, "Nit tsurik in geto, nor faroys in shlakht," *Eynikayt*, August 15, 1942, 2; Itsik Fefer, "Azoy shlogt men yidn," *Eynikayt*, October 5, 1944, 2;

Itsik Fefer, "Shloyme Gorelik, der held fun Sovetn Farband," *Eynikayt*, December 5, 1942, 2.

73 "Far a tanken kolone 'Bar Kokhba'" (GARF f. 8114, op. 1, d. 541, l. 262). However, this was not permitted and so the tank column was named Soviet Birobidzhan (GARF 8114-1-910, l. 41).

74 Livshin and Orlov, eds., *Sovetskaia propaganda*, 454.

75 Yekelchuk, "Stalinist Patriotism as Imperial Discourse," 64.

76 Fefer, "Shloyme Gorelik, der held fun Sovetn Farband."

77 D. Leytses, "A Soviet Jewish Samson" (GARF f. 8114, op. 1, d. 462, l. 132). However, in such cases one also found references to "many Russian Samsons."

78 S. Rabinovich, "Der shuster Leyb Rosin af fayer linye," *Eynikayt*, September 15, 1942, 3.

79 David Bergelson, "Der yunger sovetisher yid."

80 Sh. Persov, "Held fun Sovet Farband general-maior Yankev Kreizer," *Eynikayt*, June 7, 1942, 3; Sh. Persov, "Der yid Yankel Kreyzer" (GARF f. 8114, op. 1, d. 169, l. 56).

81 Sh. Persov, "General-maior fun artilerie Israel Beskin," *Eynikayt*, October 14, 1943, 3.

82 The collection of propaganda articles "Yidn in FSSR," edited by Shimon Dimanshtein, which was published in Moscow in 1935, followed this pattern (see the article in this collection by Abram Kirzhnits, "Di tsarishe yerushe," 183–84). The same idea was central to the exhibition "Jews in the Tsarist Russia and in the USSR" that opened in the State Museum of Ethnography in Leningrad in March 1939 (Alexander Ivanov, "'Evrei v tsarskoi Rossii i v SSSR': Vystavka dostizhenii evreiskogo khoziaistvennogo i kul'turnogo stroitel'stva v strane sovetov," *Novoe literaturnoe obozrenie* 102 [2010]: 158–82).

83 Sh. Persov, "Yidn generaln fun tanken-militer," *Eynikayt*, June 22, 1944, 4.

84 Leyb Kvitko, "Isak Kabo der kapitan fun untervaser-shif," *Eynikayt*, March 15, 1943, 7.

85 Leyb Kvitko, "Kapitan Isak Kabo," *Eynikayt*, April 5, 1943, 3.

86 Peretz Markish, "Heroik un patriotizm fun yidishn roytarmeyer."

87 On Jews and their attitude to Cossacks see also Gennady Estraikh, "Jews as Cossacks: A Symbiosis in Literature and Life" in this volume.

88 Itsik Fefer, "Yisroel Fisanovich, der held fun Sovetn Farband," *Eynikayt*, June 28, 1942, 3.

89 Hershl Polyanker, "Der veg af varshe," *Eynikayt*, October 12, 1944, 3.

90 Faivel Sito, "Der heldisher doctor Ide Epshteyn," *Eynikayt*, March 9, 1944, 3.

91 V. Pomerantsev, "Evreiskie partizany" (GARF f. 8114, op. 1, d. 170, l. 260).

92 Fefer, "Azoy shlogt men yidn"; GARF f. 8114, op. 1, d. 179, l. 349.

93 Fefer, "Azoy shlogt men yidn"; Pomerantsev, "Evreiskie partizany."

94 См. Abraham Ben Yosef, "Bibliografiya shel sifrei yidish shenidpesu bevrit hamoatsot beshanim 1941–1948," *Yad Vashem Studies* 4 (1960): 143–60.

95 For a translation of Fefer's Yiddish article into Russian, see Itsik Fefer, "Ikh vdokhnov-liala Sovetskaia armiia" (GARF f. 8114, op.1, d. 160, l. 183). For the version published in *Eynikayt*, see I. Fefer, "Zeyere gebotn," *Eynikayt*, April 20, 1948, 3.

Part II

REPRESENTATION, DOCUMENTATION, AND INTERPRETATION

Chapter 6

Foreshadowing the Holocaust: Boris Slutskii's Jewish Poetic Cycle of 1940/41

Marat Grinberg

The question of the treatment of the Holocaust in Russian Soviet poetry has remained largely unexplored. On the one hand, any examination of Jewishness in Soviet verse has inevitably turned to the Holocaust theme; according to a normative viewpoint, it was the Holocaust that prompted a number of acculturated Russian poets of Jewish origin to rediscover their Jewishness. On the other hand, analyses of such poems have not significantly drawn on the rich field of Holocaust literary studies and the critical paradigms engendered by it. Discussions of the Holocaust poems of Boris Slutskii (1919-1986) are a case in point: traditionally, they have been viewed as extensions of his pieces on the Soviet war against Nazi Germany in general.[1] Thus, their Jewish layer—intertextual, exegetical, and mythological— was ignored, being portrayed in purely factual and anthropological terms. This article, part of a larger project on the poet,[2] aims to investigate Slutskii's response to the Holocaust in a completely new critical light by focusing on his practically unknown cycle, "*Stikhi o evreiakh i tatarakh*" (Poems about Jews and Tatars), written over the period of a year from December 1940 to November 1941. This early verse demonstrates Slutskii not only responding to the horrific events of his time, but also working out through them the supreme elements of his poetics, such as translation and hermeneutic readings of Scripture.

Slutskii's poetics is a product of a Judaic genius, a potent exegetical mind, as Harold Bloom defines it: "All Jewish exegesis, from Hillel and Yeshua of Nazareth through the two Talmuds and Kabbalah on through Judah Halevi's *Kuzari* and Maimonides, and perhaps culminating in Kafka and Freud, can be termed a series of endeavors to open the Tanakh to the historical sufferings of the people Yahweh chose as his own."[3] I would add that in the Russian language, it culminates, or rather both begins and culminates, in Slutskii. His sense and reading of Scripture permeate his oeuvre's entire creative cognizance, from its reverential and groundbreaking employment of the Russian language and tradition to its knowledge of time and chaos, embodied in the poet's era—revolutionary, military, Stalinist and the later Soviet. In what Vladimir Khazan pithily defines as "one of the key features of the Jewish artist as such," Slutskii's creative modes methodically reengage scriptural "prototypes," placing the poet's programmatic generative being into "a global biblical paradigm."[4] At the same time, on the level of poetics his worldview uniquely fuses Russian and Judaic modes of thinking where the most salient points of contact between the two are quotation, interpretation of sources, rereading, re-accentuation, allusion, intertextuality, and memorialization. Indeed, for decades Russian poetry has been rightfully seen as operating under the principles of quoting, misquoting, and revising other texts, with Osip Mandelshtam and Anna Akhmatova's poetics being the prime examples of this. These poetic practices, which in Slutskii's case acquire a specific, idiosyncratic Judaic content, are what I call hermeneutics.

Slutskii performs his hermeneutic work by translation. The most fundamental fact of his creative process is Paul Ricoeur's assertion "as soon as there is language there is interpretation, that is translation."[5] An idiosyncratic concept and practice of translation defines Slutskii's poetry, transforming its biblical layer, which otherwise would have been an elusive referential and philosophical framework, into a continuous and precise hermeneutic action. It operates similarly to a "conceptual metatrope," to employ Natal'ia Fateeva's term, which "forms a realm where all threads of memory intertwine to engender a "creative memory," which ensures the translation of one "possible world" of thought and language into another and thus, generates a mechanism of producing all new "possible worlds" from the same "credo sources."[6] Slutskii locates this credo source in the Hebrew Bible, thereby transforming his creative generative process into the one of reconstruction—of *recollecting the old* [*pripominanie*], in Yurii Lotman's term.[7]

The cycle consists of three parts: "*Rasskaz emigranta*" (An Emigrant's Tale), "*Dobraia, sviataia, belorukaia...*" (Kind, holy, with white hands...), and "*Nezakonchennye razmyshleniia*" (Unfinished Thoughts). All three were dedicated to Viktoriia Levitina, Slutskii's love interest at the time, who published them, along with her recollections of the poet, in Israel in 1993 in an obscure

Russian language journal *Aktsent*, no longer in existence.[8] Considering their addressee, the poems implicitly weave the lyrical and the deeply personal, even the erotic, with the historical and the poetic. The result is Slutskii's multi-layered artistic system, what Levitina calls a "tri-part Jewish suite."

1

The first poem, "An Emigrant's Tale," reads in full:

По вечерам (хоть их никто не просит!)	In the evenings (even though none asks them to!)
В берлинских подворотнях — там и тут	In Berlin's back alleys—here and there
Они бросают глупые вопросы —	They throw stupid questions at you—
Зачем бьют?	Why? Why are they beating them?
Как быть с евреем — это не вопрос.	What to do with a Jew—is not the question.
Как бить еврея — это да, вопрос.	How to beat a Jew—that is indeed the question.
Есть мнения, что метод избиения,	There is an opinion that the method of beating
Хоть прогрессивен, но излишне прост.	Is noble, though a bit simple too.
Они травой подножною растут!	They grow like grass under one's foot!
Не укрощать, а прекращать сей люд!	We should not tame, but put a stop to this peoplehood.
Четырёхлетним молодым еврейкам	With a lancet, we are digging out lust
Ланцетом выковыривают блуд.	From all four-year-old Jewish girls.
У девочек обыкновенный взгляд.	The girls have an ordinary stare:
(Котята под трамваем так глядят.)	(Kittens stuck under a tram have such a stare too).
Но девочки не нянчат больше кукол,	But the girls do not rock dolls anymore,
А это липко видеть, говорят.	And it's better not to see their eyes, the people muse.
Я думаю, не выйдет ничего.	I think, this just won't work out.
Пусть весь народ, хоть в прорубь головой	Let the entire people be thrown Headlong into an ice hole—
Из синтеза простейших элементов	From a synthesis of the simplest elements
Воспрянет вновь Еврей как таковой.	The Jew as such will reemerge.

Foreshadowing the Holocaust: Boris Slutskii's Jewish Poetic Cycle of 1940/41

Вам, сумеркам, не затемнить зари!	But dusk cannot prevent the dawn from rising!
ЗДЕСЬ НАЧАЛОСЬ!	Here it commenced
В усталости и злобе	In disappointment and fatigue,
Еврейский Бог Адама сотворил	The Jewish God created Adam
По своему картавому подобию!	In His burring image.
Он был устал, и человек стал чахл,	God was tired, and the man became feeble,
И хилость плеч пошла по поколеньям,	And feebleness of shoulders passed on through generations,
Но звёзды заплуталися в очах,	But stars got lost in human eyes,
Сырые звёзды первых дней творенья!	Raw stars of first days of creation.
А вы, широкоплечи и крепки,	And you, broad-shouldered and mighty,
Мозгам противящие кулаки —	Who throw fists against the brains—
ВЫ просто отклоненье от Еврея.	You are simply a deviation from the Jew.
Вот кто вы такие.	Here is who you are, you are.
Я никого обидеть не хочу.	I do not want to insult anyone.
Я просто так, по глупости кричу.	I am just screaming, silly that I am.
Конечно, криком не поможешь делу.	Of course, screaming will not help anything.
Но очень душно, если промолчу!	But I will suffocate, if I just stay put

In his tale, Slutskii responds to the historical horror in a cosmic light. He does so in 1940—before either the executions at Babii Iar or the chimneys of Auschwitz, but during the period of official friendship between the Soviet Union and the Third Reich in the aftermath of the Molotov-Ribbentrop Pact. The young poet inserts a cosmological and eschatological interpretation in-between a report and a statement of poetic irony. The first part of the poem, comprised of stanzas one through five, presents a deeply felt testimony, brutal in its honesty, about the atrocities in Germany, centered on the experiments of making the Jewish girls infertile, described here before such actions would actually take place en masse in Auschwitz.[9] Here the poet serves merely as a conveyer, a transmitter of the other's story. He would perfect this reporting device in his later post-war poems on the Holocaust, most prominently in "*Kak ubivali moiu babku*" (How My Granny was Killed).[10] At the same time, he makes his poetic mark known through unobtrusive, but highly original parallel devices, such as the paronomastic usage of *byt'/bit'* (to be/to strike) in the first two lines of the second stanza.

The poem's second part consists of stanzas six through nine, presenting an intricate interlay of eschatology, historical memory and cosmogony. In 1940, Slutskii seems to have been convinced that Jews stood on the brink of a total annihilation, while the impending murder could not be stopped. Most pointedly, in reaction to this foreboding, he operates within the tradition of Jewish responses to catastrophe. In his seminal *Against the Apocalypse*, David Roskies defines what he calls "the Jewish dialectical response to catastrophe": "the greater the immediate destruction, the more it was made to recall the ancient archetype." Thus, any catastrophe that befell the Jews became "fixed in the mythic past …," transforming "the punctual … into the transtemporal."[11] In each generation, the Jews continuously compared the catastrophe of their time to various biblical episodes (most prominently from the book of Lamentations), thus ensuring that their calamity was part of the divine plan, which invariably brought the notion of redemption into history. Slutskii Russifies this biblical paradigm: the line "let the entire people be thrown headlong into an ice hole" unmistakably refers to Ivan's the Terrible massacre of the Jews in Polotsk in 1563, where three hundred Jews who refused to be baptized were drowned in the river Dvina. This episode was recounted in the famed *Encyclopedic Dictionary of Brokgauz and Efron*, published in 1893, with which Slutskii, a history buff, was undoubtedly familiar. The difference between 1563 and 1940, as Slutskii makes clear, is that the three hundred are to be replaced by the entire house of Israel. In his post-war Holocaust text, "*Cherta pod chertoiu...*" (The Pale's Impaled...), he would employ a similar, though a more radical strategy of inserting the Holocaust into Russian historical memory.[12] There he would link the Jewish annihilation with the destruction of the Russian princely families of Mstislavskii and Shuiskii, which, and this is the key element, were disseminated during the reign of Ivan the Terrible as well. Consequently, Slutskii employs both sides of Russian historical memory, the specifically Jewish and the overall Russian, to engrain the Holocaust in the Russian verse. "The Pale's Impaled..." and "An Emigrant's Tale" are thus inextricably linked both in terms of their realm of reference and, more importantly, interpretations of historical remembrance and its reconfigurations through lyric poetry's grasp of the catastrophe.

The lines "from a synthesis of the simplest elements/ the Jew as such will reemerge" are deliberately messianic. Slutskii was as a matter of principle always weary of any messianic prescience, which clashed with his sober perception of history. Only in his Holocaust verse does the reader encounter direct messianic or eschatological statements, but even there they contain a great deal of doubt. Here the entire universe, its very physical makeup, bears the irreparable impact of the Jews' forceful demise. The question is, can nature defy itself and overturn the destruction, or will it remain powerless and incapable of breaching the abyss? The two visions, the eschatological and the one deprived of messianic hope, do not cancel each other out, but simultaneously exist in Slutskii's poetics, paradoxically reinforcing each other. Stanzas seven through nine step back from the messianic pronouncement to only offer yet another mythological construct—that of cosmogony. Slutskii refashions the dialectical paradigm of responding to catastrophe once again. He intimates the notion, which will become central to "The Pale's Impaled...," that the Holocaust is a cataclysm whose totality transcends time. It is no longer sufficient to evoke the memory of persecutions past, be they from recorded historical (Ivan the Terrible) or legendary biblical times. The poet, in a task akin to that of a mystic, must reexamine the very foundations of the earth, which, to use Bialik's imagery, have "darkened" as a result of the catastrophe, and look afresh at its creation, seeking to uncover its blemishes.

Ultimately, Slutskii's cosmogony aims to resolve the problem central to his messianism as well: is there anything on the planet that can reverse the process of this historical destruction? "Here it commenced," he proclaims, arguing that the causes of both the tragedy and the eventual salvation of Jewish existence are to be found in God's imperfect creation of this imperfect universe. In stanzas seven and eight, with their creationist subject matter, he uses an appropriately high style evocative of Hebrew diction and biblical stylistics. Thus, *sotvoril* (created) in stanza seven parallels *tvoren'ia* (creation) in stanza eight, while *podob'ie* (image/likeness) quotes directly from Genesis 1:26. Reiterating his hope for the dawn of a messianic era, Slutskii delves deep into pre-history in order to display where history's pit originates. Here *byt* (history) begins in *bytie*, both in the sense of eternity and Genesis, per the Russian Orthodox title for the first book of the Pentateuch. God created man in his burring image. In the Russian context, burring is traditionally the sign of the Jew's speech. Slutskii adds this feature to the biblical vision of Adam being formed in the divine image for one and only one reason: this God is a Jew. He is not the omniscient demiurge of creation, but the tired and disappointed character of the biblical Flood story, and the Israelites' wanderings in the desert. Slutskii would carry this notion of God as a weary deity who cannot compete with the self-erected pseudo-gods of the century, particularly the Soviet tyrant, throughout his oeuvre. As in the cosmology of Lurianic kabbalah, the poet presents Creation as a troubled process fraught with fatigue, meanness, and dampness. In historical terms, this translates into Adam becoming a Jew who is beaten in the streets of Berlin. The traps of creation are embedded in his eyes and the gaze of four-year-old Jewish girls; hence their suffering in history.

To abuse a Jew is to abuse God, the poet suggests. Levitina mistakenly attributes Slutskii's depiction of Adam's frailty to either antisemitic images or Jewish self-hatred from the nineteenth to twentieth centuries. While the Jew may seem feeble, his is no ordinary weakness; it is not a sign of decline, but a secret of the Jewish and universal tragedy of existence pregnant with the hope for redemption. The stars, both signs of the grandeur of Creation and its dampness, embody this cosmic uncertainty, which can only be remedied through the messianic redoing of the Jew and thus the planet, however improbable it may seem. In stanza 11, undoubtedly weaker than the previous two, Slutskii posits the Jew as the ultimate ideal of a human being, almost a polemical substitution for Christ. These polemics would acquire their full force in the second part of the cycle. Here, indeed, taking on the cultural image of the Jew as a scholar, he makes it purely positive, pitted against the degenerates, who operate with fists.

Slutskii's cosmogony of 1940 foreshadows the Holocaust poetry of Yankev Glatstein, a major Yiddish modernist poet and one of the founders of the New York poetic Introspectivist (*In zikh*) movement. I would argue that his "Without Jews," written when the civilization of European Jews became a cause only for erecting memorials, works within a Slutskian framework. Slutskii's Jewish God, using the burring Jewish speech, creates the Jew in His Jewish image; in Glatstein's verse, the Jew shapes God in his likeness. It is thanks to Jews' existence in history that God's eternity may last; once the Jews are no more, their God perishes as well. Edward Alexander comments that Glatstein's "lines are not only an expression of the peculiarly intimate relation between the Jews and their God, or a skeptic's suggestion that God's existence is merely subjective, but a recognition that God had made the Jews the special instrument for the achievement of His purposes and their life His chief interest."[13] A similar notion is apparent in Slutskii's text when God infuses Jews with His eternal tiredness. Glatstein's poem, with its textbook-like enumeration of the Jews' relations with God prior to the Holocaust, pinpoints the catastrophe as the moment that has shattered the idyllic encounter between

God and the Jews. In Slutskii's piece, the seeds of the catastrophe as well as of redemption are planted on the very first day of Creation, making his vision resound with kabbalistic gnosticism.

The last stanza of "An Emigrant's Tale" is the poem's most significant, revealing the roots of Slutskii's mature poetics. Slutskii, as his Holocaust verse indicates, be it "The Pale's Impaled…" or "*Ravviny vyshli na ravniny…*" (The Rabbis walked out unto the plains…),[14] was haunted by the incapability of traditional symbolic and mythological schemes to express the origins, events, and consequences of the Holocaust. Producing poetry within the parameters of Russian tradition, rather than the sites of traditional or modern Jewish culture, paradoxically worked in his favor. Having composed a complex creationist poem, both deeply messianic and yet immediately historical, he assuages its purported grandeur and symbolic neatness with a statement of ironic rationality, both poignant and understated. In the finale, which switches into a fully colloquial mode, the speaker both diminishes his prophetic stature and the sense of moral certainty, while emphasizing at the same time an absolute, almost existential, need not to remain silent in the face of the historical and metaphysical horror: "Of course, screaming will not help anything./ But I will suffocate, if I just stay put." Hence, the "I" of the poem is multi-layered. In the report, the first part, it is absent, allowing the reportage to proceed unhindered. In the second section, it takes on a prophetic dimension, and in the third, becomes the self-doubting meager voice of the poet, thrown into history's whirlwind. The third element again ties the poem to "The Pale's impaled…," where Slutskii would similarly, though more solemnly, state, "A planet! Whether a good one or a bad one/ I do not know. I neither clap nor carp./ I don't know much. There is one thing I know:/ this plant burned to ashes long ago."[15]

Thus, "An Emigrant's Tale" encapsulates the principal dimensions of Slutskii's poetics. While it invites a comparative analysis with poetic responses to the Holocaust in Jewish languages by virtue of its operating either intuitively or deliberately within the same hermeneutic field, it occupies the status of a most imaginative, complete, and complex response to the Holocaust in both Russian and Jewish literatures, written uniquely on the eve of the destruction. Its analysis should reshape the current critical understanding of the treatment of the war and the Holocaust in Soviet poetry. In his insightful discussion of the war verse in both underground and semi-official Soviet literature, Il'ia Kukulin argues that while unofficial war poems almost saved

Soviet poetry from the dogma of Socialist realism, their stark naturalism and avoidance of clichés in confronting death and individual and collective suffering did not succeed in elevating the emotionally new poetic tone to an existential level.[16] It is noteworthy that in his study, Kukulin does not mention Slutskii's poetry at all. But as our analysis demonstrates, not only did "An Emigrant's Tale" present a wholly original "existential" vision, it endeavored to resolve the inherent problems associated with it through the poem's very structure.

2

"Kind, holy, with white hands..." was written in May of 1941, on the eve of the Nazi invasion of Soviet territory. It reads in full:

Добрая, святая, белорукая,	Kind, holy, with white hands
О любой безделице скорбя,	Mourning over every trifle,
Богородица, ходившая по мукам,	The Mother of God, who walked through hell,
Всех простив, ударила тебя	Having shown mercy to everyone, struck you.
И Христос послал тебя скитаться,	And Christ has sent you to wander,
Спотыкаться межи град и сел,	To stumble in-between towns and villages,
Чтоб еврей мог снова посмеяться,	So that a Jew could laugh again,
Если бы снова мимо Бог прошел.	If God again were to pass him by.
...Смешанные браки и погромы, ...	Intermarriages and pogroms,
что имеем в перспективах, кроме —	What else does future hold for us, except for that—
нация ученых и портных.	Us, the nation of scholars and tailors.
Я и сам пишу стихи по-русски —	I too write my verses in Russian,
По-московски, а не по-бобруйски,	As is the custom in Moscow, not Bobruisk—
Хоть иначе выдумал я их.	Though I have imagined them otherwise.
В этот раз мы вряд ли уцелеем —	This time we might not survive—
Техника не та! И люди злее,	The technology is different and the people meaner!
Пусть! От нас останется в веках	Let it be! What will remain of us in centuries is
Кровушка последнейших евреев —	Blood of the very last Jews—
В жилах!	In veins!
Или просто на руках.[17]	Or simply on her hands.

This poem is drastically different from "An Emigrant's Tale." It abandons the messianic layout, offering instead a more sober historical perspective.

Furthermore, in a swift polemical gesture, it places what would become known as the Holocaust into the saga of Christian/Jewish difference, which Slutskii specifies in the terms of Russian literary and mythological traditions. In a short breadth of three stanzas, he offers a profoundly original response to both Russian Christian logic and art and the impending catastrophe, while chiseling a double-edged sword of poetics and Jewish hermeneutics. Slutskii reaches deep into Russian literary history in order to indict Christendom and particularly the Russian Orthodox civilization in its willingness to let the Jews perish. At the center of his vision, not merely ironic, but deeply sardonic and even scornful, is the image of the Mother of God, the Russian *bogoroditsa*. In the third line of the first stanza, he directly references a seminal apocryphal text of Old Russian literature, "*Khozhdenie bogoroditsy po mukam*" (The Mother of God's Journey in Hell), dating from at least the twelfth century.[18] Evoked by Ivan Karamazov in Slutskii's most favorite of Dostoevsky's novels, its theme is close to that of Dante's *Inferno*: Mary walks through Hell, where she takes pity on the suffering sinners, causing her to ask God, both Father and Christ, to forgive them.[19] It is noteworthy that it is only the Christian sinners who evoke Mary's compassion. Having come upon the Jews, who burn in the river of fire for once torturing Christ, she concludes, "Let it be according to their actions," but when witnessing the torments of the Christians, she exclaims, "Let me enter and be tortured with the other Christians because they called themselves the children of my son." In Russian popular and mythological imagination, she is seen as *zastupnitsa* (protectress) of the people; Anna Akhmatova seized upon this depiction of Mary in her World War I poetry, as did Pasternak in *Doctor Zhivago*, while the Russian Orthodox Church instituted a number of holidays in her honor. Nikolai Berdiaev provided an authoritative interpretation of her unique significance for the Russian mind, "The Mother of God takes precedence of the Trinity and is almost identified with the Trinity. The people have felt the nearness of the interceding Mother of God more vividly than that of Christ. Christ is the heavenly king, but scanty expression is given to his earthly image. Mother Earth alone is given a personal incarnation ... [T]he Russian people want to take shelter ... behind Mother Earth, behind the Mother of God. "[20]

Slutskii, a Jewish, or more resolutely a Judaic poet, who argues for a Russian literary pedigree, exposes the myth of the kind-hearted and merciful mother of God on his own ironic terms, which he nevertheless solicits from this very myth. He packs his poem with the terminology redolent of the apocryphal text, embodied in the adjectival descriptions of Mary ("with white hands" is particularly scathing, as the poem's ending will illustrate), her actions through the poem's verbs, and even borrowings from Church Slavonic (*mezhi grad*). Mother of God mourns over every trifle, but beats the Jew, the fundamental human being. To recall, in the first poem of the cycle, Slutskii makes it clear that to beat a Jew is to beat God; thus, his polemics become principally hermeneutic through his argument with Christian mythology for its erasure of the Jewish deity. Slutskii's usage of the pronoun "you" in lines five and six is suggestive of this strategy, as he does not explicitly modify it, enabling it to refer to both Jews and God. The remaining three lines of the first stanza complicate this even further: "Christ sent you to wander,/ to stumble in-between towns and villages,/ so that a Jew could laugh again,/ if God again were to pass by him." Precisely because the "you" is deliberately ambiguous, the literal and yet the most revealing reading of these verses is that Christ banishes God—"you"—to stumble in the world. If the Jew, accustomed to his lot over the centuries, were to see God trotting by again, he would laugh, in accordance with the Jewish survival principle of laughter through tears. Furthermore, the usage of *proshel* (walked by) is particularly ironic as it alludes to the divine passing over Jewish houses, commemorated in the book of Exodus and the Passover Hagadah, and evocative of the saving of the Israelites' first-borns.[21] Here not only do Jews find themselves again in peril, but God's passing, or, in a hermeneutical twist, wandering, carries neither redemption nor punishment of their enemies.

Thus, Slutskii is drastically rewriting the myth of the wandering Jew, which itself constitutes a major subversive trope of modernist Jewish verse. Most prominently, in "Oracle to Europe," composed in the wake of devastation suffered by Jews in World War I, Hebrew poet Uri Zevi Greenberg depicts Ahasver the Wandering Jew as the true Jewish Messiah, nailed to the cross instead of Jesus.[22] Slutskii radicalizes this daring, though still normative interpretation—by marking God as the perpetually wandering victim of Mary and Christ, helpless and utterly incapable of staving off the destruction. In a twist of tragic irony, the Gospels acquire the characteristics of *Oedipus Rex*. I would argue that Slutskii derives this astonishing and audacious vision, both in terms of its rebuttal to Christianity and indictment of the Judaic notion of divine omnipotence and justice, from Vladimir Zhabotinskii's groundbreaking translation of Hayim Nahman Bialik's "In the City of Slaughter"

(*Skazanie o pogrome*), the key modern Jewish text of destruction, in which God proclaims himself a pauper. But if Bialik famously condemns the Jews' passive behavior, Slutskii abstains from any preaching, fully identifying with both the Jewish fate and the Jew's ironic take on the calamity.

The poem's second stanza, in defiance of any totalizing responses, brings the poet down to earth. Speaking once more from the depth and breadth of Jewish history, he concedes that nothing but complete assimilation (mixed marriages) and destruction (pogroms) await the Jews, "the nation of scholars and tailors." What follows this arguably accurate, at least as far as the Soviet Jews were concerned, though undoubtedly flat evaluation is an intimation of the cornerstone of Slutskii's artistic program, which, significantly, he begins to formulate in this measured Holocaust piece. "I too write my verse in Russian,/ as is the custom in Moscow, not Bobruisk—/ though I have imagined it otherwise," the poet confesses. Like an unfinished refrain from another text, these lines appear to be misplaced. The speaker whispers them like an incantation, which conceals the very source of his translational poetics and the primary Jewish text, which he never wrote. "Who am I to talk about these Jewish matters?" he seems to be asking. After all, he too is fully assimilated and writes his verse in Russian. Slutskii goes to the very heart of the question of whether it is possible to produce and sustain Jewish poetics, directed both inward and outward, in a non-Jewish tradition. Indeed, he writes in muscovite, not the language of Bobruisk (in other words Yiddish) or a composite Jewish language. The force, ingenuity, and openness of Slutskii's formulation demand that Bobruisk be read as a metonymy for *Yiddishkayt*. In fact, this town in Belorussia was indeed a center of Hebrew publishing and Jewish learning, both Hasidic and *mitnagdic*, secular Jewish politics, including Zionism and the Bund, as well as the birthplace of Pauline Vengeroff, author of the famed Russian-Jewish memoirs,[23] Berl Katsnelson, Zionist socialist thinker and leader, and Hebrew poet David Shimoni. Slutskii does not write in the language of Bobruisk, but he had imagined his poems differently—that is, differently from the language of Moscow. The usage of the dubious and playful verb *vydumat'* (to make up, or even to lie) positions Slutskii as a Jewish trickster in Russian tradition. Rooted in both the Bible, whose greatest swindler, Jacob, would occupy a special place in his oeuvre, and the work of Isaac Babel', whom he revered his entire life and directly called a "liar" (*vydumshchik*) in a poem-homage to the Odessan genius ("Who was Babel?..."),[24] Slutskii's creative con artistry marks his translation project as a daring, wishful, and ambiguous one, transforming his oeuvre into a polyphonic but unified system.

Slutskii demands for his verse to be translated from his underlying Jewish tongue. In adapting translation as the principle of his poetics at the moment of historical loss and destruction, he places it in a "catch-22" predicament. Slutskii is unquestionably a logocentric poet, both in terms of his poetic lineage, embodied in the figure of Velimir Khlebnikov, and his worldview. His logocentricity pledges allegiance to the Russian tongue, but what of its Jewish groundwork? While his relation to Russian was certainly not as volatile and tragic as Celan's to German, the coexistence of the two linguistic realms, for historical, literary, and religious reasons, is hardly attainable for the poet. Yet both, perpetually threatening each other, are required for Slutskii's artistic survival. Thus, his notion of translation was dramatically different from how other modern Jewish artists practiced it. Very seldom does his translation evolve into an actual incorporation of Yiddish or Hebrew lexicons into his language. Slutskii was painstakingly trying to make sure that his Russian would remain organic and unencumbered, in touch with both his era and Russian literary history. Rather, the borrowings occur on the level of both hermeneutic macro-poetics and stylistic micro-poetics, as in his adaptation of biblical parallelism for his prosody. Slutskii's Jewish language is embedded into the very fabric of his artistic thinking; it ought to be decoded.

The last stanza's tone is fatalistic. The poet expresses a resolute despondency, having managed to identify the two main features of the approaching catastrophe: its unparalleled evil, and the cold technical means through which it will be carried out. The Jews, and he among them, will perish. A faint memory of the people is to be perpetuated either through blood "in veins," referring presumably to the progeny of mixed marriages, or as bloody stains on the perpetrators' and bystanders' hands. This last line brings the poem full circle, as it makes the depiction of Mary's hands as white fully come to light: their whiteness and that of Christendom is to be soaked in Jewish blood. Slutskii exhibits the Jewish dialectical approach to catastrophe, but, as in "An Emigrant's Tale," he russifies it and, despite the last lines' bitter sense of resignation, daringly, though implicitly, locates a glimpse of redemption not in the sacred biblical past, but in the Jewish potential of his verse. The cycle's final poem would portray the pitfalls embodied in the concept of translation in stark historical terms.

Foreshadowing the Holocaust: Boris Slutskii's Jewish Poetic Cycle of 1940/41

3

Slutskii spent the first year of the war as a military prosecutor on the battlefield, until he was severely wounded. "Unfinished Thoughts" is his first catastrophe poem to be written after the start of the war. Composed in October-November of 1941, it coincided with the killings at Babii Iar but preceded the extermination in his native Kharkov, which took place in December-January of 1941-42 at Drobitskii Iar. Most likely, Slutskii learned in 1943 of the killings in his town, of which he informed his brother, who was evacuated from the city, in a letter from the front: "In Kharkov, 16,000 Jews were killed in the barracks of the machine factory."[25] "Unfinished Thoughts," the longest installment in the trilogy, is divided into two parts. The first one approximates most closely Slutskii's poetic diction, unabashedly conversationalist and starkly prosaic, features which would become a defining mark of his post-war verse. The poem is an example of what he himself would later identify as his ballads, "an explosion, concentrated in the dimension of 40+/- lines... shortened, compressed, pithy tragedies."[26]

The first 44 lines of the poem depict a scene in a crowded train car, filled with soldiers and officers headed for the front. The verse has a distinctly Maiakovskian feel, both rhythmically and visually: the lines resemble a staircase. Its allusions, however, are immediately coeval. Slutskii evokes Ehrenburg's articles of the time, which called on Soviet citizens to feel nothing but hatred toward the Nazi aggressor:

Чего нам нужно для нашей души?	What do we require for our souls?
Нам нужно злости для нашей души,	We require anger for our souls,
Столетней,	A hundred-year old
Стоялой	Stagnant
Злости.	Anger.

The cycle's title, "Poems about Jews and Tatars," is unlocked in this first part as well. A Tatar, a soldier, begins to sing on the train about the tragedy of his people, who once ruled over Russia but were later brutally defeated by it. Others have joined him in the lament and thus, "with paradoxical sadness/ the Russian people are singing about the people that once ruled over Rus'." The poet quotes from the song and later reiterates its chronicle yarn, which spans Russia's imperial history,

Здесь был Татарстан. Здесь погиб
       Татарстан.
Измена его подкосила.
  Донской порубал.
    Изрубил Иоанн.
      Екатерина казнила.[27]
	Here used to be Tatarstan. Here perished
	       Tatarstan.
	Betrayal brought it down.
	  Donskoi slaughtered it.
	    Ivan butchered.
	      Catherine executed.

In his notes from the war, written directly in its aftermath, Slutskii comments that for the first time the myth of Soviet internationalism and the friendship between multiethnic Soviet peoples was truly tested at the front. He concludes that the experiment miserably failed. The reclamation of Russian imperial history and military glory, undertaken by Stalin, fuelled Russian xenophobia. Slutskii ironically notes, "It is strange to electrify the Tatar population with the memories of Donskoi and Mamai. A military mixture of languages led to the re-acquaintance of peoples—from "the Moldovan to the Finn." [28] The situation depicted in the poem is more poignant, but it speaks to the same blemish on both Russian and Soviet histories, which Slutskii dares to give voice to in 1941.

The verse's second part returns to Slutskii's Jewish concerns, exposing the "Tatar" woe at the heart of his being, and turning a Tatar song into a Jewish *nigun*. It reads in full:

Еврейские старцы в подвал собрались,
Чтоб там над лежанкой глиняной
Случайно
  Меня
    Наректи
      «Борис» —
Татарского мстителя именем.
	The Jewish elders gathered up in a basement,
	So that there above a cradle of clay
	To name
	  Me
	    Accidentally
	      "Boris" —
	The Tatar avenger's name.

И так я родился. Я рос и подрос, А завтра из смрада вагона Я выйду на волю и стану в рост: Приму по реке оборону.	And thus I was born. I grew and grew up, And tomorrow from the smog of the train I'll exit to freedom and stand at full height: Will take on the river defense.

Foreshadowing the Holocaust: Boris Slutskii's Jewish Poetic Cycle of 1940/41

Тоскуют солдаты о смерти своей,	The soldiers are pining over their death,
А лошади требуют корму.	While horses are pleading for forage.
Убьют меня — скажут — чудак был еврей!	Should I perish—they'll say—what a nincompoop that Jew was!
А струшу — скажут — норма!	Should I chicken out—they'll say—that's the norm.
Я снова услышу погромный вой	Again I will hear the pogroms' howl
О том, кем Россия продана.	About those who sold Russia out!
О мать моя мачеха! Я сын твой родной!	O mother my stepmother! I am your native son!
Мне негде без Родины, Родина!	I am nowhere without the motherland, motherland!

The first seven lines present a Judaic nativity scene—a naming ceremony, associated with the ritual of circumcision, which takes place here clandestinely. They evoke, or perhaps even directly reference Eduard Bagritskii's poem "Origin" (1930), with which Slutskii was undoubtedly familiar, where "over my cradle rusty Jews/ crossed rusty blades of crooked beards."[29] Slutskii, however, completely alters the (ostensibly) self-hating tone of Bagritskii's expressionist verse. Levitina somewhat naively points out that in 1919, the year of Slutskii's birth, he was most likely named Borukh rather than Boris. Clearly, in the context of Slutskii's translation, the Russian Boris conceals the Yiddish Borukh and the Hebrew Barukh, with its meaning of blessing. It is important to recognize, however, that Slutskii's recollection is a construction which describes, first and foremost, not a biographical episode but the birth of a poet, imbuing the artist's name with an irreverent symbolic meaning. Thus, the poet's name is nothing but accidental; like Osip Mandelshtam, Slutskii would remain preoccupied with his name throughout his oeuvre. On the one hand, the name Boris, Slavic in origin, signifies a warrior who is blessed in battle; this element contributes to Slutskii's initiation into a soldierly life. On the other, he associates it with some Tatar avenger, thus turning his name into an intertextual cipher. The "Tatar avenger" alludes to Tsar Boris Godunov, a prominent figure, of course, in both Russian history and literature.[30] Indeed, Godunov's kin was Tatar in origin. What is more significant is that in Pushkin's drama "Boris Godunov," Prince Shuiskii describes him as "a former slave, a Tatar,

Maliuta's son-in-law, the henchman's son-in-law who is himself at heart a henchman."[31] Godunov, a profoundly troubling figure both for Pushkin and in the popular imagination, suits Slutskii's crisis. While in critical literature it is usually the false Dimitrii who is identified as an avenger, Slutskii applies the term to Godunov and thus himself in order to link his predicament with that of a Tatar soldier who mourned his people's fate in the first part of the poem. Not only is the poet's relationship with Russia ambivalent and perhaps doomed, considering again the Godunov connection, but it is also saturated with the same sense of vengeance and anger that marks the Tatar's song.[32] After all, in the cycle's second poem, it is the Orthodox Mary's hands that are about to turn bloody in the wake of the Jews' destruction. The poet directs his anger at both the Germans and the Russians, for his fate and artistic vocation are inextricably linked with that of his "Tatars"—the Jews. Thus, the terms of translation acquire a palatable historical meaning, exposing Slutskii's constructed origins—"Thus I was born"—which he has to submerge in order to now become the country's defender.

As noted by Kukulin, the best and most daring Soviet war poetry presents death in a fresh, unforgiving, and hard-bitten light; a great deal of such verse, however, was written only after the war.[33] Slutskii begins already in 1941, coolly, and yet almost apocalyptically, noting, "The soldiers are sorrowful about their death." This image of living ghosts sharply contrasts with the major themes of official Soviet war poetry—the soldiers, bound to survive, pining for the homeland. Lines 14-16 link this contemplation of death with the poet's Jewishness. He is doomed no matter what: should he be killed, he would be branded a "nincompoop" for fighting too hard for the country that had not historically shown much favor to his people; should he try to stay alive, he'd serve as confirmation that the Jews are cowards. The last stanza adopts a seer's tone. In its first line, the future tense of "I will again hear the pogroms' howl" is pivotal, as the poet foresees the antisemitic scourge that will overtake his country, as did indeed happen. The "again" of the line and the evocation of the Black Hundreds' motto about the Jews who sold Russia out reveal the poet operating within the parameters of the Jewish dialectical response to history, which, crucially, he revises in reaction to the Holocaust but leaves intact in relation to popular Soviet Judeophobia.

The poem's last two lines can strike one as platitudinous. After all, much of the thematically Jewish poetry written in Russian in the last three decades of the past century describes the relationship between Russia and Jews as that between a stepmother and her children.[34] Conversely, there is an earlier tradition of identifying the bond between a Russian poet of Jewish origins and Jews in this same manner. Ehrenburg's poem "*Evrei, s vami zhit' ne v silakh...*" (Jews, having no strength to live with you...) of 1914 is a paradigmatic case in point. The context and Slutskii's wholly original perception of Jewishness are critical for grasping his game. It is astonishing that a young poet, born and raised in a Soviet country and about to function as the accusing party at military tribunals at the front, would call his Soviet homeland *machekha* (stepmother), a term that in Russian, much more than in English, carries the connotations of wickedness and cruelty.[35] Mikhail Kul'chitskii, who to a large extent introduced Slutskii to poetry and whom Slutskii always considered to be his teacher, wrote in an unfinished narrative poem, "*Samoe takoe* (*Poema o Rossii*)" (That Very Precious [Poem about Russia]), in 1941, two years before he would perish at the front in Stalingrad, "*Ia ochen' sil'no/ liubliu Rossiiu...*" (I love Russia so strongly...).[36] Undoubtedly, Slutskii did share in this feeling, but his poetic worldview constitutes a precarious double-edged sword of Jewishness and Russianness, both historical and logocentric, polemical and symbolic. Unlike the other soldiers on the train, he has come apart: Russia is his double-headed mother/stepmother; he is fatalistically her native son. Thus, his woeful cry at the end, so unusual for his poetry, "I cannot be anywhere without the motherland, motherland," is a confession to the actual homeland, the addressee, that he cannot survive without the other native soil—his, I would argue, Jewish hearth, what in the central post-war poem "Uriel Acosta," he would define as his "kinless kin."

This "kinless kin" denotes Slutskii's poetic space. Thus, thanks to the spatial organization of his poetics, whose breadth interweaves a plethora of sources into a coherent hermeneutic whole, he manages to resolve the crisis depicted so powerfully in "Unfinished Thoughts." What might have been another normative Russian-Jewish paradigm, resulting in insolubility or the relinquishment of Jewishness, is transformed thereby into the birth of an artistic system. Slutskii's identification with Godunov, which denotes his difference, does not lead to the politics, or aesthetics of a minor literature, but positions him as a supreme voice in both Russian and Jewish traditions.

***

In the poem "Evreiskaia babushka" (The Jewish Grandmother), written most likely in the early 1960s, Slutskii personifies his Jewishness in the image of a Jewish matriarch, beautiful and benevolent:

Как еврейская бабушка, что во главе
Праздничного
      заседает
           стола,
Не идет эта строчка к угрюмой Москве.
Не идет совершенно. А шла!...
	Like a Jewish grandmother, who at the head
	Of the festive
	      Table
	           Sits,
	This line is not becoming to the morose Moscow.
	Not becoming at all. But how it used to!...

Как еврейская бабушка эта строка. Но не вычеркну, не зачеркну.[37]	Like a Jewish grandmother is this line. But I won't cross it out, will not cross over.

The poet does not and cannot erase his Jewishness, which here unequivocally refers to his poetics. The cycle of 1940-41 emerges at precisely that moment in Slutskii's creativity when Jewishness "was becoming" to the "morose Moscow," when the composite language of Bobruisk became instilled in the actual language of Moscow. Indeed, the radical terms of Slutskii's artistic myth-making were drawn then as well, but the result overpowered the potential hazards: original, profound, and powerful verse on the Jewish destruction was written in Russian. An understanding of the correlation between publishable and clandestine literature in the Soviet context requires reconsideration. In 1957, Slutskii stepped into official Soviet literature. Unquestionably, a great deal of his verse was not made accessible during his productive years; some of the poems were printed in truncated versions. He wrote, desiring to be published, but this instinctive inclination was secondary to his artistic designs. Thus, there are no poems in his oeuvre, composed *na zakaz*, to satisfy the ideological order of the day. Again this supposedly devout Soviet figure had his first collection of poems published only in 1957, thanks to Il'ia Ehrenburg's efforts, prior to that being known primarily through crumbled-up typeset pages. It would be limiting to frame Slutskii's breakthrough solely in terms of the liberalizing climate of the Thaw. Factually, it did enable his exposure to the reader, imbuing the poet with hope; but the roots of his poetics did not shift as a result, having been sown already, as this essay demonstrates, in his earliest verse on his generation's Jewish destruction. Indeed, the Jewish line would never become erased from his verse, amounting to a single uninterrupted poem, whose first word always concealed the last.

Notes

1. A vivid and most recent example of this is the first Russian-language biography of Slutskii. See Piotr Gorelik and Nikita Eliseev, *Po techen'iu i protiv techen'ia: Boris Slutskii: zhizn' i tvorchestvo* (Moscow: Novoe literaturnoe obozrenie, 2009).
2. See Marat Grinberg, *"I Am to be Read not from Left to Right, but in Jewish: From Right to Left": The Poetics of Boris Slutskii* (Boston: Academic Studies Press, 2011). This essay draws on the materials of the book, particularly pp. 86-106.
3. Harold Bloom, *Jesus and Yahweh: The Names Divine* (New York: Riverhead Books, 2005), 206.
4. Vladimir Khazan, *Osobennyi evreisko-russkii vozdukh: k problematike i poetike russko-evreiskogo literaturnogo dialoga v xx veke* (Jerusalem: Gesharim, 2001), 144, 145.
5. Paul Ricouer, *On Translation* (London: Routledge, 2004), xvii.
6. Natal'ia Fateeva, *Intertekst v mire tekstov: kontrapunkt intertekstual'nosti* (Moscow: URSS, 2007), 64.
7. Iurii Lotman, *Stat'i po semiotike i topologii kul'tury* (Tallin: Alexandra, 1992), vol. 1, 11-23.
8. Viktoriia Levitina, "Tak nachinal...," *Aktzent* (March 1993): 65-74.
9. As research presented in this volume suggests, Soviet Jews could learn of the persecution in Germany from a number of sources, such as the Yiddish press and interactions with Jews from the Western Ukraine. Most importantly, the information about the Nazi policies was disseminated in the Soviet Union at least prior to the signing of the Molotov-Ribbentrop Pact, and then later during the war as well as in its immediate aftermath.
10. See Milton Teichman and Sharon Leder, eds., *Truth and Lamentation* (Chicago: University of Illinois Press, 1994), 469.
11. David Roskies, *Against the Apocalypse: Responses to Catastrophe in Modern Jewish Culture* (Cambridge, MA: Harvard University Press, 1984), 17.
12. See Boris Slutskii, *Sobranie sochinenii* (Moscow: Khudozhestvennaia literatura, 1993), vol. 2, 340; Boris Slutskii, *Things that Happened*, trans. J. S. Smith. *Glas New Russian Writing* 19 (2000): 187-88.
13. Edward Alexander, *The Holocaust and the War of Ideas* (New Brunswick: Transaction Publishers, 1994), 27.
14. *God za godom* 5 (1989): 95.
15. Smith, *Things that Happened*, 187-88.
16. Il'ia Kukulin, "Regulirovanie boli." At http://www.eurozine.com/articles/article_2005-05-03-kukulin-ru.html (accessed October 30, 2013).
17. In Levitina, "Tak nachinal...," 73.
18. *Biblioteka literatury drevnei Rusi* (St. Petersburg: Nauka, 1999), v. 3, 306-21.

19. Slutskii's allusions to *The Brothers Karamazov* are intricate. Not only does Ivan qoute from the apocryphal text in the novel, but he also cites from Tiutchev's poem, "These Poor Villages," which describes Christ walking through Russian villages. Slutskii engages in an intertextual polemic with this poem by reversing the "poor Russian villages" into the Jewish *shtetlakh*, which, unlike the villages, are not blessed, but dispersed by Christ.

20. Nikolas Berdyaev, *The Russian Idea* (London: The Centenary Press, 1947), 6-7.

21. I am grateful to Harriet Murav for pointing out this allusion.

22. For an illuminating discussion of Greenberg, see Roskies, *Against the Apocalypse*, 266-74.

23. Polina Vengerova, *Vospominaniia babushki* (Jerusalem: Gesharim, 2003).

24. See Slutskii, *O drugikh i o sebe* (Moscow: Vagrius, 2005), 173-76.

25. "Desiat' frontovykh pisem Borisa Slutskogo," *Zvezda* 5 (2004): 166.

26. Slutskii, *O drugikh i o sebe*, 191-92.

27. The poem refers to Dmitrii Donskoi (1350-1389), Ivan the Terrible (1530-1584) and Catherine the Great (1729-1796).

28. Slutskii, *O drugikh i o sebe*, 118-19.

29. See in Maxim Shrayer, *Russian Poet/Soviet Jew: The Legacy of Eduard Bagritskii* (New York: Rowman & Littlefield Publishers, 2000), 21, 133.

30. Slutskii was quite taken with this connection. In the poem "Patria and Patronymic," he writes, "That's how it is indeed: with princely Shuiskii/ I share a surname; Boris Godunov's/ my namesake…" Smith, *Things that Happened*, 186.

31. The Russian text is available at http://www.rvb.ru/pushkin/01text/05theatre/01theatre/0837.htm (accessed October 30, 2013).

32. As Harriet Murav points out in this volume, vengeance (*nekome*) constitutes one of the key themes of Soviet Holocaust poetry. Slutskii's poem predates most of it and thus in fact foreshadows the trope.

33. This, of course, includes Slutskii's own post-war poetry, along with Alexander Mezhirov's, David Samoilov's, and the unpublishable Naum Korzhavin's. Semen Gudzenko, however, was prolific during the war, as were Ian Satunovskii and Iosif Degen.

34. Already in the 19th century, Nikolai Leskov employed this paradigm in his report on the state of Jews in Russia, benevolently arguing, "Let Russia today treat them [Jews] like their mother rather than step-mother would and they will be ready to forget everything that they've endured in the past and become her good sons" (At http://az.lib.ru/l/leskow_n_s/text_0142.shtml [accessed October 30, 2013]).

35. Of course, the major Soviet slogan unveiled at the start of the war was "*Rodina-Mat' zovet!*" (The Motherland calls on you), whose most memorable representation was the poster created by artist Iraklii Taidze at the end of June, 1941.

36. One should keep in mind the special emphasis on Russianness, as opposed to Sovietness, which was undertaken by Stalin during the war to promote patriotism among a disaffected population.

37. Ada Kolganova, ed., *Menora: Evreiskie motivy v russkoi poezii* (Moscow: Jewish University, 1993), 381.

Chapter 7

Poetry After Kerch´: Representing Jewish Mass Death in the Soviet Union[1]

Harriet Murav

Why was there no Holocaust in Soviet Russia?[2] There were killings—approximately 2.5 million Jews died on Soviet soil—but the killings did not take on the same meaning as in the West, where the Holocaust emerged as a unique and paradigmatic set of events.[3] Official Soviet history is part of the reason for the absence of the Holocaust in the former Soviet Union. Zvi Gitelman and Amir Weiner, among others historians, agree about the failure of Soviet historiography and commemoration to acknowledge the unique fate of Jews during World War II. In *Bitter Legacy*, Gitelman characterizes the dominant response to the Holocaust in Soviet historiography not as complete repression, but rather as a consequence of a universalist interpretation, according to which the destruction of the Jews was "part of a larger phenomenon … a consequence of racist fascism."[4] Weiner's *Making Sense of War* traces the evolution of the Soviet version of the "Great Fatherland War" that made Jews disappear—both as soldiers and as Holocaust victims.[5]

The term "Holocaust" itself did not have broad currency in the West during the 1940s; it was not used in Russian publications until the Soviet Union collapsed in the 1990s, and I will therefore avoid it. Nonetheless, Soviet literature, almost completely neglected by scholars and critics, confronts the impossible history of the destruction of the Jews, but not in the same terms as Holocaust literature in the West. In the former Soviet Union and post-Soviet Russia, the scholarly and artistic response to the destruction of the Jews takes on its own, distinct outline, which combines the perspectives of Jewish victim, Jewish avenger, and Jewish victor. To trace these differences, this essay focuses on three Russian-language poems by Il'ia Sel'vinskii published during the 1940s. "*Ia eto videl*" (I Saw It), first published in January 1942, describes the poet's reaction to the sight of 7,000 corpses in a ditch outside the city of Kerch'. Each of the subsequent poems—"*Sud v Krasnodare*" (The Trial in Krasnodar) and "*Kandava*" (Kandava, a city in Latvia)—returns to this scene.

The poems are among the earliest artistic responses in any language to the Nazi mass killings of Jews.[6] They form a cohesive a narrative, building from murder to trial to commemoration. Sel'vinskii's writing confronts the impossible knowledge of what was not yet called the Holocaust even within the Soviet framework of the universality of the suffering that took place under German occupation. His poetry attempts to speak the pain of the victims, but at the same time sounds the call for revenge. Finally, a distinctly Jewish voice—that resonates with Soviet Yiddish literature—emerges in his work.

The Ravine

Il'ia Sel'vinskii (1899-1968) was born in Simferopol, attended gymnasium in Evpatoriia, and fought there during the Civil War. He rose to prominence in the 1920s, when he was associated with the literary movement known as "constructivism." One of his most well-known early works, "*Uliaevshchina*," describes an anti-Bolshevik uprising and includes an anarchist named "Shtein." A narrative poem about a gangster, titled "*Mot'ka malkhamoves*" (Mot'ka the Angel of Death, 1926), uses Yiddish and Hebrew expressions transliterated into the Russian text. In this regard his early writing resembles the work of Russian language Jewish writers of the time, including Isaac Babel', Eduard Bagritskii, Veniamin Kaverin, and Semen Gekht, who employed similar heterolinguistic devices in their work. During the Second World War, Sel'vinskii served in the army in Crimea, the Caucasus, and the Baltic front, and published with several army newspapers. He achieved the rank of colonel.[7] His poem "*Ia eto videl*" (I Saw It) was first published in the newspaper *Bol'shevik* on January 23, 1942, reprinted on February 27, 1942 in the army newspaper *Krasnaia zvezda* (*Red Star*), and included in subsequent publications of his collected works.[8] The poem has been available for decades; thousands and thousands of readers during the war, in the postwar period, and in the post-Soviet period have seen "I Saw It." But no one has recognized its relation to what became Holocaust literature in the West.

"*Ia eto videl*" concerns the murder of seven thousand Jews that took place just outside the Crimean city of Kerch' in 1941, in a place called Bagerovskii rov (ravine), which was used as an anti-tank ditch (a report of this episode was entered into the Nuremberg record by the Soviets).[9] It is instructive to compare what Sel'vinskii wrote to the article that appeared in *The New York Times* on January 7, 1942. Titled "Molotoff Accuses Nazis of Atrocities," the article reported that "Soviet Foreign Commissar Vyacheslaff M. Molotoff ... charged that the Germans shot 8,000 in Kamenetz and Podolsk, 3,000 in Mariupol, several thousand in Kerch'."[10] Molotov's description of the mass killing in Kiev conforms to the emerging Soviet narrative of the universality of suffering by identifying the victims as "Russians, Ukrainians, Jews," although he uses the qualifier "a large number" when referring to the Jews.[11]

Sel'vinskii wrote to his wife on January 12, 1942 that he "visited the ditch outside Kerch', where 7000 women, children, and old people lie shot to death ... And I saw them. I don't have the strength now to write about it in prose, my nerves have stopped reacting, what I could do, I expressed in verse."[12] The key phrase is "I saw them," which the poet uses both here in the letter and as the title of his poem. The Germans completed their bloody work in December of 1941; the Soviets retook Kerch' in January 1942, leaving the Germans no time to cover the evidence, as they did at Babii Iar. Indeed, the frozen bodies of the dead could be clearly seen.

The very opening stanza claims the role of the eyewitness as offering the most credible evidence of the mass murder:

> You may ignore folk tales,
> Doubt the newspaper,
> But I saw it. With my own eyes.
> Understand? I saw it myself.
>
> Here's the road. And over there—hills.
> Between them
> Like this—
> A ravine.
> From this ravine grief rises.
> Without limit.
>
> No! you can't use words for this...
> You have to howl! Scream!
> Seven thousand shot dead in a frozen pit,
> That turned red, like rust.
>
> Who are these people? Soldiers? No.
> Partisans, right? No.[13]

The first stanza raises the question of what kind of account is credible, discarding both "folk tales" (*narodnye skazaniia*) and newspaper reports (*gazetnye stolbtsy*) as susceptible to doubt, and offering as irrefutable the evidence of an eyewitness. The distinction between evidence that is not compelling and evidence that is carries with it an obligation on the part of the witness and those who hear his testimony. The opening words "*mozhno ne slushat'*," which I translate "you may ignore" can also be rendered more literally, "It is possible not to listen to," in the sense of hearken, attend to, obey. The opening line "*mozhno ne slushat'*" (you may ignore) contains an implied commandment, "*nado slushat'*" (you must listen to): you must listen to this poem, because it speaks for the dead.

The "seven thousand shot dead in the frozen pit" have to be heard, and Sel'vinskii struggles to create an impossible language that could adequately translate the victims' pain:

К неумолимой грамматике сведен	Every cry that flies from their lips
Каждый крик, слетающий с губ.	Corresponds to an implacable grammar.
Здесь нужно бы... Нужно созвать бы вече,	Here you would have to...call an assembly
Из всех племен от древка до древка	From every tribe
И взять от каждого все человечье,	And extract from each all that is human,
Все, прорвавшееся сквозь века,-	Everything that burst through the centuries,
Вопли, хрипы, вздохи и стоны,	Shrieks, cries, sighs and groans,
Эхо нашествий, погромов, резни...	The echo of attacks, pogroms, butchery...
Не это ль	Wouldn't this
наречье	Utterance
муки бездонной	Of bottomless torment
Словам искомым сродни?	Be equal to the word that is sought?[14]

Sel'vinskii imagines an impossible language that has no words, but only inchoate cries. Each cry nonetheless corresponds to an "implacable grammar," the grammar of pain, which has no grammar, which destroys articulate speech.[15] To speak this language properly is to submit to torment, to be reduced to what is less than human. Each "correct" utterance brings the speaker closer to death. To conform to this implacable grammar means to cease speaking. Kerch' thus creates an impossible poetics.

This question of impossibility has broad resonance in the critical reception of Holocaust literature. Not only Adorno, whose essay I hint at in my title, but also Lyotard, Derrida, Cathy Caruth, and others address the problem of impossibility in relation to the Holocaust: the impossibility of poetry itself, and the impossibility of traumatic knowledge.[16] Lyotard in *The Differend* and Derrida in his writing on Paul Celan, focus on the impossibility of testimony and witnessing.[17] The differend is "the unstable state and instance of language wherein something must be able to be put into phrases yet cannot be."[18] Sel'vinskii's "I Saw It," which could easily be dismissed as mere Soviet propaganda, engages one of the central issues of Western writing about the Holocaust.

The victims, whose pain the poet translates into an impossible language, must then be listened to, and obeyed, as in the eighth stanza, in which the dead command the poet:

> Go on then! Brand them! You stand before the massacre,
> You caught them red-handed—condemn them!
> You see how the butcher's bullet
> Smashed us to pieces,
> Thunder forth like Dante, like Ovid,
> Let nature herself cry
> If
> You yourself
> Saw
> All this
> And haven't gone out of your mind.[19]

The first stanza, with its delineation of what does not have to be "listened to" anticipates this order from the dead.

In three succeeding stanzas Sel'vinskii picks out details describing three different victims of the mass murder: a young man (*paren'*) with an amputed leg; a peasant woman (*babka*), a Christian, who reproaches the Virgin Mary for what the Germans have done; and a Jewish woman with her child (*isterzannaia evreika/ pri nei rebenok*). The mention of the Christian conforms to the Soviet cliché of the universality of suffering during the German occupation. Sel'vinskii also lists as victims the inhabitants of the surrounding collective farms, whose population included a significant number of Jews.[20] Sel'vinskii, who grew up in Crimea, knew who his neighbors were. The mention of the amputee is not misleading: the Nazis had a policy of exterminating the disabled.

The description of the Jewish mother and child is the longest and most emotional:

> Next to her a tormented Jewish woman.
> With a child. Completely as if in a dream.
> With what care the child's neck
> Is wrapped in the mother's gray scarf …
> A mother's heart doesn't change:
> Going to be shot, under the gun,
> An hour, a half-hour before death
> The mother protected the child from catching cold.
> But even death is no parting for them:
> The enemy has no power over them now—
> And a red stream
> From the child's ear
> Drips into the mother's
> Cupped palm.[21]

This description of the passive Jewish mother dramatically changes in a subsequent stanza when the poet declares that the mother's hands, now a fist, will "burn through" the Germans' "blue waltzes." The image of the Jewish mother's fist transforms Jewish suffering into Jewish revenge, an important dimension of the Soviet-Jewish response to the Nazi genocide. Sel'vinskii develops the theme of revenge both in "I Saw It" and in subsequent poems.

"I Saw It" does not name its implied narrator as a Jew; nor does it explicitly identify the seven thousand corpses in the ravine as Jews, except in the vignette of the Jewish mother. Sel'vinskii's fellow Soviets, however, knew who the victims were. The mention of the Jewish mother would have been more than enough; even had Sel'vinskii used only the Soviet code for Jewish victim, "peaceful Soviet citizen," his readers would have understood. His Western readers, however, could use the absence of explicit naming to characterize the poem as too Soviet and not Jewish enough. Sel'vinskii addresses this issue in the poem I discuss next.

No Mercy

Sel'vinskii returns to the mass killing at Kerch' in a later poem, "*Sud v Krasnodare*" (The Trial at Krasnodar), first published in the literary journal *Znamia* in 1945 and republished in an anthology of the author's work in 1947.[22] The poem describes the first war crimes trial conducted by a Soviet military tribunal in Krasnodar from July 14 to July 17, 1943. The Germans had occupied the North Caucasus Krasnodar region in the latter part of 1942. They and their collaborators killed approximately 20,000 Jews, many of whom were evacuees from Ukraine.[23] Three hundred patients at a psychiatric hospital, and at least 80 wounded Soviet officers were also killed; Jews were included in these numbers. The Germans introduced mobile gas vans, known in Russian as *dushegubki*, in these locations. I. I. Kotov, who survived a gas van killing, gave key testimony at the trial. In the poem, one of the defendants accused of collaborating with the Gestapo attempts to exonerate himself by saying that he only worked for the Germans as a driver, without killing anyone. Turning on the ignition of a *dushegubka* was what released the gas into the chamber of the vehicle. Kotov identifies him as the driver of a mobile gas van (*dushegubka*):

> But Kotov's two moonbeam eyes
> stared with such force
> at the witness,
> that it seemed for a moment
> two shadows fell on the floor from them ...
> And his voice in the hysterical quiet
> of the tormented hall pronounced these words:
> —I was in the fourth group, driver.
> Don't you recognize my ghost?[24]

This defendant and seven others were sentenced to death; approximately 30,000 people came to view the hangings.[25]

The poem contrasts different responses to the verdict. A newspaper correspondent asks the first-person narrator, the poet, whether he feels pity for the condemned; the poet does not. The correspondent, skeptical about the poet's denial, characterizes it as mere propaganda ("*Etot vash otvet/ sovsem ne bolee, kak propaganda*"). For the poet, however, the sight of victims' bodies at Kerch'—"seven thousand corpses" (*sem' tysiach trupov*)—is the basis for his lack of pity for the collaborators. In the earlier poem, "I Saw It," Sel'vinskii wrote: "Whoever saw you, from now on/ Will carry your wounds in his soul" (*Kto vas uvidel, otnyne naveki/ Vse vashi rany v dushe uneset*).[26]

The wound makes itself felt in "*Sud v Krasnodare*" and even earlier; from the wound comes the poem "I Saw It." Note the relation between "Whoever saw you," and "I saw it." Earlier I remarked on the emphasis on seeing as the grounds for the poet's credibility, as if the line "I saw it" was marked "I *saw* it (*Ia eto* videl);" now another accentuation emerges—"I saw *it*" (Ia *eto videl*). It was I who saw it, and therefore I am marked, wounded by it, the victims' pain inscribes itself in me, I am implicated in it, I must answer it, I belong again and already to this community. There is something like the Deuteronomic circumcision of the heart playing just under the surface of the poem ("Circumcise the foreskin of your heart," Deut. 10:16; "And the Lord your God will circumcise your heart and the heart of your offspring" Deut. 30:6). *I* saw it and have been circumcised in my heart, I now carry your wound and therefore cannot and must not feel pity for the perpetrators.

As an eyewitness to the aftermath of the mass killing of Jews, he cannot feel sorrow for anyone who aided in other, similar killings. The exchange that follows explicitly links religious affiliation and the emotional response to the verdict. The poet's interlocutor, the correspondent, tells him that as a Christian he is obliged to pity the condemned: "*Kak khristianin, ia dolzhen pozhalet' seichas vot etikh*." The poet's extraordinary response, with which the poem ends, is worth quoting in full:

Немыслимая боль, как от удара,	An unthinkable pain
на миг оборвала мое дыханье—	stopped my breath
и тошнотой под горло....	nausea filled my throat ...
—Уходите!	Get out!
'Христианин' опешил.	The "Christian" was taken aback.
—У -хо -ди -те!	Get out!
Благодарите бога, что никто	Thank God no one
не слышал этой фразы.	heard that phrase.
Ну!	Get moving!
Ступайте!	
Мне очень жалко вашего Христа.	I am very sorry for your Christ.[27]

The poet names his interlocutor as a Christian in the line—"The 'Christian' was taken aback"—and by implied contrast, names himself as a non-Christian. He goes on to express the pity the correspondent sought for the condemned collaborators for Christ instead: "I am very sorry for your Christ." Note the possessive adjective "your." This line about pity for "your Christ" can be parsed as a Jewish response, a way that the poet names himself as a Jew. It can also be parsed as a Soviet, atheist response to the demand for Christian compassion; however, Sel'vinskii does not mention Russia, the Soviet Union,

Stalin, or communism in the passage above, just the contrast between the Christian and the non-Christian.[28] The rejection of Christ and the rejection of mercy for the perpetrators are equally Soviet and Jewish responses to the mass killings of victims whom the Soviets did not identify as Jews.

The poet's fury at the demand for Christian compassion represents one of the dimensions of the Soviet-Jewish response to the Nazi genocide. Soviet-Jewish works written in the 1940s and in subsequent periods emphasize rage and the desire for retribution, in contrast to what emerged as Holocaust literature in the West. The last stanza of Sel'vinskii's "I Saw It" hammers away at the theme of retribution:

Ров... Поэмой ли скажешь о нем?	The ravine..? Can you describe this in a poem?
Семь тысяч трупов.	Seven thousand corpses.
Семиты... Славяне...	Semites…Slavs
Да! Об этом нельзя словами.	Yes! Not with words,
Огнем! Только огнем!	But with firepower.[29]

The only language adequate to speak of the mass killing is the language of revenge. Revenge, "*nekome*," is the central motif of Soviet Yiddish literature written during the war. A document produced by the Jewish Anti-Fascist Committee on the occasion of a rally held on August 24, 1941 appealed to "fellow Jews the world over" to join the Soviet people's and the Red Army's "holy war" against Hitler: "it is not by memorial candles but by fire that the murderers of humanity must be destroyed, [n]ot tears, but hate and resistance to the monsters."[30] Peretz Markish's 1943 "*Dem yidishn shlaktman*" (To the Jewish Warrior) transforms the pain of the victims into a call for revenge: "*Un blut af ale vegn shrayt: nekome!*" (The blood on every road cries out: revenge!).[31]

Itsik Fefer's "*Di shvue*" (The Oath) was published in 1942 in the first issue of the Soviet Yiddish newspaper *Eynikayt*, the organ of the Jewish Antifascist Committee, and published in Russian under the title "*Kliatva*" (The Oath) in the mainstream literary journal *Znamia* (*The Banner*) in the same year. The poet swears that his hatred and wrath will not be spent until he feels his enemy's blood on his own flesh, and vows to fight on even if he loses both arms and grows blind. Fefer's "Oath" works by building from the consequences of his own oath and vow: the speaker swears that if he loses one arm, he will kill the enemy with the other, if he loses his other arm, his hate will give him strength to continue fighting. If he fails to erase every trace of the enemy and obliterate the memory of his enemy, if he fails in his oath and vow to the Soviet land and the Jewish people, his own name will remain forever on the roll-call of shame.[32]

The source of the revenge motif is Psalm 137, which begins, "By the rivers of Babylon, there we sat down, yea, we wept when we remembered Zion." The historical event around which the psalm is built is the destruction of Jerusalem in 586 BCE, and the subsequent Babylonian captivity—the first in a series of catastrophic destructions in Jewish history, that, according to traditional Jews, culminates in "*der driter khurbn*" (the third destruction), what the Soviets did not call the Holocaust. In the psalm, the captors demand that their prisoners sing to them; the Jews' response, however, turns compliance into resistance. The psalm begins in uncertainty, "How shall we sing the Lord's song in a foreign land?" and moves to action, first with an oath of remembrance—"If I forget thee, O Jerusalem, let my right hand forget her cunning./ Let my tongue cleave to the roof of my mouth, if I remember thee not"—and culminates in a prophecy of Babylon's destruction, depicting in grisly terms the joy of revenge: "O daughter of Babylon, that art to be destroyed; happy shall he be that repayeth thee as thou has served us./ Happy shall he be that taketh and dasheth thy little ones against the rock." The stanza is structured around a promise made by the poet and the enumeration of the consequences of its violation.

It is not only revenge that links Sel'vinskii's writing to the work of Soviet Yiddish poets. His explicit lack of "Christian" compassion for the fate of the perpetrators is another theme that connects him to the Yiddish writers. Bergelson's story *It Was Night and Became Day* (*Geven iz nakht un gevorn iz tog*), published in 1943, explicitly reserves compassion (*mitleyd*) for Jewish victims and not German perpetrators.[33] Itsik Kipnis's Yiddish language memoir *Fun mayne togbikher*, published in *Sovetish heymland* in 1965, describes his reaction to the hanging of convicted German war criminals in Kiev in 1946 as unmitigated joy. His "heart sang": "*Un in mir hot gezungen ...un in mir zingt, s'tantst unter mir.*"[34] In the West, in contrast, Jewish rage was suppressed. Naomi Seidman's comparison of the Yiddish, French, and English versions of Eli Wiesel's *Night* reveals that the original Yiddish emphasizes the theme of revenge. The original Yiddish reproaches the survivors for failing to carry out revenge; the subsequent translations into French and English praise them for transcending revenge.[35]

Where did Jewish revenge go, in what ways was it displaced and concealed in the West? This question goes beyond the confines of this paper; however, the differences between Western and Soviet (and Soviet Jewish) narratives of the Nazi genocide shed light on why Soviet Jewish responses to the destruction of the Jews remain illegible as Holocaust literature. Saul Friedlander describes the outlines of the Western Holocaust narrative in terms of passivity and heroism, catastrophe and redemption. Most Jews were led like sheep to the slaughter; the heroic few ghetto fighters and partisans mostly belonged to Zionist youth movements. The Soviet war narrative also casts the Jews of capitalist Western Europe as victims. The starring role, however, is reserved for the victorious Red Army, which united the peoples of the USSR, including Jews, Ukrainians, and others, and most heroically, Russians. The Soviet Union saved Europe from Hitler. "Implicitly, the catastrophe of European Jews," Friedlander observes, with regard to the Western narrative, "is linked to the redemption of Israel."[36] In the West, the Jewish vow, as in Fefer's "*Shvue*," went into the cry "Never again," into the struggle for Israel, struggle, which, after 1948, the Soviet Union viciously opposed, another reason that nothing written there could be seen as Jewish, or, pro-Jewish.

Quentin Tarantino's 2009 film *Inglourious Basterds* raises the specter of Jewish revenge in fantasy celluloid form. The "face of Jewish revenge" is self-conscious simulacrum, a projection on a projection, played on hundreds of movie screens.[37] The call for Jewish revenge in the Soviet Union in the 1940s, in contrast, was—dare I say it—real. Western readers brought up on the image of Jews as victims cannot recognize the work of Sel'vinskii, Fefer, Markish, Bergelson, and others as Holocaust literature because the theme of revenge is too vivid and too visceral to conform to expectations of Jewish suffering.

A Double Dream

"*Kandava*" (the title is the name of a city in Latvia) is the final and most important of the triad of poems written by Sel'vinskii in the 1940s in response to the destruction of the Jews. In this work, published in 1947, the poet describes himself both as a Jewish victim of the Nazi genocide and also as a triumphant Soviet and Jewish army officer accepting the German surrender at Kandava. Sel'vinskii in fact participated in the ceremony in May 1945 as a

Soviet officer.³⁸ The poem, remarkably, frames its account of military triumph with the Jewish nightmare of the death camp:

Мне снился накануне сон: иду с женою рядом где-то в Освенциме	Last night I had a dream: I was walking with my wife somewhere either in Auschwitz
или в Майданеке. Иду аллеей фашистских серо голубых солдат— и тысячи оледенелых глаз, презрительных, насмешливых, злорадных, а то и просто любопытных—смотрят на то, как мы идем на гибель.	or Majdanek. I was walking past a row of blue-gray fascist soldiers— and myriads of hateful eyes contemptuous, mocking, malicious and sometimes just curious—watched how we went to our death.³⁹

The opening stanza poses the question of the relation between the death camps and Kandava, the title of the work. The stanza that follows, however, does not answer the question, but introduces yet another location, the scene of the poet's childhood. The poet remembers himself as a little boy, trying to see how long he could hold his breath; this section ends with a philosophical reflection with the real suffering that dreams can inflict. The first part of the poem concludes:

Так если есть "пейзаж души" где можно бы его изобразить,— отметьте на моей: "Майданек."	If there is a "landscape of the soul" and a map, on which you could draw it— mark on mine: "Majdanek."⁴⁰

The repetition of the sounds "m" plus "e" in "*otmet'e*," "*moei*" and the first syllable of Majdanek (which I have tried to capture with "mark," "mine," and "Majdanek") embody what Roman Jakobson calls paronomasia, sound mirroring.⁴¹ The reflection of the sound of the previous word in the succeeding syllables impedes the forward motion of the line; the sound-image that is thereby formed serves to fix the place of the poet's nightmare as the death camp, pinning him down to this spot on the map and no other. The poet does not name himself as a Jew, and he never claims first-hand knowledge of Auschwitz, Majdanek, or Treblinka, all of which he mentions in the poem. However, he explicitly contrasts his own map of nightmares with that of some dreamer for whom the nightmare would take place in

Poetry After Kerch': Representing Jewish Mass Death in the Soviet Union

some other location; some other dreamer would dream of being chased by a panther in the jungle. In labeling his own space on the map of nightmares with the name of a death camp, Sel'vinskii signals his belonging among murdered Jews.

The second part of the poem dramatically changes register from dream and memory to documentary detail, giving the precise date and place, and specifying the division of the German army that surrendered. As I mentioned earlier, this section of the poem reflects Sel'vinskii's real-life experience as a Soviet officer. The poet identifies himself one of "seven Soviet officers" who enter the base to accept the surrender. The nightmare of Majdanek and other scenes of the mass killing of Jews disrupt the victory at Kandava. As he walks in front of the ranks of Germans, the poet remembers his nightmare of the previous evening and recognizes the same look of contempt in the eyes of the defeated soldiers. A German captain in particular draws his attention, because he wears a little bronze badge on his sleeve depicting the most beloved places of the poet's youth in a now destroyed Crimea. One place stands out:

И, наконец, от древности седая,	And finally, gray with age,
заваленная пеплом, как Помпея,	covered in ash, like Pompei,
забрызганная кровью и мозгами	spattered with blood and brains
вершина всех моих мучений—"Керчь"!	the height of all my torments—"Kerch"![42]

The mass killing at Kerch'—the subject of his poem "I Saw It"—which took place only three years earlier, is thrust back from the recent to the remote past; covered with ash like Pompei, it impossibly belongs simultaneously to antiquity and to the immediate present. It is covered with ash but still gory with blood and brains. Kerch' happened in the ancient past and it is still happening now. The delay in coming to terms with it and the repetition of its immediacy are characteristic of the belatedness of trauma. The poet tears the badge from the German officer's sleeve, and thinks the captain must be dreaming his, the poet's dream, from the night before—the poet's dream of Auschwitz or Majdanek, in which he and his wife were Jewish victims and the Germans were triumphant.[43] The captain must be dreaming that one of his prisoners dared to assault him, "an S. S. officer, an Aryan."

But on the day of his own surrender, however, the German does not respond to the Jew's act. He keeps quiet. The poem ends by describing what can be heard in that silence:

А в этом яростном молчаньи	And in that vivid silence
я слышал шум красноармейских стягов,	I heard Red Army banners
браваду труб и грохот барабанов,	The blare of the trumpets and the din of drums,
и ликованье мертвых голосов	and the exultation of dead voices
из пепла, из поэм, из сновидений!	made of ash, poems, and dreams![44]

The last lines of the poem bring together the incommensurable elements of the interior space of the poet's nightmare, the voices of death camp inmates turned to ash, the triumphant sounds of victory, and poetry itself, without subordinating any one voice to another. It is important that the victory of the Soviet Army—the victory of Soviet Jews—does not drown out the voices of the Jewish dead.

I conclude my discussion of "*Kandava*" by returning to the issues that I raised in the beginning of this chapter. Far from making Jews disappear as soldiers or as Holocaust victims, as Amir Weiner contends, "*Kandava*" makes Jews vividly legible in both roles. "Memory of the Jewish catastrophe," to use Weiner's language, is *not* submerged in the grand narrative of the universality of Soviet suffering.[45] The Jewish catastrophe escapes temporal boundaries in the poem "*Kandava*": it is a historically and impossibly part of the poet's childhood terror and is as ancient as the disaster at Pompei; it disrupts the poet's triumph at the place called Kandava. The poem's multiple embedded narratives of adult nightmare and "torment," childhood terror and victory, suspend the linear, teleological motion towards a single message of Soviet triumph. The poetic use of mise-en-abyme, the placement of the image of the death camp both as the frame for and at the center of the narrative of victory at Kandava, makes it impossible to decide which narrative dominates. It is this undecidability that is so crucially a part of the distinctly Soviet but nonetheless universally impossible history of what Sel'vinskii does not call the Holocaust.

Notes

1. Another version of a section of this essay was originally published in Harriet Murav, *Music from a Speeding Train: Jewish Literature in Post-Revolution Russia* (Stanford, Stanford University Press, 2011), 154-166. I am grateful to Stanford University Press for granting me permission to use this material.
2. For a discussion, see David Shneer, *Through Soviet Jewish Eyes: Photography, War, and the Holocaust* (New Brunswick, NJ: Rutgers University Press, 2011).
3. Zvi Gitelman, "Soviet Jewry before the Holocaust," in *Bitter Legacy: Confronting the Holocaust in the USSR*, ed. Zvi Gitelman (Bloomington: Indiana University Press, 1997), 11.
4. Zvi Gitelman, "Politics and the Historiography of the Holocaust in the Soviet Union," in *Bitter Legacy: Confronting the Holocaust in the USSR*, ed. Zvi Gitelman (Bloomington: Indiana University Press, 1997), 18.
5. Amir Weiner, *Making Sense of War: The Second World War and the Fate of the Bolshevik Revolution* (Princeton: Princeton University Press, 2001), 191-235.
6. For a book-length study of Sel'vinskii and "Ia eto videl," see Maxim Shrayer, *I SAW IT: Ilya Selvinsky and the Legacy of Bearing Witness to the Shoah* (Boston: Academic Studies Press, 2013).
7. I take my account of Sel'vinskii's biography from *Elektronnaia evreiskaia entsiklopediia*, s.v. "Sel'vinskii, Il'ia," http://www.eleven.co.il/article/13753 (accessed December 15, 2011); L. M. Farber, "Sel'vinskii," in *Kratkaia literaturnaia entsiklopediia*, vol. 6, ed. A. A. Surkov (Moscow: Sovetskaia entsklopediia, 1971); and Ts. Voskresenskaia, "Na voine: iz dnevnikov i pisem rodnym 1941-1945gg.," *Novyi mir* 12 (1984): 163-75.
8. The edition published in *Krasnaia zvezda* speaks of "Russian grief" ("*russkoe gore*"); subsequent reworkings in 1964 and 1971 omit this phrase and introduce other variations. I use the version found in Il'ia Sel'vinskii, *Sobranie sochinenii v shesti tomakh*, vol. 1 (Moscow: Khudozhestvennaia literatura, 1971). Unless otherwise noted, all translations from this and other works are my own.
9. Catherine Merridale characterizes the mass killing at Kerch' as providing the first evidence of the German policy of such killings; see Merridale, *Ivan's War: Life and Death in the Red Army, 1939-1945* (New York: Metropolitan Books, 2006), 291. For other discussions of the Kerch' mass killing, see Il'ia Al'tman, *Zhertvy nenavisti: Kholokost v SSSR 1941-1945* (Moscow: Fond "Kovcheg," 2002), 287; Yitzhak Arad, ed., *Unichtozhenie evreev SSSR v gody nemetskoi okkupatsii, 1941-1944: sbornik dokumentov i materialov* (Jerusalem: Yad Vashem, 1992), 183-85; and Yitzhak Arad, *The Holocaust in the Soviet Union* (Jerusalem: Yad Vashem, 2009), 402-3.
10. "Molotoff Accuses Nazis of Atrocities: Note Detailing 'Crimes' Handed to All Foreign Diplomats," *New York Times*, 7 January 1942, 8.
11. Ibid. Photographs of the Kerch' mass killing, captioned "Hitlerite Atrocities at Kerch'," were sent to Britain from Moscow. See Janina Struk, *Photographing the Holocaust: Interpretations of the Evidence* (London: I. B. Tauris, 2004), 47.
12. Sel'vinskii, *Sobranie sochinenii*, vol. 1, 678. For a discussion of the photograph that accompanied the poem, see David Shneer's essay in this volume.

13 Ibid., 352.

14 Ibid., 355.

15 For a discussion of pain and language see Elaine Scarry, *The Body in Pain: The Making and Unmaking of the World* (New York: Oxford University Press, 1985), 42-45, 60-61.

16 Cathy Caruth, *Unclaimed Experience: Trauma, Narrative, and History* (Baltimore, MD: Johns Hopkins University Press, 1996).

17 See, for example, Jacques Derrida, *Sovereignties in Question: The Poetics of Paul Celan*, ed. J. D. Caputo (New York: Fordham University Press, 2005), 65-96; Sidra DeKoven Ezrahi, "Representing Auschwitz," in *The Holocaust: Theoretical Readings*, ed. Neil Levy and Michael Rothberg (New Brunswick: Rutgers University Press, 2003), 318-22; and Jean-Francois Lyotard, *The Differend: Phrases in Dispute*, trans. Georges Van Den Abbeele, Theory and History of Literature, no. 46 (Minneapolis: University of Minnesota Press, 1988).

18 Lyotard, *Differend*, 9.

19 Sel'vinskii, *Sobranie sochinenii*, vol. 1,354.

20 Jewish agricultural settlement in this region began in Tsarist times and continued in the 1920s and '30s. See Jonathan Dekel-Chen, *Farming the Red Land: Jewish Agricultural Colonization and Local Soviet Power, 1924-1941* (New Haven: Yale University Press, 2005).

21 Sel'vinskii, *Sobranie sochinenii*,vol 1, 353.

22 Il'ia Sel'vinskii, "Sud v Krasnodare," *Znamia* (1945): 11. I take the text from Il'ia Sel'vinskii, *Krym, Kavkaz, Kuban'* (Moscow: Sovetskii pisatel', 1947), 147-55.

23 See Arad, *Holocaust in the Soviet Union*, 294.

24 Sel'vinskii, *Krym*, 147.

25 For a discussion of this and other Soviet war crimes trials, see Ilya Bourtman, "'Blood for Blood, Death for Death': The Soviet Military Tribunal in Krasnodar, 1943," *Holocaust and Genocide Studies* 22.2 (Fall 2008): 246-65; and Alexander Victor Prusin, "'Fascist Criminals to the Gallows!': The Holocaust and Soviet War Crimes Trials, December 1945- February 1946," *Holocaust and Genocide Studies* 17.1 (Spring 2003): 1-30.

26 Sel'vinskii, *Sobranie sochinenii*, vol. 1, 355.

27 Sel'vinskii, *Krym*, 151.

28 The visceral revulsion that arises in response to the demand for compassion is an important factor in resolving the question. In his study of nationalism, Benedict Anderson writes that people do not as a rule go to their deaths for the sake of an abstract idea, but rather, for the sake of a people with whom they identify; see Benedict Anderson, *Imagined Communities: Reflections on the Origin and Spread of Nationalism* (London and New York: Verso, 1991), 1-7. By the same logic, the poet's nausea stems not from his allegiance to communist atheism, but rather, from his horror and pain at the sight of the corpses outside Kerch'. These emotions, we may assume, flow both from his humanity and his particular affiliation as a Jew. However, identification with the Jews and identification with the Soviet Union do not preclude one another. The poet's sense of loyalty to the Soviet Union in the 1940s, expressed in this and other poems, arises, it can be argued, from his position as a Jew. The Soviet Union, as a non-

Christian nation, removed the disabilities that burdened Jews in the Tsarist period. The Nazis made antisemitism the cornerstone of their state ideology.

29 Sel'vinskii, *Sobranie sochinenii*, vol. 1, 355.

30 "An Appeal to World Jewry," in *War, Holocaust and Stalinism: A Documented Study of the Jewish Anti-Fascist Committee in the USSR*, ed. Shimon Redlich ([New York]: Harwood Academic Publishers, 1995), 175.

31 Peretz Markish, *Heymland: Literarishe zamlbukh* (Moscow: Der emes, 1943), 3. David Shneer explicates the link between the theme of blood and revenge in "Rivers of Blood: Peretz Markish, the Holocaust, and Jewish Vengeance," in *A Captive of the Dawn: The Life and Work of Peretz Markish*, ed. Joseph Sherman et al. (Oxford: Legenda, 2011), 145.

32 Itsik Fefer, *Roytarmeyish* (New York: ICUF, 1943), 3.

33 David Bergelson, *Geven iz nakht un gevorn iz tog.* (Moscow: Der emes, 1943).

34 Itsik Kipnis, "Fun mayne togbikher," *Sovetish heymland* 1 (January 1965): 117.

35 According to Seidman, the Yiddish *Un di velt hot geshvign* describes a scene in which surviving young men go to Weimar to steal food and clothing and to "rape German girls," but the narrator indicts them for their failure to fulfill "the historical commandment of revenge" (Naomi Seidman, *Faithful Rendering: Jewish Christian Difference and the Politics of Translation* [Chicago: University of Chicago Press, 2006], 221). Seidman does not specify a textual source for this commandment, but a good candidate is Psalm 137.

36 Saul Friedlander, "The Shoah Between Memory and History," in *Breaking Crystal: Writing and Memory After Auschwitz*, ed. Efraim Sicher (Urbana: University of Illinois Press, 1998), 347.

37 For a discussion of the debate surrounding the film, see Ben Walters, "Debating Inglourious Basterds," *Film Quarterly* 63.2 (2009): 19-21.

38 For an overview of Sel'vinskii's participation in the war and a selection of his letters and diary entries from this time, see Voskresenskaia, "Na voine."

39 Sel'vinskii, *Krym*, 209.

40 Ibid., 211.

41 Roman Jakobson, *Language in Literature*, ed. Krystyna Pomorska and Stephen Rudy (Cambridge, MA: Harvard University Press, 1987), 86.

42 Sel'vinskii, *Krym*, 215-16.

43 In this respect "*Kandava*" reworks the motif of the double dream from Lermontov's "Son." See M. Iu. Lermontov, *Izbrannye proizvedeniia v dvukh tomakh*, vol. 1 (Moscow: Khudozhestvennaia literatura, 1963), 306. I am grateful to Valeriia Sobol for pointing out this similarity.

44 Sel'vinskii, *Krym*, 217.

45 Weiner, *Making Sense of War*, 191-235.

Chapter 8

Between the Permitted and the Forbidden: The Politics of Holocaust Representation in *The Unvanquished* (1945)[1]

Olga Gershenson

In October 1945, *The Unvanquished* premiered in Moscow theaters. The Nazi crimes against the Jews that would later be known as the Holocaust were at the core of the film. One of the central characters was a Jewish doctor played by the great Yiddish actor Veniamin L'vovich Zuskin. A key scene in the film was the mass execution of Jews by an SS unit. This scene was filmed on location, in Babii Iar, a place that came to symbolize the Holocaust in the Soviet Union. For its time and place, the film was remarkable for its deeply sympathetic treatment of the Jewish catastrophe.

Because of this treatment, *The Unvanquished* has recently attracted scholarly attention. According to the Russian critic Miron Markovich Chernenko, *The Unvanquished* was the first film to depict the Holocaust on Soviet screens, and one of the first such films worldwide. He points out that several recurrent motifs in the representation of the Holocaust, such as images of Jews led to their death and characters of righteous gentiles, appeared for the first time in this film.[2] Film scholar Jeremy Hicks also approaches *The Unvanquished* as the first Holocaust film and considers it within the broader context of both the historical events of the Holocaust on Soviet territory and representations of the Holocaust in other films. Hicks provides a nuanced analysis of the film and explains why it did not become a part of the Holocaust film canon even though it was the first Holocaust film.[3] Elena Baraban reads *The Unvanquished* as a film dealing with two taboo Soviet topics: Jews and prisoners-of-war, both excluded from "the big family" of the Soviet people.[4]

Despite their different readings of the film, what underlies these scholars' interest is the fact that *The Unvanquished*, a film representing the Nazi massacre in Babii Iar, was released in 1945 and was positively received by Soviet critics—it was even chosen to represent the USSR at the Venice Biennale in 1946.[5] Seemingly, this story contradicts the widespread assumption about the Soviet silencing of the Holocaust. What does *The Unvanquished* reveal about the Soviet treatment of the Holocaust? I argue that the history of the production and reception of *The Unvanquished* demonstrates Soviet ambivalence about the Holocaust and a profound confusion about Holocaust representation. This history captures the moment of indeterminacy in Soviet discourse about the Holocaust when it was still being formulated, and thus it gives us an insight into the discourse-in-the-making.

As historians Karel Berkhoff and Kiril Feferman show, during the war Soviet attitudes vacillated between the allowed and the forbidden, complicated by the positioning of the Holocaust simultaneously as a matter of Jewish history and a part of the general Soviet war history. Throughout the war, there was no consistent policy regarding representation of the Holocaust, but despite the inconsistency the tendency was towards silencing, universalization, and externalization of the Holocaust.[6] These tendencies intensified over time: if in the early stages of the war, the Holocaust was a permissible topic (mainly because it was a matter of foreign policy), starting in 1943 the Jewish character of the Holocaust was increasingly downplayed.[7] And nevertheless, this was just a tendency. Berkoff emphasizes that "even as late as August 1944 there was no top-level decision, in writing or not to fully omit Jews from media reports about the victims of the Nazis."[8]

Despite the tendency towards silence about the fate of Jews during the war, the Jewish tragedy could still be seen in artistic productions as late as 1948, and it was directly referenced in legal discourse (mainly in the reportage of the Nuremberg Trial).[9] Taken together, this amounts to a contradictory and ambivalent picture. These tensions and ambivalence with regard to the interpretation of the Jewish tragedy permeate *The Unvanquished* on several levels—the film's narrative, as well as the film's professional and critical reception.

How a Soviet Novel Turned into a Jewish Film

In 1943, *Pravda* serialized Boris Leont'evich Gorbatov's novel *The Unvanquished*, about the fate of a Ukrainian family during the war.[10] The action takes place in an occupied Ukrainian town, where Taras lives with his extended family—his wife, his young daughter, and two daughters-in-law with children. His two sons fight in the Red Army and in the partisan movement. The novel was published when the war was still raging, but it ends on a happy note, with the liberation of the town. Among other minor characters there is an old Jewish man—a lonely doctor, who used to treat Taras's children and grandchildren. In the novel, he appears only twice: first, when Taras runs into him in the street, and second, when the doctor, along with other Jews, is marched to his death. Another Jewish character mentioned in passing is a little girl, hidden by various people in their houses, until the Nazis capture and presumably kill her.

The novel, surprisingly readable for 1943 *Pravda*, was a big hit (in the same year, it came out in book form and had dozens editions in the 1940s-1980s), and soon after its publication the great Soviet director, Mark Semenovich Donskoi, turned it into a film. Donskoi was at the peak of his fame: his then most recent film, *Rainbow* (1943), the story of a Ukrainian partisan woman, was an enormous success. *Rainbow* won not only the Stalin Prize but also recognition of American critics, and it was allegedly understood by Franklin Roosevelt without translation.[11] Donskoi was ethnically Jewish, but he was neither part of the Soviet Yiddish cultural establishment, nor did he identify publicly with the Jewish people or feature Jewish themes in his work. For instance, even though *Rainbow* takes place in occupied Ukraine, there is no mention of Jews on screen. *The Unvanquished* was a considerable departure from that position.

The transformation of the novel entailed more than the development of a Jewish plotline. For 1945 Soviet Union, the film is unusually redolent with Jewish references. This was a conscious choice: writing about the film shortly after its completion, Donskoi keeps emphasizing its Jewish characters, especially Dr. Fishman, whose story is intertwined with that of Taras's family.[12] Donskoi puts the Jewish doctor front and center: the novel opens with a scene of mass escape from town; the film opens with a close-up of Dr. Fishman. He is treating Taras's sick granddaughter to the sound of bombing in the background. Dr. Fishman cuts a sympathetic and even endearing figure. He is portrayed as a member of the intelligentsia—a balding professor, with a beard and white hair, in a suit and a tie. He speaks polite, hyper-correct Russian, in a voice that remains calm even at the most dramatic moments. His suffering is endured stoically. He doesn't lose his sense of humor—attending to his little patient under the whistling missiles, he playfully recites with her a children's poem about kind Doctor Aibolit (a Russian Doctor Doolittle, a character beloved by generations of Soviet children). He is Doctor Aibolit himself.

When the doctor leaves Taras's house, the tracking shot shows his lonely figure walking away into the devastated landscape, balancing precariously on piles of rubble, and disappearing into the smoke. This shot visually echoes the end of *Jewish Luck* (1925), when Menachem-Mendel (Solomon Mikhoels) walks away into a distance. This shot establishes that, like Menachem-Mendel, Dr. Fishman is a Wandering Jew.

After this initial interaction, Taras and Dr. Fishman meet twice more. Each encounter with the doctor constitutes an important step in the transformation and growth of Taras's character. The first such meeting takes place at a street market, where Taras runs into Dr. Fishman, who is offering his meager possessions for sale. Tracing Taras's gaze, the camera zooms on a Jewish star on the doctor's sleeve. Next to the doctor is his granddaughter, a sad and serious child with big eyes who is clutching a doll to her chest. They both are silent and motionless among the hustle of the marketplace. The doctor points to the girl: "This is my granddaughter—the most precious of what I have left." Importantly, in the novel, the doctor had no family or relations. In the film, the doctor has a granddaughter, and his line, "what I have left," hints at the prior loss of his family. Perhaps, he, like Taras, was once father and grandfather to a larger clan.

As the Germans raid the market, panic ensues, and people run away, among them the doctor. In the next shot, he is hiding in an entryway, disheveled but still clutching the girl and her doll to his body. When Taras finds them, he invites the doctor to his house. The doctor declines, but gives his granddaughter to Taras. The little Jewish girl is adopted by Taras's family, and Taras takes the place of her Jewish grandfather.

The most important encounter—and a central scene of the film—occurs when Taras and his factory comrades are burying a friend shot by the Germans for his refusal to cooperate. The funeral encounters a wretched procession of Jews with motley luggage, marched by a German convoy with dogs and guns. As the processions draw near, Taras recognizes the doctor among the figures in the convoy, approaches him, and bows. "Is this to me?" wonders the doctor. "To you and to your suffering," replies Taras (serving probably as a director's mouthpiece). "Thank you, Human Being," says the doctor, echoing Maxim Gorky's glorifying use of the word *chelovek* (human being) so familiar to Soviet audiences. The scene ends as the procession resumes to a klezmer-like melody. Later, the motif of a funeral also appears in *Commissar* (1967/1987), in a flash-forward when a procession of Jews carrying a coffin are marched to their death.

In the novel, Taras had a similar conversation with the doctor during their chance encounter in the street. In the film, Donskoi gave this conversation much more gravitas by moving it to take place on the doctor's way to death. Donskoi's script also added a reference to Gorky (whose work preoccupied Donskoi throughout his life), envisioning Jewish suffering as the universal human tragedy.

In the novel, the mass execution is depicted in a single sentence: "The Jews were shot somewhere outside of the town." In the film, the execution is depicted graphically and emphatically. Although, as Jeremy Hicks notes, the scene does not represent the execution with historical accuracy, it nevertheless pays an important tribute to the death of millions of Soviet Jews killed near or around their hometowns.[13] Moreover, in the novel, and in earlier versions of the script, the town is named Kamennyi Brod; in the later versions the town is left unnamed. Thus, even though the scene is filmed in Babii Iar—the most symbolic Holocaust site in the Soviet Union—it can be read as representing any massacre of Jews in any—and hence every—town.[14] This scene is undoubtedly the center of gravity in the film.[15]

Representing mass killing on screen for the first time must have been a challenge for the filmmaker, as there were few models to rely on. Donskoi chose to draw on images of massacres in Sergei Eisenstein's films, which were already classics. In addition to the remarkable synchronization of music and on-screen action characteristic of Eisenstein,[16] the first shots of the scene, when the camera closes in on children, women, and old men huddled in the ravine, are reminiscent of similar shots in the scene of the Pskov massacre in *Alexander Nevsky* (1938). In *Alexander Nevsky*, however, the Germans are killing ethnic Russians. In *The Unvanquished*, the victims about to be murdered are typecast to look Jewish. Among others, a bearded old man who looks like a biblical patriarch clutches to himself a young boy with curly hair (Donskoi's own son was cast in this role[17]). This shot is intercut with a close-up of Dr. Fishman, who concentrates on his silent prayers, rocking his head slightly, as the Nazis yell out orders in the background. When the shooting starts, the camera intercuts between a clouded sky and the scene of the massacre, and music grows to crescendo. In another tribute to Eisenstein, the line of Nazis who advance towards the Jewish crowd firing machine guns is reminiscent of the Cossacks in the famous *Battleship Potemkin* (1925) scene.[18]

The camera pans over the Nazi commanders who are calmly watching the execution, and then over the ravine, full of white smoke, with corpses visible in the foreground. The scene ends with a shot of a lone dead tree with a scarf caught on its branches. Although the symbolism of the image is universal, it has a particular Jewish resonance. On stage at the State Yiddish Theater, this image was used as a symbol of Judaism. It first appeared in *Wandering Stars* (1941). Later, in *Tumultuous Forest* (1947), the scarf became the scrap of a tallit (Jewish prayer shawl).[19] Another tallit was depicted blowing in the wind on a concentration camp fence in the painting by Zinovii Tolkatchev "Taleskoten," made in 1944 during the liberation of the Majdanek Extermination Camp.[20]

The execution is the end of Aron Davidovich Fishman's life, but it's not the end of the Jewish people in the film. The doctor's granddaughter was saved by Taras. On screen, the girl is shown happily playing with Taras's grandchildren, even though she has to be hidden during the Nazi raid. Eventually, the Nazis find her, still sleeping peacefully in her hiding place, clutching the doll to her chest. Her execution is only prevented by an undercover partisan posing as a *politsai*–a local Nazi collaborator—who whisks her away to safety. Again, this entire subplot was added by Donskoi. In the novel, the anonymous girl is hidden collectively—every night she is passed to another family. It is only by chance that she is captured in Taras's house; he is not solely responsible for her. Moreover, in the novel, the girl is probably killed. But for Donskoi it was important that the girl live on. With her doll, she is a little Madonna—both a reference to a powerful Christian religious symbol, and a promise of the future of the Jewish people. The Madonna-like figure is not uncommon in Donskoi's films: in a key scene in *Rainbow*, the female protagonist is persecuted, tortured, and led away by a convoy while holding a child in her arms, the same way the little Jewish girl holds her doll.

Despite such parallels, Jews and non-Jews are represented in the film with striking differences. In contrast to Taras's sons and comrades, who are actively resisting the Nazis, the Jews passively walk towards their death. Taras and his sons are men of action—grounded in their household (in the scenes at Taras's house), in their physical labor (in the scenes at a factory), and in their cultural capital (Taras's grandchild keeps reading from Gogol's *Taras Bulba*). Dr. Fishman is homeless on-screen, always with his bag and his cane, unprotected, in need of shelter, a learned but powerless man. In the patriarchal universe of Stalinist film, power belongs to men, and women are to be shushed or saved. In that context, it is significant that in *The Unvanquished* the Jews, as represented by an old man and a little girl, are emasculated.[21] This creates a dichotomous story of the Great Patriotic War, in which all victimhood is relegated to the Jews, and all heroism to the non-Jewish Soviet people (be they Ukrainians, Russians, or other titular nationalities). Obviously, there are no collaborators or traitors among those heroes.

And yet, not everything is that simple. Once Jews are gone, others take their place—at least that's what Donskoi's visual language suggests. Instead of the Wandering Jew—a doctor with his bag—Taras takes to the road. Importantly, in the novel, Taras needs to leave in order to find food, and his epic journey, including his encounters with people from all walks of life, is narratively justified. In the film, it is not entirely clear why he embarks on his journey. Taras says he is going to search for "the un-ravaged land" (*nerazorennaia zemlia*), which calls to mind "the promised land" (*obetovannaia zemlia*), an obvious Jewish reference. His lonely figure trekking through various landscapes is reproduced multiple times to show the length of his journey. On his way, Taras is joined by more and more such wanderers, until they walk in a procession like that of the Jews we've seen before. Their identities are muffled: Taras is indistinguishable from others, and it seems that the whole country, depicted by Donskoi as a vast landscape, is homeless. Now the whole people turn into wandering Jews. Their makeshift camps set up amidst the devastated landscape create striking anti-utopian images, especially in contrast to the cozy interior setting of Taras's house. All these changes to the novel—the development of the Jewish characters' subplot, the addition of the execution scene, and this reconceptualization of Taras's journey—had far-reaching consequences for the film's professional (read: censorial) reception.

Professional Reception: Ambivalent Censors

On June 21, 1945, the film was discussed at the meeting of the Artistic Council of the Film Committee.[22] The head of the Committee, Ivan Grigor'evich Bol'shakov, chaired the meeting. Among the members were such figureheads of Soviet culture as Konstantin Mikhailovich Simonov, Ivan Aleksandrovich Pyr'ev, Sergei Appolinar'evich Gerasimov, Mikhail Il'ich Romm, Igor Andreevich Savchenko, Sergei Mikhailovich Eisenstein, Nikolai

Pavlovich Okhlopkov, Boris Andreevich Babochkin, and Dmitrii Dmitrievich Shostakovich.[23] Gorbatov and Donskoi were also present.

The discussion was far from smooth. The important historical context for the film's reception was already established by Simonov, a Soviet cult poet and a scriptwriter of the popular war-time melodrama *Wait for Me* (1943), in his introductory remarks: "I went to see it with a certain trepidation … I was afraid to be biased because now one doesn't want to see and read about horrors of the war, and about frightening and difficult wartimes."[24] This is an understandable sentiment, given that the committee saw the film just a month after the long-awaited victory, a time of great euphoria. Despite his reservations, Simonov identified *The Unvanquished* as a "historic picture," and talked about its importance for the collective memory of the war crimes. He then shared this recollection:

> Once, in the streets of Prague, I saw the Czechs herding a large number of Germans through town. And they were treating them poorly…. At first, I felt this sympathy for Germans, and I stopped the car and wanted to do something…. But we shouldn't forget what happened in this war. And when I saw this film, the scenes where they march the Jews—I recalled that moment in Prague, and I thought that yes, I did the right thing by first stopping the car, and then by driving on. Let them drag the Germans however they want!

Simonov continued, "We have to keep reminding [ourselves] about this dark history."[25] From the outset, Simonov placed the Jewish tragedy and its memory at the center of the discussion. The debate that followed explicitly dealt with the larger question of the representation of the Holocaust on Soviet screens.

Indeed, the film proved divisive mainly because of its treatment of the Jewish topic: the main controversy was about the execution scene, which some committee members interpreted as privileging the Jewish tragedy above overall Soviet losses. The second point of contention, much more subtly connected to a Jewish topic, emerged in the discussion of Taras's character. The committee split over the two issues: Romm and Simonov headed the faction that advocated for the film, Okhlopkov and Babochkin led the opposition. How could cultural officials be anything but confused about how to represent the Holocaust if, indeed, they were dealing with the first cinematic depiction of the mass killings? There were no ready models, and, more importantly, no clear party line on the matter.

In his remarks, Babochkin (most famous for his lead role in the Soviet cult movie *Chapaev*) argued that the film was a failure, and among its main problems he listed the execution scene. Paradoxically, Babochkin first admitted that it was a powerful scene, but then completely denounced it: "I am convinced that this scene is unacceptable, because it does not have any elements of art. There is grotesquery (*guignol*), which cannot leave one indifferent, but it is not art. I am under the impression that we don't have the right to show to our audiences scenes like that." He continued, "audiences will not accept this picture."[26] The "representative of the people" (i.e. not a cultural producer himself) Major-General M. R. Galaktionov backed up Babochkin:

> Comrade Babochkin pointed to the execution scene. The thing is that if this scene is presented then it needs to be done 100%... But here, it is presented "halfway." If it was presented realistically, if it showed how people run in horror, how children cry, women wail, how wounded writhe with pain and so on—then it would have been deeper, more convincing. And one more thing: if it showed some sort of resistance... But here people stand calmly, timidly, and wait for their lot—to be shot... This exactly conveys stereotypical ideas about the Jewish people, who submissively accept their fate.

It might appear that Galaktionov is concerned with the more positive—and less stereotypical—representation of Jews, but in the end he comes to the same conclusion as Babochkin: "This scene of execution should be portrayed better, perhaps just leading up to it but not showing the actual shooting... This scene here is a 100% failure, and since it is so, it should be taken out completely."[27] This reaction, once again, shows a profound confusion about the scene—how can the Jewish massacre be represented? The discussants err on the side of caution: since there is no clear model, it is safer to simply take the scene out.

Film director Savchenko was silent at the meeting, but he wrote a review of *The Unvanquished*, potentially in preparation for its discussion by the Artistic Council. Ironically, Savchenko was one of the forefathers of the Soviet "ethnic" film, and yet Savchenko raises similar concerns in his unpublished review: "The facts of the physical extermination of several million Jews are so frightening, so inhumane, and so incomprehensible to a normal person, that this subject shouldn't be discussed superficially. Either it needs to become the subject of a separate picture, or it shouldn't be mentioned at all." Savchenko is equally incensed at the portrayal of Jews as "a submissive suffering herd," which according to him entirely misrepresents active and heroic Soviet Jews. He goes as far as calling the film an "undeserved insult to Jewish people."[28] The execution scene was a problem for him and others, because it portrayed the murder of innocent people outside the trope of Soviet-style heroism.

Notably, the silent Savchenko and the vocal critics apparently had the best interests of the Jewish people in mind—except for their conclusions. Since they all found Donskoi's representation of Babii Iar deficient, they felt that the Jewish tragedy should not have been represented at all. The critics felt great discomfort about the portrayal of Jewish suffering, because, with keen political intuition, they grasped that it was counterproductive both to the optimistic post-war zeitgeist and to the emerging party line.

As mentioned above, by 1945 Soviet policies regarding the events of the Holocaust already favored silencing, universalization, and externalization.[29] If there was any discussion of the Holocaust in the media, it was focused on resistance, not suffering.[30] The scene of an execution of Soviet Jews on Soviet territory did not sit well with this trend. And yet, none of these policies were formulated clearly—the discourse on the war and its victims had not ossified yet. In light of these circumstances, it is not surprising that the committee members were conflicted over Donskoi's treatment of Jewish suffering.

The camp of the film's advocates was represented most prominently by Mikhail Romm. (This was neither the first nor the last time Romm would act as an advocate of Jewish cultural producers or their work).[31] He first called such criticism of the film "unwarranted" and "unjust" and then presented his own argument: "I don't agree with Babochkin that the execution scene should not be shown… If during these years 3.5 million Jews [sic] in Europe were exterminated and we haven't yet said a word about it, haven't represented it in our films, and if in this picture, a mass execution is shown in one scene, I am convinced that this scene needs to stay there." He continued his advocacy: "Despite some shortcomings, this is a necessary film, it has to be released, and people both here and abroad will see this picture."[32] Notably, Romm cites an incorrect number of the Jewish victims. Even though the number six million had already been mentioned by Il'ia Ehrenburg in 1944,[33] it was not widely circulated in the USSR before 1955, following repeated publications of the

Nuremberg Trial documents.[34] Romm also externalizes the Holocaust. He talks about an execution of Jews "in Europe," underplaying the fact that a great many executions took place on Soviet soil. And yet, Romm makes a strong case for a need to represent Jewish suffering and leave the execution scene in.

The execution scene was not the only hurdle. Other committee members criticized the film for its overall development of the Jewish plotline as compared to the novel. Pyr'ev, a film director who in 1943 made a speech about "a lack of true Russianness in our cinema,"[35] was particularly upset about the great emphasis on the character of the doctor, which, he added, "clearly, is done on purpose." To that, Donskoi shouted from his place: "Yes!" Pyr'ev continued with his criticism, "Comrade Romm here mentioned 3.5 million Jews who perished. It's true. And it is true that this film needed to be made. But when all the peoples of our Motherland are concerned, all of them… then why separate [Jews] in contrast to the novel?"[36] Pyr'ev advocated for a particularly Soviet approach: the mass murder of Jews should not be separated into its own category, but should be part of universal Soviet suffering. Indeed, universalization was exactly the party line regarding the Holocaust for years to come. Pyr'ev's words capture a moment when this approach was being formulated.

Another debate evolved around the character of Taras. In the film, Taras is an ethnic Ukrainian, but the following discussion at the meeting was still about Jews and Jewish representation. The topic was introduced by actor and director Okhlopkov, when he criticized Buchma's performance as Taras, which he interpreted as overly emotional. Okhlopkov called Taras "a Spaniard in Africa" with "burning eyes." According to him, Buchma's Taras is "a kind of African, and everything about him is breathing fire."[37] Okhlopkov was not alone in this particular criticism. The choir director V.G. Zakharov complained that Taras is "wild and passionate."[38] Film director Gerasimov noted the character's "African passions."[39] Why were Buchma's expressive facial features and body language so disagreeable to the committee members that they reacted with over-the top orientalist imagery? Okhlopkov's own words provide an answer:

> I saw this once—a car is driving on the road, and is unable to pass two shtetl Jews who are walking right in front of it—with their hands [blocking the road] on the right and [blocking the road] on

the left—they are talking. Jews have that kind of body language. I also use gestures, but for Ukrainians it is atypical. They don't use this kind of body language… Ukrainians are in general very calm people; when it is necessary they can heat up, but to burn all the time like Taras—they don't do it. Here he looks like an African, or some sort of Spaniard.[40]

In fact, Okhlopkov doesn't like Taras's body language because it reminds him of the shtetl Jews from his anecdote. And all these "Africans" and "Spaniards" are just code words, indicating foreignness or otherness usually associated with Jews. Okhlopkov's anxiety regarding Buchma's character doesn't come out of nowhere. Buchma, in fact, grew up in Galicia, was familiar with Jewish life, and was known for his brilliant portrayal of several Jewish characters in the earlier Soviet films *On the Eve* (1928, based on *Gambrinus* by A.I. Kuprin) and *Five Brides* (1929).[41]

If Okhlopkov and others were critical of Taras's character because they saw him as a kind of Jew, then another point of contention can be explained too: nearly all the committee members, both advocates and opponents of the film, were critical of Taras's journey in the film as "incomprehensible." As Okhlopkov correctly pointed out, in the novel Taras has to take to the road to find food for his starving family. In the film, his journey is seemingly unmotivated. Moreover, his search for "the un-ravaged land" gives Taras's journey symbolic meaning derived from Judaism, which made committee members uncomfortable. Gerasimov, who was also critical of the journey, called it "the Biblical travels of Taras" and rattled against the "naïve symbolism" of the film.[42] Himself a closeted Jew throughout his career, Gerasimov was the only one who understood that Donskoi took away the perfectly reasonable and mundane justification of the journey in order to give it a symbolic dimension and to elevate it to the level of biblical parable. In the narrative logic of the film, Taras himself becomes a wandering Jew, an ambivalent symbol of persecution and perseverance.

The discussion of the film came to a stalemate, with one camp advocating for its release, and another voicing forceful opposition. A surprising remark by Eisenstein, who had remained quiet during the entire discussion, saved the day. When Okhlopkov suggests that not only the film be rejected, but even the script be rewritten and the film made anew, Eisenstein quipped, "But it's only in bad dreams that there can be such a punishment!"[43] Everyone laughed, and somehow this resolved everything. Eisenstein's support is not surprising. His solidarity with the Jewish people was evident both in his activity with the Jewish Anti-Fascist Committee, and in the widely circulated anecdote that Eisenstein said about himself that although he was not Jewish, he had "a bit of a Yid" in him (*s prozhid'u*).[44]

After the laughter died out, Bol'shakov, who had also been silent up until that moment, simply dismissed the suggestion to re-make the film, despite Babochkin's and Okhlopkov's still virulent opposition. Bol'shakov then recommended the film for mass release, with minor revisions. It is hard to know for sure what led to such a dramatic turn, and to Bol'shakov's decision. Perhaps Eisenstein's authority was much greater than Babochkin's and Okhlopkov's taken together—at the time, Eisenstein's star was still shining brightly (this was before the 1946 banning of the second part of his *Ivan the Terrible*). Or maybe Bol'shakov knew something that Babochkin and Okhlopkov did not. Either way, Bol'shakov aligned himself with the film's advocates and his choice saved the film. Once again, the controversy demonstrates the ambivalence in Soviet policy regarding the representation of the Holocaust.

The meeting concluded with a resolution: "The novel's adaptation to film is paler than the original." The problem was that the authors "got carried away with the development of the secondary characters" (read: Jewish). Still, the text praised the mastery of the director in the scene identified as "the execution of peaceful residents" (a Soviet euphemism of choice for Jews). The text also lavished praise on Zuskin and Buchma for their performances as the doctor and Taras (who is described as "a complex character"). The ultimate resolution was to permit mass release.[45]

The deliberations of the Council reflected the ambivalence of the Soviet policies towards the Holocaust at the time. During the war, the Soviet attitude vacillated between the allowed and forbidden, complicated by the positioning of the Holocaust simultaneously as a matter of Jewish history and a part of the general Soviet war history. Although there was no consistent policy regarding the representation of the Holocaust during the early stages of the war, by 1944-45 the Holocaust was increasingly silenced. And yet, it was still present in both artistic productions and legal discourse. No wonder that Jewish suffering became such a bone of contention at the Council meeting. The members were confused about the party line. Is it permissible to show murdered Jews, and if yes, how? Therefore, the film's opponents made such contradictory pronouncements. While recognizing Jewish tragedy, they also voted against the execution scene and against explicitly Jewish characters, labeling them "a misrepresentation."

Critical Reception: Confused Critics

Released in October 1945, *The Unvanquished* was greeted by a number of overall positive reviews, which especially praised Zuskin and Buchma. The film's media reception, however positive, nonetheless reflected the already familiar confusion and ambivalence over representation of the Holocaust. The Jewish topic proved to be most controversial. Controversy arose even over the way of addressing it: some reviewers mention Jews verbatim, some refer to them euphemistically.

Only one review (in *Sovetskoe iskusstvo*) chose to avoid Jewish references completely, without even mentioning Zuskin.[46] Not coincidentally, this was the most critical review of the film, pointing out its many shortcomings, while giving lukewarm praise. Most of other reviewers in one way or another dealt with the Jewish topic, without using the word "Jew" explicitly. A review in *Moskovskii bolshevik* described the scene of the last meeting between Taras and the doctor in great detail, noting that it "embodies a lofty idea of national equality and brotherly respect among Soviet people" in contrast to "fascist hatred and racist obscurantism."[47] This hinted at Nazi antisemitism without actually spelling it out.

Similarly, the major newspapers *Izvestiia*, *Vecherniaia Moskva*, and *Trud* praised the doctor's character as one of the most memorable and significant in the film, especially in comparison to the novel.[48] *Izvestiia* commended the powerful scene of mass execution. *Trud* mentioned Babii Iar and Trostianets (a place of mass executions of Jews near Minsk), but carefully called it "a place of mass execution of the populace." Thus, even though these reviews referred to the events of the Holocaust, the reviewers never mentioned anything Jewish directly. Their message might have been coded, but it was still clear. A review in the most authoritative newspaper, *Pravda*, echoed similar themes.[49] The reviewer praised Zuskin but was critical of the doctor's "submissiveness." *Pravda* also did not approve of the execution scene: "On screen, our people go to their death submissively, but from real life experience we know that in such cases even the timid ones would rip bricks out of pavement and throw them at their murderers." Here the reviewer raised the much debated question of Jewish resistance (or lack thereof), and yet he completely evaded direct Jewish references.

Some reviews did bring up the Jewish topic, at least in passing. Discussing the doctor's character, *Moskovskii komsomolets* pointed out that he was murdered only for being a Jew (the reviewer scolds his portrayal as "doomed"). *Krasnyi flot* mentioned the Nazi persecution of the "little Jewish girl."[50]

But two reviewers, I. Sokolov (*Komsomolskaia pravda*) and I. Kruti (*Literaturnaia gazeta*), specifically focused on the Jewish themes in the film. Sokolov discussed every instance in which the Jewish topic is treated in the film. He pointed out the Star of David on the doctor's sleeve, which marks him as a Jew. With great sympathy, he described both the scene of the little Jewish girl's capture, and the last meeting of Taras with the doctor, again not shying away from the Jewish content.[51] Similarly, when Kruti praised the image of the two death processions coming toward one another, he described one of them as "procession of Jews, herded towards their execution at Babii Iar." Moreover, unlike some other reviewers, Kruti appreciated the doctor's character and saw in it an alternative model of courage: "V. Zuskin, with his customary precise and unobtrusive artistic mastery, creates an image of a great intellectual and moral power. He is not a victim, but a judge. This man goes towards his death unvanquished, as those who remain alive with weapons in their hands are unvanquished."[52]

This warm reception should have guaranteed the film's wide circulation and long run, especially during a time when few films were made. However, after its widely publicized premiers, *The Unvanquished* did not stay in theaters for long.[53] Even as the film was shown at the Venice Biennale, its screening at the Mariánské Lázně International Film Festival was substituted at the last moment with a Stalinist tableau, *The Vow* (1946).[54] After Zuskin's arrest in 1948, *The Unvanquished* disappeared from screens completely. However, even then it was not scratched out from Soviet film history. In 1948, Bol'shakov (who had served as chair of the Council meeting) published a brochure: *Soviet Cinematic Art During the Years of the Great Patriotic War*. He dedicated a generous two pages to the account of *The Unvanquished*, praising mainly its portrayal of heroism and resistance of the Soviet people in "proletarian Donbass." Zuskin is never mentioned, although amazingly Bol'shakov praises such "scenes as the execution of peaceful citizens, the raid at the market, and the journey in search of bread" as "well-made by the director and actors."[55] Like most newspaper reviewers, Bol'shakov here talks about the Jewish scenes in the film, without ever identifying them as such. Even in the 1950 edition of the same brochure (re-issued mainly to add a few jabs at "rootless cosmopolitans"), a discussion of *The Unvanquished* remained in place, and did not change in tone.[56] The film was never ostracized, but it was not endorsed either.

In sum, the film's reception reflected the ambivalent Soviet policies of the time, when the topic of the Holocaust was neither completely suppressed nor fully acknowledged, but vacillated in the grey area between the allowed and the forbidden. Its history—from the publication of the novel in *Pravda*, through its transformation into a film and the subsequent battle at the Artistic Council meeting, to its inclusion into the official party brochure—today provides insight into the shifting Soviet cultural politics regarding the Holocaust and its representation.[57]

* * *

In the 1960s, Soviet audiences had a chance to see *The Unvanquished* on TV.[58] However, in contrast to the other Donskoi classics shown in their entirety, only excerpts from the film were allowed (it is easy to guess which excerpts were excluded). *The Unvanquished* returned to Russian audiences only relatively recently, when it was released on VHS and DVD. And so, decades after it was made, the film was salvaged from obscurity, and today occupies its due place alongside other Soviet cinematic classics. Moreover, the key scene of *The Unvanquished* stands today for the Babii Iar massacre. In a remarkable Russian documentary about Holocaust survivors, *Children from the Abyss* (2000, dir. Pavel Chukhrai), the scene from *The Unvanquished* is used as a substitute for missing archival footage of the mass execution in Babii Iar. Thus, despite its historical inaccuracy, this scene constitutes a source of visual memory for audiences both in Russia (where this documentary was broadcast on the state TV channel) and worldwide (*Children from the Abyss* was a part of the TV mini-series *Broken Silence*, produced by Steven Spielberg and widely circulated). In the same way in which the storming of the Winter Palace in Eisenstein's *October* (1927) became an iconic image of the Russian Revolution, the execution scene in *The Unvanquished* is becoming an iconic image of the Holocaust in Russia.

Notes

1. This article is a version of previously published chapter "How a Soviet Novel Tuned into a Jewish Film: The First Depiction of the Holocaust on Soviet Screens, *The Unvanquished* (1945)," in Olga Gershenson, *The Phantom Holocaust: Soviet Cinema and Jewish Catastrophe* (New Brunswick: Rutgers University Press, 2013), 40-57.
2. Miron Markovich Chernenko, *Krasnaia zvezda, zheltaia zvezda: Kinematograficheskaia istoriia evreistva v Rossii, 1919-1999* (Moscow: Tekst, 2006).
3. Jeremy Hicks, "Confronting the Holocaust: Mark Donskoi's The Unvanquished" *Studies in Russian and Soviet Cinema* 3.1 (2009): 47.
4. Elena Baraban, "Semeinyj krug: traktovka rodstva, evreev i voennoplennyh v stalinskom kino o voine," *Ab Imperio* 3 (2009): 476.
5. According to many sources on the Russian Internet, *The Unvanquished* received a Golden Medal at the Biennale (e.g. http://russiancinema.ru/template.php?dept_id=15&e_dept_id=6&text_element_id=37 [accessed October 30, 2013]). However, according to the archives of the Venice Biennale *The Unvanquished* did not receive any official prizes.
6. Karel C. Berkhoff, "'Total Annihilation of the Jewish Population': The Holocaust in the Soviet Media, 1941-45," *Kritika* 10.1 (2009): 477-504. Kiril Feferman, *Soviet Jewish Stepchild: The Holocaust in the Soviet Mindset, 1941-1964* (Saarbrücken, Germany: VDM Verlag Dr. Müller, 2009).
7. Feferman, *Soviet Jewish Stepchild*, 27.
8. Berkoff, "Total Annihilation," 93.
9. Feferman, *Soviet Jewish Stepchild*, 44.
10. Boris Leont'evich Gorbatov, "Nepokorennye (Sem'ia Tarasa)," *Pravda*, May 17, 19, 20, 21, 22, 23; September 25, 26, 27, 30; October 2, 3, 4, 6, 7, 8, 9, 10, 11, 1943.
11. For a detailed recollection of this anecdote, see Oleg Iakubovich, "Voennye fil'my Marka Donskogo," in *Kino i vremia*, vol. 4 (Moscow: Iskusstvo, 1965), 92.
12. Mark Semenovitch Donskoi, "My Work on the Film *Unvanquished*," *Cinema Chronicle* 10 (1945): 9-16. Thanks to Jeremy Hicks for sharing this document with me.
13. Hicks, "Confronting the Holocaust," 41-43.
14. Thanks to Jeremy Hicks, who drew my attention to the composite nature of the execution representation in the film.
15. To watch this scene (with English subtitles), see www.phantomholocaust.org.
16. Anne Nesbet, *Savage Junctures: Sergei Eisenstein and the Shape of Thinking* (London; New York: I.B. Taurus, 2003), 173.
17. Milena Musina, "Ischislenie Roda," *Kinovedcheskie zapiski* 51 (2001): 197.
18. See also Hicks, "Confronting the Holocaust," 43.
19. According to the memoirs of Zuskin's daughter: Alla Zuskin-Perel'man, *Puteshestvie Veniamina* (Moscow: Gesharim, 2002), 262.
20. Zinovii Tolkatchev, who was ethnically Jewish, served as an official artist of the Red Army, attached to the forces liberating Majdanek and later Auschwitz. Tolkatchev depicted terrible scenes he witnessed in the camps.

21 *The Unvanquished* is not unique in that regard. Judith Doneson notes that many Holocaust films portray Jews as feminine to express weakness and victimization. Annete Insdorf adds that with the same purpose Jews are also portrayed as children. Judith Doneson, "The Jew as a Female Figure in Holocaust Film," *Shoah: A Review of Holocaust Studies and Commemorations* 1.1 (1978): 11. Annette Insdorf, *Indelible Shadows: Film and the Holocaust* (Cambridge and New York: Cambridge University Press, 2003), 77-92.

22 The Artistic Council of the Film Committee was at the time a new organ, established in 1944 in order to "elevate the quality of films" and to ensure that the films are "wholesome aesthetically and of the highest ideological content" (Valerii Ivanovich Fomin, *Kino na voine: dokumenty i svidetel'stva* [Moscow: Materik, 2005], 431). The Council was entrusted with screening the scripts and approving the films for mass release, and as such it had a censorship function.

23 Shostakovich remained silent during the meeting, but years later, in 1961, he set a part of his Thirteenth symphony to the words of Evgenii Evtushenko's poem "Babii Iar."

24 Rossiiskii Gosudarstvennyi Arkhiv Literatury i Iskusstva (RGALI) f. 2456 (Komitet po delam kinematografii pri SNK SSSR, Ministerstvo kinematografii SSSR), op. 1, d. 1056 (Stenogramma, protocol i zakluchenie zasedania khudozhestvennogo soveta pri komitete po delam kinematografii po fil'mu Nepokorennye). Here as elsewhere the translations are mine.

25 RGALI f. 2456, op. 1, d. 1056.

26 Ibid.

27 Ibid.

28 RGALI, f. 1992 (I. A. Savchenko, "Retsenziia na Nepokorennye"), op. 1, d. 160.

29 Berkhoff, "Total Annihilation," and Feferman, *Soviet Jewish Stepchild*.

30 Berkhoff, "Total Annihilation," 70.

31 For more examples of Romm's advocacy, see Fomin, *Kino na voine*, 538-46, and Mikhail Romm, *Kak v kino: ustnye rasskazy* (Nizhnii Novgorod: Dekom, 2003), 120-34.

32 RGALI f. 2456, op. 1, d. 1056.

33 Il'ia Grigor'evich Ehrenburg, "Pomnit'!" *Pravda*, December 17, 1944, 3. Cited in Berkhoff, "Total Annihilation," 70.

34 Feferman, *Soviet Jewish Stepchild*, 44.

35 Fomin, *Kino na voine*, 550-551.

36 RGALI f. 2456, op. 1, d. 1056.

37 Ibid.

38 Ibid.

39 Ibid.

40 Ibid.

41 Iurii Morozov and Tatiana Derevianko, *Evreiskie kinemotagrafisty v Ukraine, 1917-1975* (Kiev: Duch i Litera, 2004), 174.

42 RGALI f. 2456, op. 1, d. 1056.

43 Ibid.
44 Fomin, *Kino na Voine*, 537.
45 RGALI f. 2456, op. 1, d. 1056.
46 S. Burov, "Nepokorennye," *Sovetskoe iskusstvo*, October 26, 1945, 2.
47 D. Kalm, "Nepokorennye," *Moskovskii bol'shevik*, October 21, 1945.
48 N. Zhdanov, "Nepokorennye," *Izvestiia*, October 23, 1945; M. Beliavskii, "Nepokorennye," *Vecherniaia Moskva*, October 22, 1945, 3; M. Ilushin, "Nepokorennye," *Trud*, October 21, 1945, 2.
49 S. Borzenko, "Nepokorennye," *Pravda*, October 24, 1945.
50 A. Kamenogorskii, "Nepokorennye," *Moskovskii komsomolets*, October 20, 1945, 3; A. P. Shtein, "Nepokorennye," *Krasnyi flot*, October 21, 1945.
51 I. Sokolov, "O Neprimirimykh i Nepokorennykh," *Komsomolskaia pravda*, October 21, 1945.
52 I. Kruti, "Nepokorennye na ekrane," *Literaturnaia gazeta*, October 20, 1945.
53 Hicks demonstrates that at least in Moscow and Kiev the film was shown in theaters for less than two months ("Confronting the Holocaust," 45).
54 Iakubovich, "Voennye fil'my Marka Donskogo," 99.
55 I. G. Bol'shakov, *Sovetskoe iskusstvo v Gody Velikoi Otechestvennoi voiny, 1941-1945* (Moscow: Goskinoizdat, 1948), 51-52.
56 Ibid.
57 For analysis of the Holocaust representation on Soviet screens throughout the Soviet era, see Gershenson, *Phantom Holocaust*.
58 Iakubovich, "Voennye fil'my Marka Donskogo," 100.

Chapter 9

From Photojournalist to Memory Maker: Evgenii Khaldei and Soviet Jewish Photographers

David Shneer

About half the Russian photographers who documented the construction of the new Soviet society and its near destruction at the hands of the Nazis during World War II were Jews.[1] Arkadii Shaikhet, Aleksandr Grinberg, Mark Markov-Grinberg, Dmitrii Baltermants, Max Alpert, and Evgenii Khaldei all moved to the capital of the Communist world, Moscow, from their towns and cities throughout Ukraine and Belarus to document the revolution, and later to bear witness to the Holocaust. The connection between war photography and Jews was so natural in the wartime Soviet Union that several pop cultural references explicitly make the connection. Konstantin Simonov's *Zhivye i mertvye* (*The Living and the Dead*) features a heroic frontline Jewish photographer, and the popular film *Zhdi menia* (*Wait for Me*) focuses on another heroic, martyred Jewish photojournalist. Among the most well-known real-life wartime photojournalists was Evgenii (Efim) Ananievitch Khaldei. This paper will examine how changing responses to Khaldei as a Soviet and Jewish photographer changed Khaldei's own sense of himself as a Soviet citizen, a photojournalist, and as a Jew.

To understand Khaldei's trajectory, it is necessary to go back a generation to the beginning of Soviet photojournalism. In the first two decades after the 1917 Revolution, photography became a craft and art form that was deeply embedded in the Soviet revolution. In the same period, Soviet photography was also defined by the social revolution transforming Russian Jewish society. Many young Jews from the provinces were at the forefront of Soviet photography, because it was a new technology that required entrepreneurialism and experimentation, something with which Jews in Russia had much experience.

Fig. 9.1. Soviet Photo- and Print Journalists at Reichstag, May 1945.
Courtesy of Evgenii Khaldei and the Fotosoyuz Agency.

It was an easy-to-learn art form that did not have art councils, salons, and schools to restrict Jews' access, as had been the case for other forms of art for much of the tsarist era. Perhaps most important, it was a new means of making a living in a society that put new visual technologies, like film and photography, at the center of socialist culture.

Photography had a rough start in the new Communist country. With the impoverishment of Russia as a result of World War I, revolution and civil war, and closed borders that prevented the import of most photographic material, the field of photography, which had been well established in Russia since the mid-nineteenth century, shriveled and nearly died.[2] In 1923 Mikhail Koltsov (who, like many other Soviet Jewish intellectuals, changed his name from the more "Jewish"-sounding Fridliand) founded *Ogonek*, the most important illustrated magazine in the new country, dedicated to describing life and the news for a mass audience through the lens of the modern, hand-held camera. Koltsov was just one of many starry-eyed Jews from the provinces, who moved to Moscow looking for work and escaping the impoverishment of war-ravaged southern Russia. It was a privilege of mobility that most Jews, and most Russians for that matter, were experiencing for the first time, because the fall of the tsars meant the temporary end of residency restrictions.

Koltsov's Moscow photographic operation, which grew from one magazine into an entire conglomerate of newspapers, magazines, and publishing houses, was not only popular with readers, but also with budding photographers.[3] The magazine quickly garnered a reputation as the first stop for young, culturally and visually curious, but relatively uneducated Jewish migrants. Abram Shmuelovitch Shoykhet was born in 1898 in Nikolaev, in the Odessa region, and moved to Moscow in 1920. Like Mikhail, young Abram Shmuelovitch changed his name to Arkadii Samoilovitch Shaikhet, in his attempt to take on a revolutionary, and less provincially Jewish, persona. In 1923, Shaikhet met Koltsov and showed him some of his retouched work and his own photographs that had been published in another popular Soviet newspaper that employed many Jewish migrants, *The Worker's Newspaper* (*Rabochaia gazeta*), and Koltsov was sold. Many others would follow Shaikhet into Koltsov's office. Thus began a trend of budding Jewish photographers, arriving in Moscow desperate for work, and a sense of community among other Jews who left their homes to be part of the revolution. One of the first stops was always to meet Koltsov and hopefully find an internship or work either at *Ogonek* or at one of the other publications connected with the magazine.

These two 25-year-olds quickly became the leaders of a cultural phenomenon—the emergence of an institution called Soviet photojournalism. Although photojournalism emerged worldwide in the 1920s due to technical improvements in camera size, means of transmitting images, and printing techniques, photojournalism also emerged in the Soviet Union as a new society was taking shape. Soviet photojournalism, then, was documenting the "building of socialism" more than it was a new tool to capture the day's news visually.

Max Alpert, born in Simferopol in 1899, ended up in Moscow in 1924 and worked for *The Worker's Newspaper* too. For two years he served as photo editor of *Pravda*, the voice of the Communist Party and most important newspaper in the country.[4] Eleazar Langman, born in 1895 in Odessa, moved to Moscow to study music before finding his way into photography with the avant-garde photography group October. Semen Osipovitch Fridliand, born in 1905 in Kiev, moved to Moscow in 1925 and immediately started photographing for *Ogonek*. It could not have hurt that Mikhail and Semen were cousins.[5] A very young Mark Markov-Grinberg, born in 1907 in Rostov, moved to Moscow in 1926 and interned with several trade union newspapers.[6] And Georgii Zelmanovitch, born in Tashkent, made a name for himself in the 1920s photographing the ethnic diversity of the Soviet empire. He too moved to Moscow, and in the 1930s, was a collaborator on one of Maxim Gorky's magazines, *USSR in Construction*, probably the most important illustrated magazine of the 1930s.

This group was the first generation of Soviet photojournalists. Among them were many young Jews raised in the tsarist empire, some of them steeled in war and revolution, who had moved to Moscow to flee poverty and to be at the center of the revolution. Through the 1920s and into the 1930s, they argued about the nature of Soviet photography and photojournalism on the pages of the magazines and journals that they themselves created. And all of them were dedicated to laying the groundwork for a profession that would become young Evgenii Khaldei's life.

This first generation of photographers attracted and mentored the second generation of Soviet Jewish photojournalists, born between 1910 and 1920, who came to Moscow as *Soviet* Jews, and became photographers in the Stalinist 1930s. These photographers, like Evgenii Khaldei, Dmitrii Baltermants, Iakov Khalip and others, had a different relationship to photography. They did not grow up in the "fire of revolution," they did not have to build a profession, and they did not have to fight on the pages of photo magazines about what Soviet photography was supposed to be. In fact, unlike the first generation, which wrote prolifically to answer the question "what is Soviet photography," the second generation inherited the answer. They entered a well-formed, stable profession called photojournalism, passed down from the "fathers," now ancient at the age of 40. (There were virtually no "mothers" in this burgeoning field. The only well-known female Jewish photographer, Olga Lander, is of the second generation.)

Khaldei's life story is one of the most well known among this group of Soviet Jewish photographers. In the 1990s, after the fall of the Soviet Union, he gave interviews, told stories, and even had a documentary film made about him in which his Jewishness played a central role in his life story. Born in 1917 in the eastern Ukrainian city of Iuzovka (later Stalino, and later still Donetsk), Khaldei was raised in a Yiddish-speaking Jewish family on the cusp of modernity. His grandfather ran a traditional Jewish school known as a *heder*. During the Civil War that wreaked havoc on Russian society, a wave of pogroms broke out across Ukraine. Hundreds of thousands of Jews were killed,

Fig. 9.2. Khaldei's Family in 1920.
Courtesy of Evgenii Khaldei and the Fotosoyuz Agency.

and perhaps millions more were forced from their homes or migrated abroad. Young Zhenia watched his mother and grandfather get killed in one of these pogroms; he was too young to remember the experience, but the memories of these anti-Jewish riots had a powerful influence on him and his family.

Khaldei did not excel at academics, and as a young teenager he had to choose where to apprentice for his future profession. He started working as a metalworker in a factory, but he quickly became more interested in photography and began playing with cameras. One of his earliest photographs was of the destruction of a local church during the anti-clerical campaign of the Cultural Revolution in 1931-32. The earliest evidence of Khaldei's professional photographic career comes from 1932, when he freelanced for the Donetsk division of the press photography unit of the Ukrainian Photo Union. He also faked his birth date in order to start working earlier than he was allowed. All of his official documents give his birth date as 1916, a fiction invented in a job interview in 1932.[7] He worked for several local publications as a photographer but got his big break in 1935, when he was invited to Moscow to attend a photography seminar at Soiuzfoto, what would become Fotokhronika TASS, the largest photography wire service in the country.[8] In 1936 he moved from Stalino to Moscow, which he would call home for the rest of his life.

Khaldei entered a Stalinist system of cultural production, in which photography was less about creative genius than it was about doing a job as outlined by an editor. In 1934, socialist realism had been enshrined as the official aesthetic of the Soviet Union, and modernist aesthetics were in theory decried as putting form ahead of content and politics. In addition to a changed political and aesthetic framework of photography, Khaldei entered a centralized system for producing culture, in this case the process of training photographers, organizing publications, establishing editorial policies, making photographic assignments, and shaping the process from camera-click to published image. Stalinist-era photography production was defined by large, overarching professional unions under Communist Party control and through centralized bureaucracies that controlled photographic subject matter and editorial policies.

Fig. 9.3. Evgenii Khaldei, "Raising the Red Flag over Reichstag."
Courtesy of Evgenii Khaldei and the Fotosoyuz Agency.

Khaldei trained as a photographer in this world, but he became well known only during World War II, an event that catapulted all of the second-generation photographers into the ranks of the most important photographers in the country. Khaldei photographed the war from beginning to end, from the Arctic to the Black Sea, from Berlin in the West to the Chinese border in the East. His work with the Black Sea fleet was deemed so important that in 1942 the 26-year-old Khaldei was promoted to a higher rank.[9] His most famous photograph, "Raising of the Red Flag over the Reichstag," crowned his career as a military photographer, even though he continued photographing the war with Japan in August and September 1945. Khaldei was at the peak of his career when he was invited to photograph the post-war Nuremberg Trials and the Paris Peace Conference in 1946.

In addition to his relatively well-known career as a photographer of Soviet victory, Khaldei also photographed the darkest story of the war—Nazi atrocities against Jews, what we now call the Holocaust. Everyone in the Soviet Union knew about the Nazi atrocities, which were widely publicized in the Soviet press from the first days of the war. *Ogonek* published its first photo of such horrors on June 25, 1941, its first edition following the invasion, and a gruesome image it was.[10] At first, the Soviet press published perpetrator photographs, like the one above—those taken by the Germans, Nazis, and other collaborators themselves, which were then captured and made their way to Moscow as "trophy photographs." But it did not take long for the Soviet press's own photographers to bear witness to Nazi crimes. In January 1942, Khaldei, Baltermants, and Mark Redkin photographed the southern city of Kerch', where the Nazis killed thousands of Jews. The city had been held by the Germans for only six weeks, from mid-November until late December 1941, but in that time, much of the city's Jewish population had been rounded up, sent to the outskirts of town to a trench near the suburb of Bagerov, and shot.[11] Kerch' would very quickly become one of the earliest and most important symbols of Nazi brutality in the Soviet Union. This happened through literary representations of the event like Il'ia Ehrenburg's 1943 book *Russia at War*, which talks about the "terrible pit near Kerch' in which the children of Russians, Tatars and Jews are buried"; Il'ia Sel'vinskii's "*Ia eto videl*" (I Saw It), the subject of Harriet Murav's essay in this volume; and through photographs published in all of the major press.[12]

The photographers were on the scene shortly after liberation in early January and photographed an unbelievable scene of mass murder. Khaldei

Fig. 9.4. Evgenii Khaldei, "Sonits Dig a Grave."
Courtesy of Evgenii Khaldei and the Fotosoyuz Agency.

writes in his diary about how he, as a photojournalist, collected stories from survivors and family members of the dead, who told him about the mass murder of Kerch''s Jews.[13] (See Figure 9.4.) Although Khaldei's photographs did not appear in the central press at the time, Baltermants' and Redkin's photographs were splashed across the pages of *Ogonek*, the most important illustrated journal in the country.

The caption beneath Redkin's photographs, which appeared on February 4, 1942, suggests how he and the *Ogonek* editors placed atrocity photographs into an evolving narrative of the war: "Hitler ordered his bandits to annihilate the peaceful Soviet population. Wherever the Germans found themselves, they murdered thousands of women and children. The bodies of the murdered were dumped in a pit (see top photograph). Among the murdered were many women and children (see bottom photograph). The Hitlerite thugs showed no one any mercy." The caption obscures the perpetrators of the crimes. In one sentence they are followers of Hitler; in another, Germans. No mention is made of the fact that most of the dead women and children so grotesquely splashed across the pages of the magazine were Jewish.

One month later, *Ogonek* followed up its earlier Kerch' images with a two-page layout of photographs by Dmitrii Baltermants and Israel Ozerskii and an article by the journalist I. Antselovich, all three of whom were Jewish. The headline reads: "These photographs were taken after the German occupiers drove [the people] out to this place. 7,500 residents, from the very elderly to breastfeeding babies, from just a single city were shot. They were killed in cold blood in a premeditated fashion. They were killed indiscriminately— Russians and Tatars, Ukrainians and Jews. The Hitlerites have also murdered the Soviet population indiscriminately in many other cities, villages, and in the countryside." (See Figure 9.5.) Although they appear as just one of several, Jews were clearly named among the murdered Soviet nationalities. But the captions of the Redkin and Baltermants photographs obscure a fact that all of these photographers knew—that the Nazis targeted Jews above others.

For Khaldei, the events of the Holocaust moved from the professional to the personal when he visited his hometown of Stalino shortly after the city's September 1943 liberation. There he discovered that many members of his family had been murdered, killed in mine shafts on the outskirts of town. According to Khaldei's daughter, Anna, only his brother and sister, who

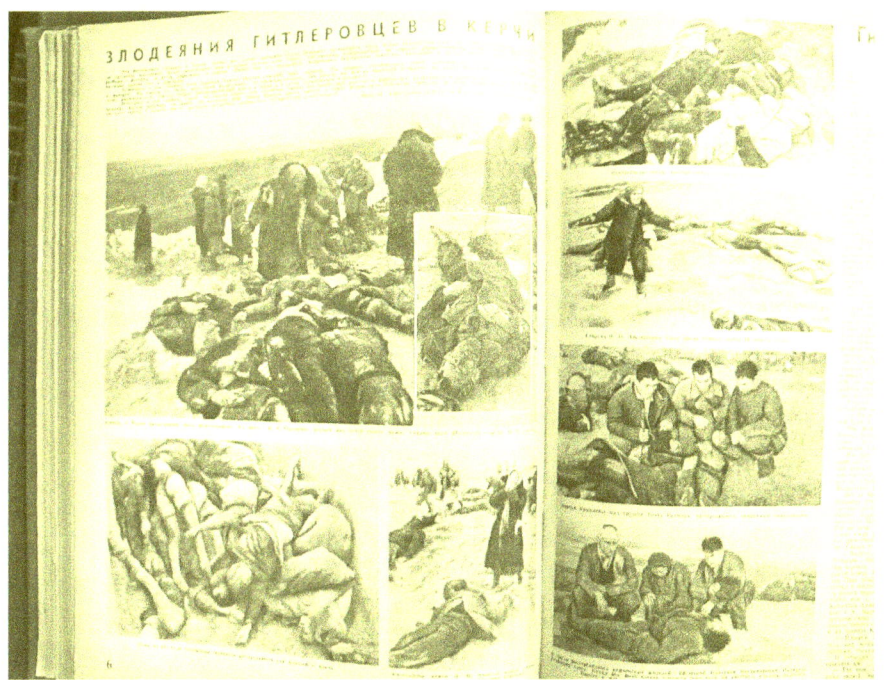

Fig. 9.5. Dmitrii Baltemants and Israel Ozerskii, "Hitlerite Atrocities in Kerch'," *Ogonek*, March 2, 1942. Courtesy of Evgenii Khaldei and the Fotosoyuz Agency.

were evacuated before the Nazis reached Stalino, survived the war.[14] Khaldei was transformed by the experience of seeing the violence first hand. In one interview, he claims that when he entered Germany with the troops in 1945, he sought out opportunities for revenge, and even set a German's house on fire in order to photograph it burning as Soviet troops marched by.[15]

But Khaldei's most powerful photographs that engaged the Jewish story of the war are of the Budapest ghetto. Khaldei accompanied the Red Army on its path of liberation through southern Russia and the Balkans, and he found himself in Budapest, Hungary in late January 1945. Khaldei made an unusual trip to the Jewish ghettoes to photograph the specific tragedy of European Jewry.[16] It is not clear if he was doing this on assignment from his TASS editors.[17] His trip to the ghetto was obviously more personal than his usual work at sites of liberation. He intended to bear witness to one of the last extant ghettos in all of Europe, where he could photograph Jews who survived Nazi occupation. He took many photographs of what had taken place in the Budapest ghetto in late 1944. His archive has more than a dozen images of corpses with stars sewn onto jackets, makeshift killing rooms, and mountains of destruction as the city was seared by battle in the Soviets' months-long attempt to take the city.

On March 3, 1945, about three years after the appearance of the first Holocaust liberation photographs from Kerch' in the Russian press, and about a month after he took the photographs in Budapest, a Soviet media outlet published some of Khaldei's ghetto photographs. However, they were not published in *Pravda*, *Izvestiia*, or *Krasnaia zvezda*, the army newspaper for which Il'ia Ehrenburg and Vasilii Grossman worked. Instead, Khaldei's photographs appeared in the central Soviet Yiddish newspaper published during the war, *Eynikayt* (*Unity*), which ran a grim layout of Khaldei's photographs from the Budapest ghetto on the front page.[18] Why the Russian-language press did not publish these images is a matter of speculation. The Russian press obviously published images of what we now call the Holocaust from the first day of the war until the last, including photographs of the extermination camps liberated by the Soviet army on Polish soil, like Majdanek and Auschwitz. But the editors of those papers, who were often Jewish themselves, were more invested in universalizing the Nazi atrocities by labeling victims as "peaceful Soviet citizens," most of whom were, of course, Jews, as we saw with the Kerch' photos. Photographs of empty burial pits, disfigured corpses, barbed wire, or gas canisters could easily be read as images that would speak to any reader of the Russian-language Soviet press. But Khaldei's Budapest photographs were harder to universalize. After all, most of those in his grainy black and white pictures, whether dead or among the survivors, were wearing a six-pointed Jewish star instead of the five-pointed Soviet one.

From the first weeks of its publication in June 1942, *Eynikayt* "judaized" the war for both its domestic and international Yiddish-reading audiences.[19] Throughout 1942, *Eynikayt* published graphic photographs of German violence committed against Jews. There were pictures of Jewish burial sites, the Warsaw ghetto, and other images whose captions clearly noted that the people in the pictures were Jews. Unlike the Russian-language press, whose purpose was to create a nationally unifying narrative of the war, *Eynikayt*'s role was to build support for the Soviet Union by creating connections among Yiddish-reading Jews *across* national borders. If the Russian press marked victims as "peaceful Soviet citizens" or "citizens of one particular nationality," a subtle way of singling out Jews without saying so, *Eynikayt*'s identified victims unambiguously as Jews.

Since the Soviet press did not simply tell the news but always also interpreted it, the captions for individual photographs had to both describe the awful scene and help readers understand it:

> Jews in Budapest. Hitlerites drove tens of thousands of Jews from all over Hungary into Budapest's ghetto region. [Pictured here is] the first building that served as the beginning of the ghetto and the store in this house, which the fascists transformed into a torture room in which they used to inflict all kinds of things on Jews, shoot them, and then toss their bodies onto the square. Thanks to the hate-driven attack of the Red Army, thanks to the fact that Soviet forces quickly encircled the city, a significant part of Hungarian Jewry was saved from murder.
>
> In the pictures (from right to left): 1. Budapest is liberated. Jews go in every direction back to their places of permanent residence. 2. A mother and daughter whom the fascists dragged out from their cellar, beat in the middle of the street, and then shot. Next to them sits their husband and father. 3. Jews with yellow Stars of David. The fascists forced them to wear these on their chests. 4. A store in which Jews were shot. 5. Slaughtered Jews whom the Germans and fascists murdered before retreating from the city.

This text, along with the captions to the individual photographs, told readers that by 1945 the Soviets were liberators of Jews from Nazi atrocities, not victims themselves. There was no discussion of the murder of "peaceful Soviet citizens," especially given the obvious fact that Soviet troops were now in Hungary, not the Soviet Union. In addition, *Eynikayt*'s editors chose to express both a Jewish and Soviet story. Through the use of active verbs such as "murdered," "forced," and "dragged," rather than the passive constructions that would have been more common in both Yiddish and Russian, the caption articulates a clear perpetrator, the fascists/Hitlerites/Germans, and a victim, the Jews. In *Eynikayt*, the Soviets' role was as heroic liberators who saved Jews—not "peaceful Hungarian citizens"—from murder and destruction. The third photograph in the series would become one of Khaldei's signature images. The photograph's caption describes the act of visually identifying people with a Jewish symbol that the Nazis had turned into a grotesque icon that flattened individual identity.

Shortly after the liberation of Budapest, Khaldei was a lead photographer documenting the conquest/liberation of Vienna and, in May 1945, of Berlin. His "Raising the Red Flag over the Reichstag" photograph is probably his most famous image, and it circulated widely in the 1960s, 1970s, and 1980s, when Soviet war memory became a monumental industry. But this photographic success during and shortly after the war did not protect him during the anti-cosmopolitan campaign of the late 1940s and early 1950s, when Jewish doctors, writers, artists, editors, journalists, photographers, and others were fired from their jobs, or even murdered, for having been "too Jewish" during the war. Those connected with *Eynikayt*, the newspaper that published Khaldei's Budapest photographs, and with the Jewish Anti-Fascist Committee were suspected of being at the center of a Jewish/Zionist nationalist conspiracy. Many of the most important Jewish culture-makers were killed.[20] In this case, it's a good thing photographers were not considered important culture-makers.

Khaldei's story of running into trouble with his superiors actually began during the war in 1943. That year, David Ortenberg, editor of *Red Star*, was fired, as were other editors of lesser-known newspapers. And historian Gennadii Kostyrchenko marks 1943 as a point at which the state's relationship to its Jewish population took a turn for the worse.[21] Although he never talked about it, in 1943, Khaldei was nearly dismissed from serving as a photographer with the Black Sea fleet for publishing photographs that had not passed through the local military censor. Only a petition from Khaldei's top boss, the head of Fotokhronika TASS, to TASS headquarters kept him at his job. In 1946, after returning to Moscow from his glory days in Germany for the

Nuremberg Trials and Paris for the Paris Peace Conference, he was taken off of an assignment for refusing to turn in some photographic equipment that he needed to use. In 1947, he was brought before a Communist Party board to be reprimanded for his "low cultural level," and in 1948 the bombshell hit. On October 7, he received notice that he was being terminated from TASS after 12 years of employment due to "staff downsizing."[22] Khaldei was one of several Jewish photographers who lost their staff positions in 1948 and worked through the late Stalin period as freelancers. Khaldei had commissions from *Labor* (*Trud*), *Soviet Woman* (*Sovetskaia zhenshchina*), *VOKS* (*All Union Society of Foreign Cultural Relations*), and others. After Stalin's death, *Pravda* rehired him, and Khaldei remained an important photographer for the rest of his career, especially in the 1960s, when Soviet war memory became big business. But Khaldei's photographs of the Budapest ghetto lay dormant, unpublished since the war. Although it worked as Yiddish-language news in 1945, the "Jews with Yellow Stars" of Budapest had become too Jewish for public Russian-language Soviet war memory. Khaldei never regained the prestige he had in May 1945 when he took his famous Reichstag photograph, and he died in 1997 living in a tiny apartment, poor but absolutely not forgotten.

If, during the war and in the 1960s, Khaldei was an important *Soviet* photographer, in the 1990s, after the fall of the Soviet Union, Khaldei became relatively famous internationally as a Soviet *Jewish* photographer. Just before his death in 1997, the Jewish Museum in New York and the one in San Francisco each mounted a large solo exhibition of Khaldei's work, firmly embedding him and his work in a Jewish context, and a Belgian filmmaker made a documentary about him.[23] It was in this context, as part of the institutionalization of Holocaust memory in the West in the 1990s, that the Jews with Yellow stars from Budapest made a wildly successful return in the post-Soviet period as "The Jewish Couple." The stories Khaldei told about the photographs show how he refigured wartime photojournalism documenting Nazi atrocities into iconic Holocaust photography adorning the walls of museums around the world.

Khaldei loved to talk about the Jewish couple photograph. This quote is from an interview he gave to scholars Alice and Alexander Nakhimovsky, who helped organize Khaldei's launch in the American photographic market:

> I saw them walking down the street. I was in a black leather coat, and at first they were afraid—they thought I was from the SS. I walked

over and tore off their stars, first the woman's, then the man's. She got even more frightened. She said, "No, no, you can't do that, we have to wear them!' I told them that the Russians were here. I told them, "Shalom." Then she cried.[24]

Khaldei positions himself very clearly as a Jewish photographer—emphasized by him speaking to the couple in Hebrew, at least according to this version of the story. Another version of the interview suggests that Khaldei did not say "Shalom" in Hebrew, but that he said in Yiddish "*ikh bin oykh a yid. Sholem-aleykhem*" (I'm a Jew too. Hello.), a more likely scenario. Khaldei also positions himself as the Jewish couple's liberator. As he tells the story, he was in fact the one who carried out their symbolic liberation by tearing off their stars. Obviously, in the photograph, the couple still has the stars, showing that Khaldei did not, in fact, tear off the stars. I am more interested in how he refashioned his role in the scene fifty years after the fact, as the photographer-liberator of his Jewish brethren on the war-torn streets of Budapest.

The photograph of the encounter, called "Jewish Couple," has adorned the walls of art galleries and Jewish museums around the world, but it is dif-

Fig. 9.6. Evgenii Khaldei, "Jewish Couple," 1945.
Courtesy of Evgenii Khaldei and the Fotosoyuz Agency.

ferent from the version published in *Eynikayt* during the war. First, the faded photojournalistic image in *Eynikayt* had a descriptive caption rather than a pithy title like "Jewish Couple." If the emphasis during the war was on the Nazis' violent act of fixing identities—marking Jews by putting yellow stars on them—then in the 1990s, the story was about the Jews themselves. The composition of the photographs is different. In the published 1945 photo, the stars are at the center of the frame. The woman looks away from the camera, suggesting disengagement with the photographer. The image is cropped close on their bodies, so the viewer sees little of the buildings and streets of the grand, but ruined city of Budapest. In the exhibition photograph of the 1990s, our gaze is directed into their faces and into the endless street behind them that suggests the long journey they have traveled and through which they have travailed. The exhibition photograph—the more compelling of the two—tells a more intimate and more profound story. "Jewish Couple" made the people, and not the wartime antisemitic laws about wearing yellow stars, the central theme.

Khaldei's story about photographing the couple shows just how invested he was in the Jewishness of his work as he presented it late in life to American, and often Jewish, audiences. His 1997 *New York Times* obituary talked in detail about Khaldei being raised in an "Orthodox Jewish family."[25] In fact, the word "Soviet" disappeared from his description of the photograph entirely, and the focus became the Jewishness of the encounter. (Note how he says the "Russians," not "Soviets," had arrived in Budapest.) Khaldei's photograph lost the Soviet wartime liberation story as it became an icon of Holocaust memory to the many Western audiences who lauded him and his work in the last years before his death.

However, Khaldei's post-Soviet legacy in Russia is quite different from the one in the West. As the official Soviet war narrative became the post-Soviet war memory, with Jews the ever-present absence, Khaldei rarely presented himself, or his story of the Budapest ghetto, as Jewish. Rather, he presented himself and the photo as part of the heroic Soviet war memory, not as images representing the tragedy of the Holocaust. This is how Khaldei recounted the story of the Budapest photograph to a Russian journalist in the 1990s:

> I was walking along a side street and I ran into these two. Although people knew that Soviet troops had entered the city, the woman

stopped and looked distressed. I began to explain to them in German that I was Russian, Soviet. The woman began to cry. I photographed them, and then they immediately began to rip off the stars that had been sewn onto their coats.

In this interview, Khaldei does not use the word "Jew" once and instead describes himself as Russian and Soviet. He does not speak Yiddish or Hebrew to the couple, but says that he spoke German. Perhaps most important, he says that the couple tore off their own stars, rather than him doing the symbolic liberating. In framing the Holocaust for a post-Soviet Russian audience, Khaldei was Soviet, not Jewish. In the 1990s, Khaldei presented different selves and different frameworks for his photograph to audiences who, fifty years later, had very different memories of the war. In post-Soviet Russia, because of the universal memories of the war that absorbed Jewish suffering into general Soviet and human suffering, his photograph was not embedded in a separate memory of the Holocaust. It was a part of the Soviet war experience. To Western audiences, not only did he speak Hebrew or Yiddish to the Jewish couple, but he proudly proclaimed a traditional Jewish heritage.[26]

In all stories about the photograph, Khaldei emphasized one important point—that because of the Jewishness of the image, the photograph had never been published in the Soviet Union. As the Nakhimovskys relate in their description of the "Jewish Couple," "The image of the Jewish couple was not [publishable]. The photograph of the Jews in the synagogue appears here for the first time."[27] (Why it was not publishable is not mentioned.) Both photographs, of the Jewish couple and an image of dead Jews whose bodies were strewn about a makeshift synagogue in the Budapest ghetto, were, in fact, published during the war on the pages of *Eynikayt*. However, more interesting than the historical truth of the publication of these photographs is Khaldei's and subsequent scholars' interest in crafting this particular history for them. The Russian journalist ended his Khaldei interview with the statement that the photograph had never been published and laid in reserve for sixty years.

In fact, every source that discusses this image and every person I interviewed for this project insisted that because of the Jewishness of the photograph, "Jewish Couple" never appeared in the Soviet Union, neither in a newspaper as photojournalism, nor in an exhibition as an art photograph recalling the war.[28] We know that it did appear in *Eynikayt*, so why would

Khaldei and all of these commentators tell a story of wartime censorship and repression of his Budapest photographs?

Since Khaldei was, in fact, persecuted as a Jew in the post-war period, and it was true that after the war, discussion of the Holocaust—the specific persecution of Jews by Nazis and their collaborators—was silenced, it made sense to craft a life story showing how he, his photographs, and the story of the Holocaust were repressed under Stalin. He may even have forgotten that his photographs were published during the war, since that fact was difficult to incorporate into the narrative of his post-war life. The irony is that his photographs appeared during the war, under Stalin, but they were suppressed under Khrushchev and Brezhnev, as part of the creation of Soviet war memory.

In the 2000s, two exhibitions attempted to return Khaldei and his photographs to their original context in time and place. In 2005, at the Russian State Historical Museum on Red Square in Moscow, the late Khaldei and his son Leonid, a budding photographer in his own right, had an exhibition titled "Budapest through the Eyes of Two Generations." It was the first major showing of a wide range of Khaldei's Budapest photographs and included several taken in the Budapest ghetto. Leonid went to Budapest in 2005 to take photographs for the exhibition, nicely contrasting the elder Khaldei's historic photojournalism of violence and destruction with contemporary documentary images of the newly bourgeois capital of a European Union country. Following Khaldei's self-presentation to Russian audiences as a Soviet, not Jewish, photographer, the online catalog for the exhibition makes no mention of the fact that both photographers are Jewish. In the biographical description of the elder Khaldei, it mentions nothing about pogroms or an Orthodox Jewish upbringing, like the *New York Times* mentioned, and says that he was fired in 1948 not because he was Jewish, but "because of what was written under 'nationality' in his passport." It is true that most visitors would know this was the same coded reference to "Jewish" as had appeared during and after the war, but as befits the Soviet and post-Soviet memory of the war, the word "Jew" never appears.[36]

In 2008, the German photography agency Voller Ernst mounted the largest solo show of Khaldei's work in the august Martin Gropius Bau in the center of Berlin. The exhibition included hundreds of beautiful exhibition photographs, ephemera from Khaldei's archive, and even his old camera, which was shipped from Moscow for the occasion. The German organizers produced an expensive glossy, several-hundred-page cloth-bound catalog with articles by several scholars, myself included. The organizers asked me explicitly to frame his story as a Jewish story, and so I titled my article "When Photography was Jewish." The title works in English as a statement about the social history of photography for an American audience that has read much scholarship and popular literature showing how migrant Jews helped build much of twentieth-century visual media.[29] In German, however, the title echoed with a Wagnerian, antisemitic presumption that there was something called "Jewish photography" and, potentially, its opposite, Aryan art. It simply would not fly in that cultural and linguistic context. So in German, we titled it simply "Evgenii Khaldei and Soviet Jewish Photographers."

The comparison between the two exhibitions and the three linguistic and cultural universes represented shows how history and memory always operate in tension with one another. It is a fact that Khaldei was Jewish and that his Budapest photographs were published during the war. However, 60 years after their publication, different national memories read his photographs through different lenses. In a post-Soviet Russian context, the war against the Soviet Union is still a more powerful memory than the Holocaust is, even (or perhaps especially) for Soviet Jews who fought in the war. According to Zvi Gitelman's study of the Soviet Jewish war generation, most elderly Russian Jews understand the importance of the Holocaust to Jewish identity, but when asked about the Holocaust's role during the war, Soviet Jewish veterans told Gitelman that "they did not fight in the war as Jews but as Soviet citizens."[30]

In the US and Israel, Khaldei is celebrated as an important photographer and as an oppressed Soviet Jew who was persecuted despite having been a Soviet patriot who took some of his country's most important war photographs. In Germany, these stories are even more complex than the distinction between Russia's emphasis on the Soviet war and the American and Israeli reading of the images as Holocaust photographs. The Martin Gropius Bau exhibit opened on May 8, 2008, the day marking the Soviet victory over Germany and the end of the Nazi war against the Jews. How odd it was to be in Berlin, just walking distance from the new, glass-domed Reichstag, at the largest, most expensive Khaldei exhibition in history, whose primary icon was a Soviet flag flying over the ruined Reichstag, and whose catalog opened with an article originally titled "When Photography was Jewish"!

Returning iconic photographs to their original news context shows how they function in the creation of narratives and memories. Soviet Jews,

Khaldei among them, saw the war as many tragedies in one—personal, familial, communal, and national. And when he shot his Budapest photographs, he was taking news photos of particular aspects of this Soviet and Jewish war. His employer, the Soviet press, was the first institution to publicly develop a narrative of and an interpretive framework through which to understand Nazi atrocities, in both Russian and Yiddish. When we see these photographs in all of their historic complexity, the distance between Soviet and Jewish, and the war and the Holocaust collapses.

As for our photographer, Khaldei's story reminds us that, like the photographs, people's identities change over time and place. During the war, Khaldei was an up-and-coming Young Turk of Soviet photography. On the one hand, he ran into trouble with censorship that had nothing to do with Nazi atrocities. On the other hand, he was king of the profession, standing on top of the Reichstag and in the courtroom at Nuremberg. And, retrospectively, we now see that during the war he was one of the most important photographers of what we now call the Holocaust. In the late 1940s, he was persecuted as a Jew; in the 1960s and 1970s, he was celebrated as a Soviet hero. In the 1990s and now, he is all of these things and more.

Notes

[1] I base this number on reviews of dozens of lists of Soviet war photographers and attempts to determine which ones of them were Jewish. In interviews with many family members of these photographers, they estimated that at least 50 percent of photographers were Jewish.

[2] See David Shneer, *Through Soviet Jewish Eyes: Photography, War, and the Holocaust* (New Brunswick: Rutgers University Press, 2010), Chap. 1.

[3] On Kol'tsov see A. Rubashkin, *Mikhail Kol'tsov* (Leningrad: Khudozhestvennaia literatura, 1971); S. V. Iakovleva, "Predislovie," *Mikhail Kol'tsov, Vostorg i iarost'* (Moscow: Pravda, 1990).

[4] Maks Al'pert, *Bespokoinaia professiia* (Moscow: Planeta, 1962).

[5] "Biographical Information," *The Semen Fridlyand Archive*, Denver, Colorado. See also Rupert Jenkins, ed., *Photography of Empire: Semyon Fridlyand Photographs* (Denver: University of Denver Press, 2007). A third member of the Fridlyand family became one of the most important makers of Soviet visual culture—Boris Efimov, the country's most famous cartoonist. See Stephen Michael Norris, "The Visual World of Communism: Boris Efimov (Fridlyand) and the Soviet Century" (paper presented at the Association for the Advancement of Slavic Studies, Boston, MA, November 2009).

[6] On Markov-Grinberg, see Paul Harbaugh, video interview with Mark Markov-Grinberg, June 1997, private archives of Teresa and Paul Harbaugh, Denver, CO.

M. Markov, "Seria eshche ne zakonchena," *Sovetskoe foto* 11 (1937): 15-16. For more information on Markov-Grinberg, see David Shneer, *Through Soviet Jewish Eyes*.

7   Khaldei talks extensively about being born in 1917, but his sources reflecting his official, professional Soviet biography give 1916 as his birth year. See for example his official biographical form, in which he outlines his work history, and gives his birth year as 1916. Evgenii Khaldei Archives, housed at Agenstvo FotoSoyuz, Moscow. The files are not catalogued.

8   His work history is documented in archival records showing hiring and firing dates from his days in Iuzovka. These uncatalogued biographical records can also be found in Evgenii Khaldei Archives, at Agency FotoSoyuz, Moscow. See also David Shneer, "Jewgeni Chaldej und die jüdischen Fotografen der Sowjetunion," in *Jewgeni Chaldej: Der bedeutende Augenblick*, eds. Ernest Voller and Heinz Krimmer (Leipzig: Neuer Europa Verlag, 2008).

9   See TASS *prikaz* 119, October 19, 1942. Uncatalogued document in the Khaldei Files of the Voller Ernst Archives, Berlin.

10 *Ogonek* June 25, 1941, no. 18. On how the Holocaust unfolded on the pages of the Soviet press, see Karel Berkhoff, "Total Annihilation of the Jewish Population: The Holocaust in the Soviet Media, 1941-1945," *Kritika* (Spring 2009): 61-105.

11 See David Shneer, "Picturing Grief: Soviet Holocaust Photography at the Intersection of History and Memory," *American Historical Review* (February 2010): 1-25.

12 Il'ia Erenburg, *Russia at War* (London: Hamilton, 1943), 130-31.

13 Dnevnik Evgeniia Khaldeiia, ianvar' 1942g., in Evgenii Khaldei Archives, Agenstvo FotoSoyuz. Much of Khaldei's diary was recently published in German and lavishly illustrated. See Jewgeni Chaldej, ed., *Kriegstagebuch* (Berlin: Das Neue Berlin, 2011).

14 Interview with Anna Khaldei, September 2007.

15 Evgenii Khaldei, *Icons of War: Evgenii Khaldei, Soviet Photographer, World War II* (Tel Aviv: Beth Hatefutsoth, 1999).

16 See Timothy Cole, *Holocaust City: The Making of a Jewish Ghetto* (New York, London: Routledge, 2003).

17 On orders to editors about Nazi atrocities, see, for example, "Direktiva Glavpu RKKA voennym sovetam i nachal'nikam politicheskikh upravlenii frontov o prisylke v Glavpu RKKA fotodokumentov," Tsentral'nyi arkhiv Ministerstva oborony (TsAMO), f. 32, op. 920265, d. 3, l. 157 (August 1, 1941), as printed in V. A. Zolotarev, ed., *Velikaia Otechestvennaia* (Moscow: Terra, 1996), 55.

18 "Yidn in Budapesht," *Eynikayt*, March 3, 1945.

19 Dov Ber Kerler, "The Soviet Yiddish Press: *Eynikayt* 1942-1945," in *"Why Didn't the Press Shout?": American and International Journalism during the Holocaust*, ed. Robert Moses Shapiro (New York: Yeshiva, 2003), 221-50.

20 On the anti-cosmopolitan campaign, the Doctor's Plot, and other examples of postwar state-sponsored antisemitism, see Joshua Rubenstein and V. P. Naumov, eds., *Stalin's Secret Pogrom: The Postwar Inquisition of the Jewish Anti-Fascist Committee* (New Haven, CT: Yale University Press, 2001). See also David Brandenberger, "Stalin's Last Crime?: Recent Scholarship on Postwar Antisemitism and the Doctor's Plot," *Kritika* 6.1 (Winter 2005): 187–204; Jonathan Brent and Vladimir P. Naumov, *Stalin's*

Last Crime: The Plot against the Jewish Doctors, 1948–1953 (New York: Harper Collins, 2003); G. V. Kostyrchenko, *Tainaia politika Stalina: vlast' i antisemitizm* (Moscow: Mezhdunarodnye otnosheniia, 2001). Joshua Rubenstein, *Tangled Loyalties: The Life and Times of Ilya Ehrenburg* (New York: Basic Books, 1996), 372–76. See also Louis Rapoport, *Stalin's War against the Jews* (New York: Free Press, 1990).

21 See G. Kostyrchenko, ed., *Gosudarstevennyi antisemitizm v SSSR, 1938-1953* (Moscow: Materik, 2005) and Kostyrchenko, *Tainaia politika Stalina*.

22 The materials documenting Khaldei's relationship with TASS authorities can be found in the Khaldei Archive housed at Agenstvo FotoSoyuz in Moscow. The archive is not organized or catalogued. See for example "Zav Fotokhroniki TASS P. Serebriannikov Tov. Khavinsonu, Otvet. Rukovoditeliu TASS" (June 1943); or a letter from Khaldei requesting to challenge the order to return his photographic equipment (November 16, 1946), or N. Kuzovkin, "Predsedatel' attestatsionnoi kommissii i chleny kommissii attestatsii, tekst attestatsii Khaldeiia" (December 1947). The archive also holds the document telling Khaldei he has been "downsized." See Spravka, October 25, 1948.

23 The Jewish Museum of New York mounted an exhibition in Spring 1997, and the Jewish Museum of San Francisco in Summer/Fall 1997. For the documentary, see "Evgueni Khaldei—Photographer Under Stalin" (dir. Marc-Henri Wajnberg, 1997).

24 Alice and Alexander Nakhimovsky, eds., *Witness to History: The Photographs of Yevgeny Khaldei* (New York: Aperture, 1997).

25 Douglas Martin, "Yevgeny Khaldei, 80, War Photographer, Dies," *New York Times*, October 9, 1997.

26 See http://cityscan.ru/catalog.php?view=687 (accessed October 30, 2013). The original Russian reads: "Ia idu po ulochke, a eti dvoe mne navstrechu. Khotia v obshchem-to znali, chto sovetskie voiska voshli, zhenshchina ostanovilas', i kakoe-to napriazhenie pochuvstvovalos'. Ia nachal po-nemetski im ob'iasnit', chto ia russkii, sovetskii. Zhenshchina rasplakalas'. Ia ikh sfotografiroval, a potom oni priamo u menia na glazakh stali sryvat' zvezdy, kotorye u nikh byli nashity na pal'to." In my September 2007 interview with Khaldei's daughter, she insisted again that the photograph had never been published in the Soviet Union, until I showed her scanned images of the Yiddish newspaper from March 1945.

27 Nakhimovsky, *Witness to History*, 10.

28 For this project on Khaldei, I interviewed many family members, collectors, and others who were familiar with these photographers. In the following interviews, the issue of the "Jewish Couple"'s unpublishability came up: Anna Khaldei, Andrei Baskakov, Paul Harbaugh, Ernst Volland, and conversations with the Nakhimovskys.

29 See, for example, Neil Gabler, *An Empire of Their Own: How Jews Invented Hollywood* (New York: Anchor, 1989). J. Hoberman and Jeffrey Shandler, eds., *Entertaining America: Jews, Movies, and Broadcasting* (Princeton: Princeton University Press, 2005). Max Kozloff, "Jewish Sensibility and the Photography of New York," in *New York: Capital of Photography* (New Haven: Yale University Press, 2002).

30 Zvi Gitelman, "Internationalism, Patriotism, and Disillusion: Soviet Jewish Veterans Remember World War II and the Holocaust," in *Holocaust in the Soviet Union*, occasional paper, US Holocaust Memorial Museum, Washington, DC, November 2005.

Chapter 10
MEMOIRS

The Story of Gershel'man, a Jew
Boris Slutskii
Translated by Dariia Kabanova
From Boris Slutskii, *Zapiski o voine* (St. Petersburg: LOGOS, 2000), 135-48

One morning, a short, dried-out, lean person came up to me. His gray hospital gown was not doing a good job covering his rank of Private. He asked me for an unheard-of favor: "Comrade Captain, I would like to tell you the story of my life." Five minutes later, we were sitting by ourselves, and Private Gershel'man, casting anxious glances around, began his story.

I lived in Kharkov, I knew your father. For 22 years I was a Party member. My life was good. For many years, I was in charge of a print shop. I married a Russian. I have a daughter, Katia, she is 14. My life was so good, he repeated pensively, I completely forgot I was a Jew.[1] In July 1941, I joined the People's Volunteer Corps. I advanced in rank to become the company's political instructor; I was at the front lines. Then, our army group was surrounded. I was near headquarters at that time. One could see from there exactly how this took place. First, motorcycle troops separated the unit from its headquarters. They did not even shoot anymore, and our commanders did not shoot either, they just buzzed with tension. Then, long-standing relationships—those of duty, of respect for rank—began to dissolve. It was apparent that people moved away from the previous system of subordination. New hubs were formed around people whom nobody knew but who now spoke louder and louder. The logistics unit, the field kitchen—those were still functioning by inertia. Then a German officer arrived. He was alone, without guards, and then everyone realized that there was no Soviet headquarters anymore, that they were not part of a political unit, and not a military unit either; they were instead prisoners, just a lot of prisoners. Soon everyone would be sent to a camp.

From complete uncertainty began to emerge the fate of Jews, of counterintelligence officers, of commissars. Many destroyed their Party cards openly. Others, in the same open manner—in a foolishly open manner—buried their papers under comically obvious markers, like isolated trees. They wrinkled their foreheads in the effort to commit these locations to memory.

I was watching a group of commanders, young Jews, very handsome, majors and lieutenant colonels. Everyone was already clearly avoiding them, but nobody was yet brave enough to laugh at them. Beside the inertia of hunger, which sustained the existence of the field kitchens, the inertia of fear continued to operate.

Suddenly, six men from the group stepped aside—not too far, just to have enough space around them. They kissed each other. Then they suddenly pulled out their revolvers from their holsters, hitting themselves in the temples with the cold barrels of their guns, and the sounds of these little blows were lost in the sound of the shots.

Others stared into the small circle of the barrel crowned by the front sight, and when the last cold beads of sweat covered their foreheads, they hit their target. This mass suicide made the officers extremely anxious. More single shots were heard. In the political department head's tent, someone was crying inconsolably, openly. And the Germans were coming at us from all sides, green and silent. We were surrounded, herded into one crowd. It was too late for me to shoot myself; besides, I had nothing but my rifle—and to try to shoot myself with a rifle was a rotten business, anyway. I thought—I'll crawl out of this somehow, but I couldn't think more than two, maybe three days ahead. I was scared to think further. I speak Ukrainian well, I know all the terrain from Kiev to Kharkov, and I have a lot of friends in the villages. "I'll crawl out of this," I thought, and I was relieved.

When the Germans herded us together to send us to the registration office, I was in one of the columns. I was silent all the way. I thought up a name for myself: Grigorii Mikhailovich Moskalenko. My name is Grigorii Moiseevich, but they always called me Grigorii Mikhailovich at work, especially the Russians. I was most afraid that I'd betray myself somehow, out of pure absent-mindedness. For three days, we were quartered at some kolkhoz yard. We regained some of our courage. We began to share things with each other. There was this one orderly—he did not leave the side of the commissar of his regiment, an old, sickly man.

On the fourth day, the Germans came to register us and send us to camps. First, they selected the Jews. I remember the desperate wail of an Armenian doctor when they pushed him into the crowd where our people were standing silently. They pushed him in anyway.

I did not confess, shrunk in the corner, and waited until it was over.

Three people were registering us, one Ukrainian, who looked like he would have been a Petliura supporter, a girl with a very pleasant face, and an indifferent German. Their desks were next to each other. There was just one line. I realized: if I get the Petliura guy, I'm done for, he has already given away two of our people. If I get the girl or the German—I'm saved. I counted people in the line and divided the number by three; then I got confused and had to count again. At last, everything was clear, just two people were left in front of me, and I was definitely getting the Petliura guy. So, I tried to loosen my puttee inconspicuously, stepped aside and adjusted it for a very long time. Then I went straight to the girl. I heard the words coming from somewhere: name, patronymic? And then I heard my own voice: Grigorii Mikhailovich Moskalenko. Did I succeed?

I told them I was a railroad worker from Kiev railway station—they were letting people like this go first. In two hours, I was already on my way to Kiev, showing my brand new papers to the German patrols on my way.

I had lived in Kiev for six years. I had a lot of Russian and Ukrainian friends. I used to help them. They used to help me. My wife and daughter were in Kiev. Now, in my mind I was sorting through all my friends and acquaintances. I asked everyone in my mind: "Will you let me in? Will you give me a change of clothes?" It was impossible to go see my family downtown while I was still wearing my Red Army uniform.

I gave it a lot of thought, and then I went to the rail inspector Pasechnik, who lived on the outskirts of the city. I had known him for many years, we would see each other six or eight times a month, and he always seemed like a good person to me—an honest person, that is. He was a very old man, a dusty man. Jews of this sort are often called "scabby." But Pasechnik was not a Jew, so I could go to his house. It was already getting dark when I knocked on his window—very timidly, so that nobody would get angry. The old man looked out of the window and started back: "Gritsko, is that you? Go away! You'll get both of us killed! They are looking for your kind all over the city." But I understood that the old man would not turn me out of the house. Moreover, I had nowhere else to go. And I said: "Take everything I have, I will be in your debt for the rest of my life. But I need to change my clothes and go to the center of the city, to my family. I can't do anything until I know what became of my family."

New times were coming, times of slavery. Later, when I remembered Pasechnik, I thought that my words about my being in his debt for the rest of my life could be well construed as an actual obligation, not as a figure of speech.

Pasechnik's wife, a buxom woman who grew fat on potatoes with sunflower oil from her own vegetable patch, was peeking from behind his back. She was completely dazed with fear and could only repeat "Kick the kike out! Kick the kike out!" Still, I spent the night at the old man's house; in the morning, he gave me an old suit and shoes. I took out three 30-ruble bills (out of the five I had), but the old man refused. Fear had left him, and he wanted his sacred cause to remain sacred to the end.

Later, the Germans banned those 30-ruble bills with Lenin's portrait, and allowed only small bills—with the image of a worker and a peasant. Such was their policy.

Pasechnik told me about how the house manager and "activist" neighbors put together lists of Jews. He told me about hysterical bargaining for the converts, for Jewish wives and Christian husbands. He told me about Jews walking down the street—not in any formation, but in an endless line to the store where death was distributed.

I said goodbye and went to my apartment without much hope. We lived on the third floor. I met no one in the courtyard. I ran up the stairs and saw the door open, the furniture in disarray, the lacquer finish torn from the wardrobe in large stripes.

Kondrat'evna, a severe old woman, my neighbor, came out to investigate the noise. She just shook her head: "Well, Grigorii Moiseievich, you're a lucky man. Your wife left for Tashkent on the last train—all of your people are going there now." This is how I gained my first goal in life—to survive, to wait it out, and to see my wife and Katia.

Kondrat'evna also told me that three whole blocks in the street were now managed by Korsunskii. He was *that* Jew. In Kiev, they thought he was an Odessa native. He was tall, dignified, and bespectacled; he looked like a professor. He was engaged in some shady business and edited the apartment complex wall newspaper. He got on with all local officials. Now, he thought up something incredible—he called himself a Karaite, talked to some learned

German about it and obtained some paperwork that would protect him, to his neighbors' great anger.

I was already walking down the stairs to see Korsunskii, when suddenly a woman threw herself at me, an acquaintance of mine, who lived in the same complex. "Ah, the kike!" she shouted, "you came for your trash, your trash is in Gestapo hands!" She yelled to the boy who played in the yard to go fetch the Germans so they could arrest the kike. "Anna Romanovna," I said to her softly. I had never called her Anna Romanovna before; nobody in our complex did. Everyone knew she was a prostitute: at the age of 45, she would sleep with anyone for five rubles; her son, a seaman, came on leave once and repudiated her. He went to spend the night with neighbors and in the morning went back to his ship.

But I said, "Anna Romanovna!" and tears swelled in me, going straight into my head from somewhere below, and my legs gave way, and I understood: just a little longer, and I, a Party member, a member of the State Council, a distinguished person, would fall on my knees and plead with her to grant me a little more life in this world.

But the yardman was already rushing down the stairs, and I wrenched my arm from her hand, hit her in the face, and jumped out of the window. I ran down the street, and the yardman, the neighbor, and the boy chased me, yelling, "Kike! Kike! Hold him!" For two years after that, whenever I ran in the streets, I would hear, "Kike! Kike! Hold him!" behind my back. But the passers-by were not helping to catch me. It seemed that some watched me with pity.

In two hours I was at Korsunskii's apartment and drank tea with milk. All confidence was stripped from this man, and he now actually looked like an elderly professor. Before the war, we did not get along. I always thought that a Jew ought to work and not trade—everyone is always accusing us of being a "commercial nation," no need to add to the stereotype. But now we were sitting together as brothers. I understood that I could ask a lot from him. He knew that I would make no extensive demands, and that he needed to give me everything that I requested.

"The situation is as follows," Korsunskii said. "The Germans distributed fifty thousand sets of property among the local population. This property belonged to the Jews who escaped or were executed. It consists of fifty thousand sets of furniture, tableware, linens. In place of your community activists, they now have activists of their own—the Jewish Property Distribution

Committees. There are a lot of those former activists in these new committees. For two more months, until Kharkov is captured," (Korsunskii was sure that Kharkov would be captured) "the highways will be patrolled. For those two months, you stay here. Contact the Distribution Committee. You have papers. They will give you an apartment. Maybe two apartments. There were so many Jews that they could only collect the best stuff—watches, lengths of fabric, leather coats. In two months, you'll be able to sell enough at the market to have money to cross the front." Then he shoved me out of his door and gave me a wad of bills as a farewell. It was two thousand rubles in thirty-ruble bills.

The Distribution Committee consisted of six old, neat, polite men. There was an accountant, a proofreader, and a master from a tailor's artel. For twelve hundred rubles, they gave me two apartments that used to belong to a Shapiro and a Bronshtein. Five rooms in all. Luckily, I did not know either one of them. I had to compile an inventory of their property, mostly, the property that would be hard to move—nobody kept track of the rags. The committee members gathered at one of my apartments three times. They ate honey, drank their tea from saucers, so very clean, bespectacled, and in suit jackets. Then they would approve the inventories I compiled and would assign ridiculously low prices to the rugs, the pianos, and the books. Twenty-five percent of the difference went to them, and I took the rest—for my hard work. Little by little, the contents of both apartments relocated to the market. At first, I shuddered whenever I saw white stickers on the doors that said "Bronshtein—Jewish property" and "Shapiro—Jewish property." Then I got used to it. In a month, I had two suits, an Italian kit-bag, six thousand rubles in Soviet money, and some valuables in gold. With all of this, I planned to go to Kharkov, where my Russian mother-in-law lived with her sons. My departure was sped up by a visit from one of the committee's old men. He was a little drunk; he looked at me and sat down—at that time, I was already well-fed and had begun to lose my obsequiousness. He said: "Grigorii Mikhailovich, oh Grigorii Mikhailovich… Aren't you Jewish, Grigorii Mikhailovich?" I laughed out loud and said I had a mother and two sisters in Poltava, and that everyone knew them, and that I myself had suffered from Jews. I gave him six hundred rubles and a watch.

In half-an-hour, I was walking down streets with few people about. I stopped at Korsunskii's place on my way. I knocked and then suddenly was taken aback: I saw the white sticker on the door that said, "Korsunskii—Jewish property".

At that time, Kharkov was half-empty. The defense of Kharkov lasted for so long that everyone who wanted to leave could. Jewish corpses were already rotting in Losevskii quarries. Those who survived were crawling away, spreading out across all of Ukraine with their carts and wheelbarrows—there was famine in the city. Only next year would the people in Kharkov think of growing life-saving corn. During the first winter of war, thousands upon thousands faded away in the unheated apartments. The men swelled up, lost their sexual potency for a long time. Women went to streets where the German officers from the nearest units poked about, and the entire front—from Orel to Rostov—knew of the infamous Kuznetskaia Street, where the brothels and other houses of hospitality were located.

For a long time afterwards, for many weeks after the second liberation of Kharkov, the girls hid their Parisian hairdos under modest headscarves, trying to forget their German and remembering how they cried at nights at the assembly points where people were sent to Germany; they remembered how their SS friends would come flying, getting rid of the guards, tracing the flashlight beams over tear-soaked faces, taking their girlfriends to the barracks.

Free trade was proclaimed. Trade artels sprang up. Informers were recruited, mutely hated by the native population. The city council officials begged the Commandant for ten trucks to carry Jewish rags to Poltava to exchange them for food. The truck party commander was a certain Iashchenko, a small man, a cashier. In two months he was a millionaire—he bought houses and dealt in hard currency. There were five or six such millionaires in Kharkov.

Kharkov was empty. I would enter houses. I would ring the bells. I would break the bells' strings—three stories of the house would hum with sound, as if the big church bell tolled. From some cellar or other, an old woman would appear and whisper, "Everyone left," or, "Everyone's in jail," or, "Everyone's been taken to a ravine."

I went to spend the night in Klochkovskaia Street, where my mother-in-law, Maria Pavlovna, lived with her adult son, Pavlik. She wrung her hands weakly and looked at me, so pitiful and hungry that I thought, "There *are* people who have less luck than I do." A youth came in, her son, Pavlik—before the war, I would often lend him beer money. But now I stood up and tensed before him.

"Go away, kike," Pavlik said. "I'm giving you 30 minutes. After that, I go to the police." He looked at his watch demonstratively, and I realized that he had already made his decision, a long time ago, and that he would not change it; I knew that it was no use to talk about God or kinship, and that I needed to go away, into the blizzard and into the night. And I bowed to Maria Pavlovna, bowed to the ground, and said politely to the youth: "Good-bye," and I went, not waiting for those 30 minutes to be up.

All night was I strolling over the Kholodnaia Mountain, where there were no patrols. I thought that I bore Maria Pavlovna no ill will. And I realized that I now had another goal in life, the most important one. Once the Red Army was back, I would go through Kharkov once again, I would go to Kiev and pass through the whole Ukraine—I would go everywhere where they persecuted me and would yet persecute me. I would knock on every familiar window. I would reward all of those who ever helped me, either with bread, or silence, or a kind word. And I would punish all of those who betrayed me, who refused me bread, silence, or a kind word.

In the morning, exhausted and chilled, I went to a tea house. There I talked to a group of young women—soldiers' wives, who planned to go to Poltava to exchange goods. At four o'clock, after I slept for a short while, I was already walking with six women along the Zmievskii highway.

When we were leaving the city, I came across someone who I will never forget. It was Savelii Andreevich N. He was the director of a big print shop where I had worked for many years.

The women stepped aside, and Savelii Andreevich, quickly, casting around anxious glances, shared his thoughts with me, the most important thoughts that he had carried inside for the last three months.

"I realized that the Germans came not for just several years. They came to stay, forever. It is pointless and wrong to resist them. One has to live with them. Of course, you, as a Jew, would have it much harder than I will. But I decided—I will go work in the council."

I was looking at this well-fed, well-dressed man, and I thought: "We worked together for a very long time, and you were my superior, and it seemed to me that it was because you were Ukrainian and I was Jewish. And when we would meet, I would bow to you, and you would just slightly nod to me. Now, I am the lowliest of the low, a scabby Jew, just a sliver of wood in the stormy sea, but I'm larger and better than you, Savelii Andreevich." And I looked him straight in the eye, and I said, "It is not entirely unlikely that the Soviet power has more of a chance than you are willing to afford it!" And we parted ways.

For three months I roamed Poltava, exchanging goods, sometimes trading, waiting until spring would come so that I could cross the front lines under its green cover. I grew used to many things; I became smarter and more cautious. Once in February, while drunk, I mounted one of the soldier wives, and we lived together till April. One night in April, the woman told me, laughing, "You're a Jew all right, hide it or not—I took a peek and saw everything." We laughed together, and in about two hours, after she finally fell asleep, I took the remnants of my things and left following my nose. I trusted no one; it was not the time to trust anyone. The ground was already dry, you could sleep in the woods for a night. I found a fellow traveler, a young worker from Kharkov, and we started off for the front.

For two weeks we prowled along the Donets River, and then grew desperate and parted ways. On our way we'd met a group of three defectors—young Jews, typical, effete, their feet bloody from all the walking. Those types were normally caught about 20 kilometers from the front line. The best outcome would be for them to blow themselves up on mines.

In June, the front moved far to the east, and I settled down as a *priimak*, or temporary member of a household, in the Krasnograd region, where I had some trade connections from the previous winter. There were many of those *priimaks* in Ukraine—from Chernigov to Balta. They were Russians, people from occupied territories, those who were lucky to escape from the camps, sometimes senior officers, and very seldom, Jews. They entered the everyday life of a Ukrainian village as a large, close-knit group. Ukrainian police feared them and left them largely alone. Many of them married soldiers' wives and girls, either in church or "the common way." The *priimaks* were not in the habit of asking too many questions. I was not asked any questions, either. My "wife" was a widow of about twenty-eight who liked to laugh a lot. She had two children and was a sister of the village's blacksmith, a famous strongman and entrepreneur. I lived with her for only four months.

Once I went to Krasnograd for the first time—I was buying salt. When I passed by the city council, I noticed a small, white-bearded old man. His shabby frock coat and something in his profile told me he was a Jew, and a Jew who was not in hiding. I ran up to him, forgetting any precautions. We went to a tiny room in the council's cellar. Here, I heard the story of the Jews of Krasnograd.

When the Germans came, they went to greet them—to meet cultured people. The Rabbi was in the front, with bread and salt. This surprised the Germans and made them curious. The Commandant gathered the whole community—120 people—and said that Hitler would not forget the welcome given to the German troops by the Jews of Krasnograd. They took our property, they moved us to the ghetto. But we are alive. Yet, it would have been better if we hadn't brought that bread and salt.

When I was approaching one of the villages, I was told that my widow with whom I had lived the winter came to visit. My heart sank. Soon, a boy came running—the blacksmith, her brother, asked me to come by.

He sat alone, under the icons, a bottle of moonshine on the table.

"So, Grigorii Mikhailovich, it has come to my attention that you are a Jew. We will not report you—we're not like that. You did not treat us wrong—we won't either. You can't stay here, though. If they learn about you—neither you nor my sister will be spared. Now, you slept with a woman for four months—so leave your things here, and those three watches, leave them too. Take the jacket so you don't freeze."

We drank together and parted, bearing each other no ill will. It was late autumn, and the jacket did not keep me very warm. I did not know where to go; I felt miserable and lonely. I roamed around for some time, and then went to work at a sugar factory, about 50 kilometers from Krasnograd.

I had to live in the factory's dormitory and use the communal bath house. For many Saturdays I wriggled, trying to be on duty during the bath day, to be the last one to wash. Once, late in the evening, when I was ready to get dressed, my roommate Petro ran into the bath house. He butted in with a flashlight and shouted triumphantly, "A kike! I knew he was a kike!" He then ran out of the room.

Petro had graduated from high school, he read Vlasovite[2] literature and wrote poetry in Ukrainian. People in the factory were scared of him, believing he was a secret informer. I realized I was in mortal peril. I had to leave everything again and go away. But at that point, I had been running for a year and a half. My body was overcome by a warm, viscous exhaustion. I decided: what will be, will be. In the morning, the police woke me up. They marched me to the regional authorities—to the Head of Police. The Head of Police listened to my oaths very calmly and ordered that I be brought to the hospital for "the scientific corroboration of Jewishness."

In the hospital, I was shoved into an office where I discovered a young woman. She was the wife of the Head of Police.

When I saw her eyes, when I heard a polite request to undress, when the cold of death blew into my ears and crept under my clothes, I understood: "It's now or never." I fell down on my knees, I crawled, biblically embracing her legs, I cried silently and said, "Don't examine me. Yes, I am a Jew. Save me!"

This woman had graduated from medical school just before the war started. She came to live with her relatives and was taken as a wife by the first man of the community—by the Head of Police. And now, with maidenly embarrassment, she was consoling me, raising me up from my knees. Then she took a deep breath, filled out a standard form and said: "Now run! Tomorrow, today—do not delay, or we will both perish!" The same night, I ran from the factory.

Now we are sitting here, comrade Captain, but what I want is to be there at the hospital, to go to the NKVD, to the city council, and say: "This woman is not just the wife of the Head of Police, she is a human being, and she saved my life!"

The rest of it is not as interesting.

I went to be a *priimak* again. For the third time. First, I was taken in as a day laborer. Then as a husband.

In August, I heard the cannonade approaching and left to the east. In two days, I came across our scouts. And I ran up to them and cried. They were laughing and saying: "Hello, gramps!" I am just 45 years old, comrade Captain, and I was 44 then. And I told them I was Jewish, and I told them of my sufferings. And they told me: "Jews are people, too."

Now I serve as a baker at the division's bakery, but I want to get back to the front lines, whatever it may take. I want revenge. I want to survive. I want to come back and walk through the villages, knock on the windows and give everyone their due—for the good and for the evil they did me.

And do you know what I think about the people, if I were to sum it up? There are ten times more of those who helped me than of those who betrayed me, comrade Captain.

Notes

[1] Slutskii does not use quotation marks, moving between Private Gershel'man's narrative and his own interjections without distinguishing the two. We preserve this feature of his style (Editors' note).

[2] The narrator refers to the propaganda literature in Russian that was distributed by the Russian Liberation Army's Headquarters.

The Question of the National Question, or A Rally for a Genuinely Russian Cinema

Mikhail Romm
Translated by Dariia Kabanova

From Mikhail Romm, *Kak v kino: ustnye rasskazy*
(Nizhnii Novgorod: DEKOM, 2003), 120-29.

Until the year 1943, as we know, we had no antisemitism, comrades. Somehow, we managed without.

Well, that is, we had antisemites all right. But they concealed the fact, so nobody really noticed.

It was not until 1943, then, that something began to brew. At first, quite unobtrusively.

For example, war reporters began to have their last names changed: Kantorovich became Kuznetsov. Rabinovich became Korolev, and some Abramovich or other became Aleksandrov. Something like that.

Then everyone began to change their last names.

And then, more signs appeared. And more sprouts of antisemitism. Antisemitism began to grow. Soon, some antisemitic notes were heard on the official level.

At about that time, I sent an editor to Alma-Ata, to a joint studio—Lenfilm and Mosfilm were both evacuated there.

The studio's art director was an Ermler, and his deputies were a Trauberg and a Raizman. One can see how having last names like that was not entirely tactful in the light of *that* whole ticklish issue.

At that time, I was the art director of the Department [of Movies] in the Ministry.[1] So, I send the editor there. He comes back, shows me the report.

And the report is all about Pyr'ev: deputy art director Ivan Aleksandrovich Pyr'ev ordered this, Ivan Aleksandrovich canceled that, Ivan Aleksandrovich instructed, Ivan Aleksandrovich began, Ivan Aleksandrovich completed, comrade Pyr'ev noted, and so forth.

I say, "What does Pyr'ev have to do with anything? Since when is he the deputy art director?"

My editor looks me straight in the eye, ever so calmly, and says, "Don't you know? He was appointed."

I say, "Appointed officially?"

"Not officially, no. I haven't seen the appointment letter, but it is a fact."

I say, "Well, until I receive the letter, please be so kind as to consider Ermler to be the art director, and Raizman and Trauberg to be his deputies.[2] Rewrite the report to reflect this and show it to me."

He looks at me, his eyes so peacefully, heavenly blue, and asks, "Is that your order, Mikhail Il'ich?"

I say, "Yes, that would be an order."

"All right, I'll rewrite it."

Next day, I send for him and ask, "Did you get a chance to rewrite the report?"

"No, didn't have time. I was working," he says. And his eyes are heavenly, enigmatically blue again.

"All right," I say, "you have until tomorrow."

Next day I come into the office and ask him, "Where is the report?"

He asks, "Have you, Mikhail Il'ich, had a chance to read today's mail?"

And then he shows me the orders: "Hereby, Pyr'ev is appointed as art director of the Alma-Ata joint studio."

There's more; the same orders contained a note from Ivan Grigor'evich Bol'shakov.[3] He informed me that well, you have asked many times, Mikhail Il'ich, to be relieved of your duty, and you have felt unhappy occupying an administrative position… So we have decided to relieve you and make sure you go back to creative work; in that light, we suggest that you go make the opera, *Sadko*, together with Ivanovskii,[4] using the props and sets that were left after *Ivan Groznyi*.

Well, of course I didn't go to make *Sadko*, but I did turn my duties over.

By that point, the sprouts sprouted well—we had an exemplary gardener, as everyone knows. So, whatever grew, took root.

I went to Moscow to have a talk with Ivan Grigor'evich, but even before that I wrote a huge letter to Stalin complaining about these circumstances. I said episodes like this could make one believe we have antisemitism in our country. Dear Iosif Vissarionovich, I would like to draw your attention to these incidents, etc., dear Iosif Vissarionovich etc., please help…

The Question of the National Question, or A Rally for a Genuinely Russian Cinema

So I come to Moscow, and the situation in Moscow is not the same anymore. Bol'shakov has taken a severe tone with me.

I had to choose what I would do next then, never mind what it was, the main thing was that I was offered work in Tashkent, not in Moscow—I could only *finish* the film in Moscow, and that was it.

I learn that a "Rusfilm" studio is being organized in Moscow. One crew director said to me, "Mikhail Il'ich, we're organizing a studio to be called 'Rusfilm.' Only Russian directors will now work at Mosfilm."

I go to Bol'shakov again and say, "Who will work at Mosfilm?"

He says, "Well, comrades Aleksandrov, the Vasil'ev brothers, Ivan Aleksandrovich Pyr'ev, Pudovkin … who else … Babochkin, Dovzhenko, some other comrades."

I ask, "Excuse me, what is the factor that you take into account when assigning people to Mosfilm, exactly? I'm just curious."

He says, "Hm, the factor … I'll leave you to be the judge of that."

I went to Aleksandrov, to the Central Party Committee.

Georgii Fedorovich Aleksandrov was at that time Head of the Propaganda Department.[5]

I tell him, "I sent the letter."

He says, "Well, here it is on my desk."

I look, and I see the letter's scribbled all over with questions and exclamation marks, in blue pencil, and, in the bottom, instructions are appended: EXPLAIN THE ISSUE.

So, Aleksandrov had to begin explaining.

I got mad and got up.

Aleksandrov had great manners. He also got up.

I sat down. He sat down as well.

I got up. He got up.

I say, "Forgive me, Georgii Fedorovich, I can't sit still, I've got a weak nervous system. But you don't have to get up all the time."

He says, "Well, I can't remain seated when my guest is standing."

We remained standing for a good hour and a half.

I shouted at him, and he explained things to me, very calmly. What exactly he explained to me, I forget. At least he promised to me that Eisenstein and I would be back at Mosfilm, along with some others.

This was what I had to take back to Tashkent.

I won't tell other stories—for example, the one when Iusupov tried to send me to Moscow; we had an interesting conversation.[6] There other things I won't tell either.

In a year I was back in Moscow. I had half of the feature, *Man Number 217*, done. And what do I see? The whole business is in full bloom, and indeed, the project of organizing this "Rusfilm" studio at Mosfilm is in the works.

And it is then that the meeting of the activists' committee is scheduled.

So the activists gather, Bol'shakov was the one who chaired the session, someone reported something—I forget what.

The main event was the report by a certain Astakhov, I don't remember his first name. He had a limp, and he was hideous, angry as a dog, and a raving Black-Hundreder. He was a director of a script studio.

He came to the rostrum, limping, and delivered his great presentation.

"There is," he says, "Ukrainian cinema, there is Georgian cinema, there is Armenian cinema; there is Kazakh cinema, too. But Russian cinema did not exist until this day. Only separate instances of it existed. Now we need to create Russian cinema. And Russian directors will make this cinema Sergei Appolinar'evich Gerasimov, for example. He is a true Russian filmmaker."

Little did poor Astakhov know that Gerasimov's mother was Jewish. Shklovskii, for example, was considered to be Jewish, because his father was a rabbi and his mother was a priest's daughter. Gerasimov, on the other hand, was considered Russian, because his patronymic was a Russian patronymic. Some way or the other, the fact that his mother was Jewish did not see the light of day.

"Here is Sergei Appolinar'evich Gerasimov. Have a look at the way the actors work—all of this breathes Russianness. Or take the Vasil'ev brothers, or Pudovkin (etc., etc.). These are Russian filmmakers, they all breathe of Rus', the Rus' of old.[7] We must pull together these forces and create Russian cinema."

Then, the floor was given to Anatolii Golovnia. He also delivered quite an oration—mostly, by attacking me.

There are, he says, filmmakers and cameramen who seem to make Russian films, but are they really Russian? Take the birch-tree. It may be a Russian birch, but it may be a non-Russian birch—a German one, for example. A person must possess a Russian soul to be able to distinguish between a Russian birch and a non-Russian birch. Romm and Volchek lack this soul.

The Question of the National Question, or A Rally for a Genuinely Russian Cinema

True, in *Lenin in October* they somehow managed to fake this Russian spirit; but the rest of their films, so to say, breathe of France, not of Russia.

French breath it was, not Jewish breath. But of course I'm sitting right there, and grinding my teeth in anger.

To be fair, Igor Savchenko gave a speech right after Golovnia. Savchenko was a great guy, a stutterer, fair-haired—an amazing man. So he started talking about national art and, in particular, rebutted Golovnia as follows.

"Whe-e-n I," he said, "um, made the fi-irst film of mine, *Acco-o-ordion*, um, *Acco-o-ordion*, one man came up to me and said, 'Why would you spend time on crap like that? Those birches and the rest of it? One must emulate the German expressionists.' This man was comrade Go-o-olovnia, currently present," Savchenko said to everyone's delighted laughter.

Of course, someone responded to Savchenko right away. And the discussion went on and grew, all about filmmakers who were supposed to smell like Russians.

Finally, they gave me the floor. I came to the rostrum and said (here's the outline of this speech, I managed to keep calm and did not shout):

"Well, as long as the Russian cinema employing Russian filmmakers who smell like Russians is in the works, I, of course, should be looking for another job. But, I ask myself, where would the director of *Battleship Potemkin* work? Where would the directors who made *The Great Beginning* and *Baltic Deputy*, Kheifits and Zarkhi, work? What studio would employ the director of *The Last Night*, Iuli Raizman? Would Ermler, the one who made *Great Citizen*, be unemployed? Would Kozintsev and Trauberg? Would Lukov, who made *Big Life*? Where would we all work? Clearly, we would all work in Soviet cinema. I would gladly work with these comrades. I do not know what spirit they breathe, I did not smell them. Comrade Astakhov, on the other hand, did, and affirms that Babochkin, the Vasil'ev brothers, Pyr'ev and Gerasimov smell as they should, while we do not. Well, we the un-smelly ones, if I may, will continue making Soviet cinema. And you, the smelly ones, are welcome to make Russian cinema."

You know, when I was speaking, the audience was deadly silent. When I finished, they roared with delight and I received the kind of applause that I'd never experienced before or after. As I went to take my seat in the audience, I saw that many on the panel were very scared.

That night, Lukov called me and said, "Misha, we all want to shake your hand and give you a hug."

The next day, all of the Central Committee attended the Activists' Committee session. They began to back up cautiously. Not really drastically, but they did begin to back up. And Gerasimov softened it all for us. He gave a very roundabout, soft speech, saying that comrade Astakhov, of course, did not mean the national origin, but rather, the national essence of art. And, so to say, art has a right to be national. And I understand Mikhail Il′ich's concern, an understandable concern, but the question is more complex, it goes deeper, this question does, it is the question of national character etc., etc..

Then the meeting was over. I was told, "They're going to chew you up and spit your bones out."

In about three days, I received a phone call from Grigorii Vasil′evich Aleksandrov, not from Grigorii [sic] Fedorovich but from Grigorii Vasil′evich, the film director.

He says to me, "Mikhail Il′ich, my congratulations, you're awarded a personal fixed wage."

I ask, "How?"

He says, "We were at the Central Committee with Ivan Grigor′evich [Pyr′ev], reporting to comrade Malenkov about those film directors who are worthy of receiving an extraordinary wage increase. We say, these are Eisenstein, Pudovkin, Chiaureli, and then we give him some more names. And then Malenkov says, 'What about Romm? Keep in mind, comrades, that not only is he a good filmmaker; he is also a very smart person.' So, Ivan Grigor′evich says, 'We wanted to waitlist him.' And then Malenkov says sharply, 'No waitlisting Romm.'"

This was how I suddenly received an extraordinary wage increase for my speech.

That's how it turned out for me. But as far as *that* question goes, things did not get easier.

Appendix
A Letter to I.V. Stalin

Dear Iosif Vissarionovich!

I wanted to write this letter to you for a very long time. But, having in mind the enormous magnitude of the work that you shoulder on a daily basis, I never found the courage. However, the situation has been aggravated to the extent that I can no longer delay writing this letter.

Dear Iosif Vissarionovich! Have you ever asked yourself the question why, during the war, you did not seen a single feature film by Eiseinstein, Dovzhenko, Ermler, Kozintsev and Trauberg, or by me, by Aleksandrov, by Raizman (given that his *Mashen'ka* was began long before the war), by Kheifits and Zarkhi (as *Sukhe-Bator* is also, in essence, a pre-war film), and by some other prominent filmmakers? Is it possible that these people, bound to the Party with blood ties, brought up by the Party, the people who created, before the war, such masterpieces as *Battleship Potemkin*, *Alexander Nevsky*, *Great Citizen*, *Shchors*, *The Maxim Trilogy*,[8] *Lenin in October*, *Lenin in 1918*, *Baltic Deputy*[9] and others—is it at all possible that such people would not or could not work for their Motherland at this time that called for great civic responsibility? No, it is not possible—the fact of the matter is that your favorite brainchild, Soviet cinema, has found itself in an unheard-of state of disorder, confusion and decline.

I will begin with my own story, though my personal story is not the reason I am writing. A little more than two years ago, I was appointed as art director of cinematography in the Ministry. At the same time, other filmmakers were appointed as art directors of studios. We, the creative workers, enthusiastically hailed this change, an obvious result of the Central Committee's and your own decision. We accepted this change as evidence of the new era in Soviet cinema. We took these administrative jobs with which we were not entirely comfortable, we took this difficult and thankless task, and, if I am allowed to speak frankly, by the sweat of our brow we corrected numerous mistakes that Bol'shakov made before us. Little by little, we filled in the chasm that for many years separated filmmakers from other creative workers.

Yet, in the last couple of years, I began finding myself in a very confusing position. I have to work in the atmosphere of distinct hostility emanating from Bol'shakov and his deputy, Lukashev. Moreover, I am under the impression that I have fallen into some secret disgrace. All of the most crucial questions concerning art directing are decided not just without me, but even without informing me about the outcome. Scripts are approved without my opinion; production is launched and directors are appointed without my approval; completed films are either given a green light or rejected without my input. My own staff, together with other workers of the cinematographic industry, including art directors, are appointed or relieved of their responsibilities without any notification. All my questions, conceptual and practical, are not even acknowledged by comrade Bol'shakov: I do not even know when I myself will get a chance to make a film, and what film that will be.

It has come to the point when my own staff looks at me with frustration and disbelief, not understanding what is going on. My directors, cameramen, my actors come to me with many pressing creative issues, but I cannot give them any answer, as my answers often do not correspond to the instructions given by Bol'shakov (about which I uninformed), leading to more confusion.

If the interests at stake were just my own, if the difficult position in which I have found myself were the only instance of this kind, I would have never found the courage to write to you. But what is at stake is not my personal career. Ermler, the art director of the Alma-Ata studio, finds himself in an equally deplorable position. Everything that I have written about myself applies equally to him. He has no voice in the most crucial decisions that define his studio's creative methods and practices. The last straw was that, on Bol'shakov's orders, Ermler's deputies Trauberg and Raizman were relieved of their duties, with Pyr'ev appointed in their stead. Ermler was not consulted about a decision of this magnitude; moreover, he was not even informed about it. I had a conversation with Ermler in Tashkent. His condition, morally and psychologically, is deplorable. Similar feelings are shared not just by art directors but also by a whole cohort of our most prominent film directors. Today, I received a tragic letter from Kozintsev, the creator of the *Maxim Trilogy*. He complains about being treated in a manner that is hardly bearable, about being disoriented; he speaks of feeling like a "former" person, he speaks of feeling that he is about to perish. His story, which is indeed disgraceful, is not unique to him.

Dear Iosif Vissarionovich! We ask ourselves: what is the matter? How have Ermler, Romm, Kozintsev, Trauberg—and many others whom I do not mention here only because they have not spoken to me personally and have not written to me, yet their situation and state of mind I do know—how have they sinned against the Party and Soviet power? There is not a single one among us who did not make numerous requests to be assigned to Moscow or to go to the front. Yet, we remain in the rear, severed from the Party's chief administration, receiving, instead of the guidance we seek, only orders, bureaucratic peremptory shouts and streams of murky, hostile guidelines from the Central Committee. The dark atmosphere of slander, of bureaucratic enigma, which seemed to have gone away in the last four to five years, is beginning to return to life in new forms, accompanied by all of its typical "delights": by favoritism, sycophantism, enigmatic rearrangements, conceit, petty tyranny and vindictiveness. We watch workers in other areas of labor with jealousy, as they live their lives to the fullest and notwithstanding all the hardships of the wartime, as they cheerfully give the full extent of their labor to our Motherland.

As you know, one month before the war, the Central Committee of the Communist Party held a meeting devoted to the questions of cinema, lead by comrades Andreev, Zhdanov, Malenkov, and Shcherbakov. The speeches by the Committee's Secretaries contained a number of guidelines: about increasing and strengthening art directorship, reducing and eliminating bureaucratic red tape that presents an obstacle to cinema's operation, simplifying the economics of cinema, increasing the engagement of youth, promoting young directors, and so on. Some of these guidelines were given in the form of practical proposals, but none of them were implemented, while the practices of the Cinema Affairs Committee are in direct opposition to the guidelines given at that meeting. This cannot be explained by the war alone, as the war should have pushed the Committee to implement the Secretaries' guidelines as soon as possible, given the distinct pre-war atmosphere of the meeting.

I would not allow myself to keep your attention any longer by dwelling on more facts that illustrate bureaucracy, organizational confusion and superficial problem-solving. People are perishing. The most prominent filmmakers, whose names are not just known to every Pioneer in our country, but also known in the United States, in Britain, and all around the world—these filmmakers find themselves in such a deplorable position that, if nothing changes very soon, the country might lose these masters forever. It might not be possible to put them back on their feet again. As far as the younger generation of filmmakers goes, it may be too late. Our few successors are half gone.

I ask you, Iosif Vissarionovich, to summon the art directors of the major studios, Ermler, Yutkevich, Chiaureli, Aleksandrov, and me, to Moscow, to the Central Committee. I also ask to summon the directors: Eisenstein, Kozintsev, and Trauberg. Dovzhenko, who is currently in Moscow, can represent Ukrainian cinema.

I might end my letter here, because I am convinced that this meeting would clarify all of the pressing issues and give us political and creative guidelines for a long time to come. But there is one more question remaining; this question I cannot address to anyone but you. In the last few months, there was quite some reshuffle in the cinema—15 to 20 prominent figures (art directors, members of the Script Studio's editorial board, deputy studio directors, and heads of script departments) were either transferred or relieved of their duties. This entire reshuffle cannot be explained by any political or administrative considerations. Given that all of those relieved of their duties turned out to be Jewish (and that all of those replacing them are non-Jewish), some people, having overcome their initial perplexity, began to reason that the reshuffle is best explained by the anti-Jewish trend in the leadership of the Cinema Affairs Committee. As appalling as it sounds, new directives of the Committee only feed the rumors, which became too pervasive to counteract.

I caught myself at being convinced that in the last few months I am often reminded of my Jewish origin, though in the 25 years of the Soviet rule I was never reminded of it, having been born in Irkutsk, having grown up in Moscow, where I spoke only Russian and have always felt Russian, a truly Soviet person. If even I am plagued by such thoughts, then the situation is much worse in the cinema as a whole, especially in light of the fact that we are currently fighting Fascism, which has inscribed antisemitism on its banners.

Dear Iosif Vissarionovich! Twice in my life I have appealed to you at a dark hour. If I am wrong now, if you find that I do not understand something, I ask you to explain to me, as a party member and a filmmaker, the error I have committed.

I apologize for this letter taking your time, so valuable for all progressive humankind.

Signature

January 8, 1943,
Tashkent

Stalin Award Laureate
Mikhail Romm

Notes

1. During that time, the "Ministry" was called State Committee for Cinematography.
2. Ivan Pyr'ev (1901-68), Fridrikh Ermler (Vladimir Breslav, 1898-1967), Iulii Raizman (1903-94), and Leonid Trauberg (1902-90)—film directors.
3. Ivan Bol'shakov (1902-80) was head of State Committee for Cinematography.
4. Alexander Ivanovskii (1881-1960)—a film director.
5. Earlier, Romm mentioned the film director Grigorii Aleksandrov (Mormonenko).
6. Usman Iusupov (1900-66)—First Secretary of the Central Committee of the Communist Party of Uzbekistan.
7. Translator's note: Romm refers to a line from Aleksandr Pushkin's 1820 poem, *Ruslan and Ludmila*, an example of Romantic nationalism: "There, in a mortar, onward sweeping/ All of itself, beneath the skies/ The wicked Baba-Yaga flies;/ There pines Koshchei and lusts for gold..../ All breathes of Rus', the Rus' of old/There once was I…"
8. *Great Citizen* (Velikii grazhdanin) is a film by Friedrich Ermler (1939, Lenfilm); *Shchors* is a film by Aleksandr Dovzhenko (1939); *The Maxim Trilogy* (*The Youth of Maxim*, "Iunost' Maksima" [1935]; *The Return of Maxim*, "Vozvrashchenie Maksima" [1937]; *New Horizons*, "Vyborgskaia Storona" [1938]), directed by Grigorii Kozintsev and Leonid Trauberg (Lenfilm).
9. *Baltic Deputy*, "Deputat Baltiki," is a film by Iosif Kheifits and Aleksandr Zarkhi (1937, Lenfilm).

A Novel of Memoirs

Anatolii Rybakov
Translated by Dariia Kabanova

From Anatalii Rybakov, *Roman-vospominanie* (Moscow: Vargius, 1997), 222-45.

24.

Before the war, in Ryazan, my friend Robert Kupchik told me the story of his parents. In the last century, his grandfather moved to Switzerland from Simferopol, graduated from a university there, and got married. His oldest sons became doctors, too, and when his youngest was about to enter the university, he decided to take him to Russia, to show his son the land of his ancestors. It was the year 1909.

In Simferopol, the young Swiss fell in love with a beautiful young Jewess, a shoemaker's daughter; he married her and took her to Zurich. She did not like it there; she returned to Russia and her husband, Robert's father, came with her to stay in Simferopol, where he worked as a shoemaker, like his father-in-law. In the thirties he, a "suspicious foreigner," was, naturally, incarcerated.

This story amazed me. For the pre-war generation, "Switzerland" was something like Mars, or the Moon. It was another world. Yet, the man left his land, his rich parents, and his career—all for love.

After the war, I came across Robert. His father was freed in 1940: his Swiss passport survived, his mother turned out to be German, and Stalin was friends with Hitler then. But, in 1942, Robert's father and mother, along with the rest of the Simferopol Jews, were executed by the Germans. Their corpses were thrown into a common grave on the road to Sudak. This was the story Robert told me.

At that point, I was already an author of many books, and I seized the plot like that: I had wanted to write a novel about love for a long time. Moreover, I myself was in love with my future wife then.

I met Tanya in 1950, when she was 21 and I was 39. I would have never let her go; the circumstances of that time led us apart. She was a daughter of an "enemy of the people." Her father, Mikoyan's deputy, was executed in 1938, her mother was sent to the camps, both brothers died in combat during the war. Could I, with my "Article 58" past, have protected this girl, could I have been a good partner for her? This past hung over me again: it was then that Stalin said about me, "He is not a sincere person." I had no right to enter into any serious relationship. Tanya listened to me, her head hung low. She did not believe that I loved her.

In several years, we came across each other in Peredelkino, by accident. She was with her charming two-year-old daughter, as beautiful and joyful as before, she nodded to me and immediately turned into the side alley. Her husband was a famous poet: I came across his poems every once in a while, poems dedicated to her—so, she looked reasonably happy. I, too, was quite well: I was rehabilitated, and a popular writer. But it was clear: Tanya was avoiding me. Both of us had lives of our own, and the rest was seemingly past us.

Yet, we had a chance to see each other again. We met twenty years later, in Crimea, in Koktebel. We were in the House of Arts at the same time. I walked along an alley, Tanya walked in the opposite direction, and there were no side alleys this time, so she could not avoid me. She had to stop and exchange a couple of phrases. The next day, we came across each other again, and again, and again … Tanya's flight to Moscow was before mine, there were only a few days left, and now we were scared of parting even for a short while. We swam far into the sea, and I looked at Tanya's dear, sweet face, and the whole world ceased to exist…

We have been together for nineteen years—my happiest years. A loyal, loving person, my first editor and critic, is at my side. I like to talk to her about the things I plan to put on paper tomorrow. My thoughts rush forward; this is called "occupying a territory." But … a funny detail—we never discuss Tanya's corrections. We both are too emotional; we would start arguing right away. She writes her suggestions on the margins of the manuscript, or composes a whole review letter to me. I read these, railing. Then I re-read, think it over, calm down and have to agree with what she says—Tanya's taste is impeccable. I bring the corrections to the room where she sits at her computer and joke, "The things I do to preserve peace in the family."

But at times, when Tanya is especially pushy, I want to even the score and I read something to her that is appropriate for the moment, for instance, from the Goncourt brothers: "Catching fleas stultifies even the major talent. Polishing a phrase using a magnifying glass is a distraction from all the power, grandeur, and warmth that give life to a book."[1]

We laugh together.

In 1975, when I was thinking over my novel, *Heavy Sand*, I told Tanya: "Now I know what love is, now I will be able to write about that."

Another thing has driven me to the story Kupchik told…

Stalin laid the foundations of Soviet state's antisemitism. He himself became an antisemite in his youth, in conflicts with other members of the underground and exiled revolutionaries who were smarter, more educated than he was, and often, Jewish. They were as intolerant in their political discussions as he was. His antisemitism was strengthened by his jealousy of Trotsky during the Civil War, and later—by his struggle for power with Zinoviev and Kamenev. Many Jews were members of the Bolshevik Party, decimated by Stalin in the late thirties.

When Hitler exterminated six million of their compatriots, the Jews' national consciousness was sharpened. The creation of the state of Israel and its heroic struggle for existence created a feeling of national pride. The grief for the dead and the pride for the living—Stalin understood how explosive this mixture of feelings might become. Soviet Union voted for the creation of Israel, hoping to make it into the Soviet outpost in the Middle East. These plans fell through. Israel aligned itself with the United States. The lay of the land became clear to Stalin: the United States, where there are enough Jews in politics and economy, is the chief enemy; the United States' ally is the Jewish state of Israel. Whom would the Soviet Jews support? Of course, Israel and the United States.

Antisemitic policies on the state level came flowing: literary critics and writers became "rootless cosmopolitans" and anti-patriots. The members of the Jewish Anti-Fascist Committee became spies and saboteurs. The Jewish doctors became "murderers in white-coats." An insolent antisemitic campaign in the press molded and sustained the "people's wrath." The Jews had to be "saved" from this wrath by being deported to the Far East.

Stalin died, not having completed what Hitler started. The doctors were freed, the guiltless were rehabilitated. Yet state-level antisemitism persisted during Brezhnev's rule, having transformed into the fight against Zionism. The Jews were now treated as potential emigrants, all too ready to move to Israel. An anecdote from those times: filling in the paperwork, a Jew writes in the space for his nationality, "Yes!" The Jews' access to higher education was limited; Jews could not hold state, party, or military positions of any significance. Numerous books and articles were published by all the Evseevs, the Beguns[2] and the rest of the Black-Hundreders of that time, accusing Zionists of being anti-Communists and counter-revolutionaries. In this way, those Black-Hundreders were different from the contemporary ones, who accuse Zionists of Communist propaganda and blame them for the October Revolution itself. Even Savitsky, the People's Artist of Belarus, painted a pit where the corpses of the executed Slavs were thrown, two executioners by its side: an SS-trooper and a Jew.

Nowhere was the horrifying catastrophe of the European Jewry ever mentioned; even the mass graves of the killed Jews were inscribed with "Victims of the Fascist German occupants" only. The persecution of Jews who wanted to move to Israel, of the famous "refuseniks," the persecution for learning Hebrew—all of those were markers of the Brezhnev times.

Such was the situation in the seventies.

I grew up in Moscow, in a Russified family; I did not know Hebrew; I lived, I worked, I roamed around Russia and never felt any antisemitism against me personally. I fought for Russia, I was born in Russia and in Russia I will die.* But I am a Jew. I was appalled by what was going on in my country, in the country which, at the dawn of the revolution, proclaimed the universal brotherhood of nations. I gave Biblical names to the characters of my new novel: Jacob and Rachel. "And Jacob served seven years for Rachel; and they seemed unto him but a few days, for the love he had for her."

In Simferopol, where the parents of my Ryazan friend lived, everything seemed alien. It was not my city, it did not stir any memories; it did not jolt my imagination. I decided to move the setting for my novel to the land of my ancestors, to the land of my grandfather and grandmother, to the Rybakov family, to the town of Snovsk, later renamed Shchors.[3] The only person surviving from this side of the family was my mother's younger sister, Aunt Ania, who lived in Preobrazhenskaia Street in Moscow.

She was well over seventy, yet her mind was clear and bright; her memory was strikingly sharp and her sense of humor inexhaustible.

Why are we the Rybakovs? Where did this last name come from? We began thinking of it only in Moscow. Oh yes, only when we came to Moscow. So we come to the Vostryakovskoie Cemetery, to their office, and ask them where the grave of David Rybakov is. (This was her brother, my uncle). And one man in the line says suddenly: "Look, they're taking our last names already." Well,

---

* He died in New York on December 23, 1998, and was buried in Moscow.

how about that! We take their last names! Things like that—only in Moscow can you hear such things. There, in Snovsk, the Rybakovs were always the Rybakovs. Everybody knew that. In Snovsk they knew, and around Snovsk they knew all right. Where did the last name come from? Who knows where last names come from? Nobody knows! The Rybakovs are the Rybakovs, the Kuznetsovs are the Kuznetsovs, and the Sapozhnikovs are the Sapozhnikovs. My grandfather, your great-grandfather—he lived in a village, he was doing something, they drank vodka; fights follow the vodka, you know, and murder follows the fights. Somebody killed someone, I don't know who, I don't think it was my grandfather, but he ran away to Snovsk anyway—just in case. He was the forefather of the Rybakovs of Snovsk. He was nicknamed "Bolt," because he bolted from that village to Snovsk. How did Snovsk come to be? I'll tell you. They were building the Romenskaia railroad and they had to build a bridge across the river Snov, so the river gave name to the settlement. Your grandfather worked there. He lugged ties. Do you remember the fists your grandfather had? One can write novels about your grandfather. When the New Economic Policy was abolished, they sealed off your grandfather's store. The goods, the money—everything was in the store. Other stores were sealed off too. Everyone remained silent. But your grandfather did not…

She eyed the tape recorder suspiciously.

Should I keep talking?

"Of course," I said. "It's just for me."

So, what does your grandfather do? He takes Isaak, my husband, and Tolia, his eldest son, and goes to the store with them, at night. Isaak and Tolia are afraid of the police, but they are even more afraid of your grandfather. Behind the store, there was … what do you call it? The thing you use to go down to the basement?

"A hatch?"

Yes, exactly, a hatch. So your grandfather goes down to the basement through this hatch, and through the basement he enters the store. Isaak and Tolia follow him. And, what do you think? They take the money and the priciest goods, several boxes of them, they take them out through the hatch and hide it with someone. Who would dare to do something like that? Only your grandfather would.

In a month, Aunt Ania recorded eight tapes. I have to repeat, her memory was strikingly sharp. Her speech was full of imagery, and I passed her intonation onto the narrator of *Heavy Sand*. I learned the story of my family and of other families, my plot was growing with events, fates, legends—it was in this milieu that I placed Rachel and Jacob. The novella about love was turning into a family chronicle.

In the seventies, Belarusfilm studio produced my television films: *Dirk, Bronze Bird, The Last Summer of Childhood*. Every film had three episodes.

The principal photography took place in Belarus, so I went to Minsk and to other towns. I went to where ghettos were established under Germans, where the Jews were exterminated; later, Tanya and I went to Vilnius, to the infamous Ponary where tens of thousands Jews perished. A horrifying picture of the catastrophe of European Jewry rose before me. I read everything that was published in the Soviet Union, but nothing really *was* published, with the exception of the Nuremberg trial transcripts. Sarra Babenysheva, a literary critic and an acquaintance of mine, a courageous woman who lived in Peredelkino, had connections among dissidents and would often give me the issues of an underground journal, *Jews in the USSR*, where I would find the materials I needed.

"The least we can do … is to prevent this [Slavic] alien blood from rising higher in the national body. I admit that this danger will not be diminished if in the near future we occupy regions with a high proportion of the Slav population, which we shall not be able to get rid of very quickly … *We are obliged to depopulate* … as part of our mission to preserve the German population … We shall have to develop a technique of depopulation … I mean the removal of entire racial units … If I can send the flower of the German nation into the hell of war without the smallest pity for the spilling of precious German blood, then surely I have the right to remove millions of an inferior race that breeds like vermin! […] It will be one of the chief tasks of German statesmanship for all time to prevent, by every means in our power, the further increase in the Slav races. Natural instincts bid all living things not merely conquer their enemies, but also destroy them."[4]

Extermination of the whole ethnic groups, Slavs first and foremost—such was Hitler's general program. Killing six million Jews was just a lab, where Germans became skilled hands at extermination, where they accumulated experience.

Let this be a thought for those who fall for the propaganda by the contemporary Fascist-minded goons who call Hitler "Adolf Aloizovich."

So I went to Shchors and stayed in the House of the Kolkhoz Worker. They gave me the only room with a telephone they had—of course, I was a writer from Moscow!

A small, half-Russian, half-Ukrainian town, the same two markets—the old one and the new one, just like I remembered them from my childhood; a cafeteria near the railway station where one can have a cheap and satisfying lunch of borscht and beef Stroganoff; a fire-lookout tower, grandfather's spacious house on Bolshaia Alekseevskaia Street, these days occupied by the City Council; familiar streets and alleys. Yet, new people live here now; two hundred are left out of the three thousand Jews that used to live here. I introduced myself to the local officials, and asked the District Committee Secretary to drive me around the partisan sites.

In the evening, several old Jews who knew my grandfather came to visit me.

Avraam Rybakov, said one of them reverently. Who didn't know him? Everyone knew him. There is not a single person who did not know Avraam Rybakov.

They came to ask for a favor. Some combine driver went past the cemetery and struck the fence with his combine. The fence fell down, they wanted to repair it, but it turned out that the rails rotted to the core and need to be replaced, there is no money … Who are the Jews that stayed? Old people, children … The younger people work at the depot, at the saw mill, at the tannery, how many of them? Few and far between. They turned to the officials—no help there. Who cares about the Jewish cemetery?

I promised to go there and have a look. I told them when I would be coming, and decided to take the District Committee Secretary with me.

I remembered one of the old men, a former local barber Bernard Semyonovich, from my childhood visits to Snovsk. He was an elegant, dignified gentleman; his barbershop used to be something like a club for the local intellectuals. Even now he was energetic, tidy, gray-haired, and handsome; he remembered everyone who lived here and died here; he remembered those who moved away, and those who came back. During the war, he evacuated; he returned right after the town was liberated. Together with other old men, he would go around the town, around the empty lots, along the roads; they would roam the woods and the fields, collecting the remains of the killed into sacks. The corpses decayed, but Bernard Semenovich recognized some people by their hair. They buried those remains in the communal grave at the cemetery, though there was no Jewish cemetery anymore: the tombstones were pilfered and the cemetery itself was ploughed up on the orders of the German Commandant. The cemetery was restored, the Jews could bury their dead again, but—tough luck—the fence fell.

Bernard Semenovich spent several days with me; he told me about the fate of every resident of Snovsk. After the war, the combat soldiers were back, and the evacuees were back too: they asked the locals about their relatives, they collected even the tiniest grains of truth. People, who were saved from the execution by some miracle, people who crawled out of the graves, people who joined the partisans—those turned up too. Bernard Semenovich committed their stories to memory and told them to me; he took me to the survivors, to the witnesses, he took me to the "half-breed" women who were not executed only because the executioners spent too much time determining how much Jewish blood they had.

Little by little, a picture of what happened in Shchors assembled in my mind; I remembered my grandfather and my grandmother well, I remembered my uncles and I could now see Rachel and Jacob clearly. And I knew what they would have done under those circumstances. All that happened to these people happened to me, too. The night fell upon the town, and I was wandering these streets in the dark. And the shadows of the martyred walked by my side from one house to another.

We went to the forests with the Regional Committee Secretary. I asked him to drive by the cemetery on our way. The Jewish residents of the town were waiting for us there: the old people, the middle-aged, and the young people. There were some children, too, and those who were born here after the war. Some of them knew my grandfather and grandmother; most of them did not. But here, in the communal grave, their grandparents lay along with their parents, their brothers and sisters. Unarmed, defenseless, helpless, they stood here when the Germans shot them.

It was a deserted cemetery with a collapsed fence, with almost no tombstones, no monuments. Where were my ancestors laid to rest, where were my grandparents? There was no answer: only the young birches rustled their leaves softly over the graves that bore no names.

A large black granite tombstone over the communal grave bore the inscription: "We will always remember the victims of the Fascist German occupants." The inscription was in Russian. Under it, there was an inscription in Hebrew.

I came up, laid my flowers to the grave, kneeled and kissed the ground in which my tortured people lay ... Those around me were wiping tears from their faces.

I pointed the Secretary to the broken fence, and he ordered his driver to go back to the District Committee to have it restored. Then we went to the forest.

We came back in the evening, following the same route. The cemetery had a new fence. In the Soviet Union, when they want to work, they can, I thought.

The old men came late at night to thank me for my help.

Tell me, I asked them, how did you translate the inscription, "We will always remember the victims of the Fascist German occupants," into Hebrew?

Bernard Semenovich smiled.

"We didn't. The inscription says something else entirely."

"What exactly?"

"It's from the Bible: Now should I cleanse, their blood I will not cleanse."[5] All is forgiven; shedding of the innocent blood is never forgiven.

I came back to Moscow and told Tanya:

"I have the closing lines of my novel."

25.

I sent the novel, entitled *Rachel*, to *Novyi mir*. Tvardovsky was gone from *Novyi mir*, and his successor, Kosolapov, a party newspaper administrator, a decent man who published Evtushenko's "Babi Yar" in *Literaturnaia gazeta*, was also gone. Now, a poet, Narovchatov, was at the helm of the journal.

Narovchatov was not stupid; he was educated, and had studied at the Institute of Philosophy, Literature and History. In the past, he had drunk quite a lot, but he quit. The Party leadership liked people like that. He would treat any novel suspiciously, and would print it only after he would receive a firm approval "from above."

Where else would I go? Two of my novels were printed in *Novyi mir*; they announced the publication of my *Children of the Arbat*, even if they did not end up publishing it. Moreover, Diana Tevekelian, a progressive (at least according to my Peredelkino neighbor, Aleksandr Kron, a playwright), headed the Department of Prose. In 1962, she took active part in the public campaign against N.V. Lesiuchevskii, chief editor of the publishing house

"Sovetskii pisatel'," who informed on Boris Kornilov and Nikolai Zabolotsky in the thirties.

I sent the manuscript to her and began to wait for the answer.

I gave the manuscript to my friends to read, too.

Vasia Aksenov read it and came to see me in Peredelkino. He stood by the window and said with reserve, looking out to the street, not meeting my eyes:

"They will never publish it here, and if they do, they will hush it up. In the West, though … that's a whole another business. They would appreciate it there."

In his restraint, in his posture by the window, in his unwillingness to meet my eyes, I sensed the possibility of getting help from him. It looked like he had connections to the Western literary circles and opportunities to smuggle my manuscript there, which he was now cautiously communicating to me. My suspicions were confirmed when *Metropol*[6] was released.

"There is more than enough of literature of this sort in the West," I said. "We must break the wall here."

"As you wish," he said.

Semen Izrailevich Lipkin liked the novel, too. I valued his opinion tremendously. He was a great poet, who also went on to become a classic of poetic translation, a man of spotless reputation. The authors of Aksenov's almanac, *Metropol*, stated that if even one of the authors faces any kind of repressions, they will all resign, in protest, from the Union of Soviet Writers. However, when Viktor Erofeev and Evgenii Popov were persecuted for their contributions to *Metropol*, only two of them—Lipkin and his wife, Inna Lisnianskaia, a poetess—kept their word; Aksenov himself does not count, as he was in the United States by that time.

Iura Trifonov's reaction to *Heavy Sand* was much more complex. We were friends, and I, who was much older than he was, understood how difficult it had been for him to have become a son of the "enemy of the people" at 13, how difficult it had been for him to lose his father (who was executed) and mother (who was sent to the camp). He concealed these parts of his biography when he applied to the Literary Institute, and when it all came to light, a scandal unfolded. Yet, Trifonov was in the prose seminar taught by Konstantin Fedin, a conformist and a timeserver. Fedin wrote well in his youth, however, and could appreciate good literature. Fedin appreciated Trifonov's talent and nominated his novella, *Students*, for the Stalin Award.

Iura received this award in 1951. There was official recognition, but I doubt that it brought him happiness. I think that, among us, Trifonov suffered the most from an inability to reveal who he really was. And his time finally came. In the late sixties, several of his short stories appeared and became hot points of discussion right away. Then his *Exchange*, *The Long Good-Bye*, *Another Life*, *House on the Embankment*, and *An Old Man* were published. His books raised the level of the Soviet prose drastically; he had found his language, his form. The right-wing would throw at him, snarling, but the intellectuals would buy up his books in the stores and rush to the Taganka Theater to see his *Exchange* and *House on the Embankment* on stage. He published a novel, *Impatience*, in the Politizdat's "Ardent Revolutionaries" series. The novel was about the terrorist members of the People's Freedom organization, and it was praised by the West German critics (who understandably reacted to the proliferation of the "red brigades" terror at that time); even Böll said he liked the novel.

In the evenings, Trifonov would sit in the Central House of Writers' restaurant, showing the praising reviews from Germany to his friends. He would smile. He would enjoy himself. The world had acknowledged him. This was his childish tribute to the long-wounded pride. Having read *Heavy Sand*, Iura said, with his condescending smirk:

"Tolia, don't flatter yourself! Your novel received much praise, but it's not a pinnacle of literary craft yet."

When he returned the manuscript of *Children of the Arbat* to me, he never even said anything. He only mused:

"I gave the manuscript to Sasha Gladkov [the author of the play *The Hussar Ballad*; Gladkov was incarcerated for many years.—AR], he was surprised how well you remember that time."

I was not hurt by Trifonov's remarks. I loved and understood him. His path to success was long and hard; he was jealous of others' successes, too. His talent grew. But suffering, while sharpening writer's skill, often shortens their lifespan. Trifonov passed away in 1981. He was fifty-six.

On June 20, 1977, I received a letter from *Novyi mir*. "In acknowledgement of our conversation, I would like to inform you that, unfortunately, we have to return the manuscript of your novel, *Rachel*, as it does not fit within the publishing plans of our journal. D. Tevekelian."

The conversation indeed happened; or, rather, it was not a conversation, but Tevekelian's monologue about the impossibility of publishing the novel at that time. The monologue was somewhat aggressive: I was put at fault for writing a piece that would never go through censorship.

I took the manuscript to *Druzhba narodov* [Friendship of nations]: the novel's themes would fit well with their intellectual direction, I thought. The head of the Prose Department, Inna Sergeeva, refused even more flatly that Tevekelian did: "We will not publish this. It is about the year 1937. The depiction of the war is one-sided—not only the Jews suffered in the war, but other nationalities, too".

What was I supposed to do? Where would I go now? I had an inkling about another journal, *Oktiabr'*, which once had published my short novel, *Drivers*.

After Panferov's death, Vsevolod Kochetov took the helm of the journal. Kochetov was a Stalinist, and, under his leadership, the journal turned into a bulwark of reactionary forces. In the early seventies, Kochetov passed away, and Anatolii Anan'ev was appointed as Chief Editor. Anan'ev was a writer of the war generation: they said he was not half bad. He selected the new editorial board, and tried to attract progressive writers to his journal. But all his attempts to change the journal's reputation were in vain—the very word *Oktiabr'* remained synonymous with reactionary views. I was counting on Anan'ev's desire to have a novel that would be talked about.

I did not know Anan'ev personally, but I did know one member of the editorial board, Grigorii Baklanov, who also belonged to the war generation. I asked Baklanov to show the manuscript to Anan'ev. Baklanov read the novel.

"You know, Tolia, I'm afraid it wouldn't work. It's not even about the year 1937. But Jews ... It's too big of a risk for Anan'ev."

"I only ask you to give the manuscript to Anan'ev and tell him Rybakov asks him to read it."

"Anan'ev is on vacation right now."

"That's even better. Put the manuscript on his desk."

Baklanov took the manuscript to Anan'ev and put it on his desk. When Anan'ev was back from his vacation, he discovered the novel on his desk, read it and gave me a call. He invited me to stop by his office; when I came, he said he would print it if I agreed to accept the corrections. What kinds of corrections? Well, other comrades on the editorial board should read it, they'll write the report, and then we'll see.

I would not burden the reader with the description of the novel's trials and tribulations in *Oktiabr'*. I will simply quote some points from the surprisingly long report (three pages!) that I received:

"The Editorial Board's recommendations in connection with A. Rybakov's novel, *Rachel*.

In every part of the novel, the Great Patriotic War will be characterized as multiethnic, all-national suffering, while Nazism will be characterized as an ideology directed against all of the mankind, not just against the Jews.

All mentions of Stalin, Molotov, and Dostoevsky will be removed from the novel, as well as all and any discourse in conjunction with these names.

The story of arrest and death of Lev Rakhlenko, as well as all and any mentions of the political trials of 1937-38, are to be removed from the novel.

Rachel's call is to be directed towards not just male Jews, but towards all mankind.

The city of Zurich is to be replaced by any other Germanophone city in Switzerland.

September 3, 1978. *N. Kriuchkova*, Head of the Prose Department."

The rest of the "recommendations" were very similar: remove, replace, not "just Jews" but "all mankind," etc. The report was authored by the Deputy Chief Editor, Vladimir Zhukov. Little did he understand that no matter how many instances of using the word "Jew" were removed from the novel, the novel would still remain a novel about Jews.

I changed the title of the novel into *Heavy Sand*. I took it from the Bible, from The Book of Job: "my grief and calamity would be heavier than the sand of the sea: therefore my words are swallowed up."[7]

It was much harder for me to compromise on the ideological plane. Do I agree to cut out the political trials of the thirties; do I get rid of characterizations of Stalin and Molotov? It was like cutting away my own flesh. Lev Rakhlenko is executed in the novel as an "enemy of the people"—I had to throw him under the train instead. I had to replace the quotes from Dostoyevsky on the antisemitic leaflets (which the Germans distributed on the front lines) with quotes from Knut Hamsun. But I'd still have a chance to tell something, I thought. Even the very number of Jews who were killed—six million—was being kept secret at that time, my novel was first to cite this number.

Because of all the edits and corrections, the novel grew poorer, of course, but I managed to save its main pathos.

Oktiabr' [October] had one substantial advantage. When *Novyi mir* [New world] would plan to publish a novel in three issues, the censor would ask them to give the whole text to him, and would approve the first issue only after having read the whole text. In the compliant, respectable *Oktiabr'*, the censor would read the current issue, not asking for the whole novel. This was exactly what happened in my case. The censor read the first part and found nothing seditious: a small Ukrainian town before the revolution, nothing special. He gave his approval; only later was the second part sent to him. Of course, he began to fuss, but it was too late—I would not accept any further corrections, and nobody would dare to suspend the issues of the journal. Suspending publishing would mean another huge literary scandal.

In 1995, in my collection of works, I restored everything that I had to cut out of *Heavy Sand*.

The funniest part was when they asked me to replace Zurich with any other city; they did it because Solzhenitsyn's book, *Lenin in Zurich*, was released not long before. They were scared of any association. One could not even have been born in Zurich! I replaced Zurich with Basel.

Later, when the novel was already about to be published as a book, I was invited to the Central Committee of Communist Party, and a colorless official very much like Maslov (who once received me there) read some comments on the novel to me. He added, with deference:

"Those are Mikhail Andreevich's comments."

At first, I did not get who Mikhail Andreevich was, and only afterwards I realized it was Suslov, the Party's chief ideologue. I was surprised he had time to read the novel. On the other hand, everyone was reading *Heavy Sand* at that time; one had to get in line at the library to get it.

Suslov studied in the Institute of Red Professors. A mousy, ordinary student, he was known only for having created his own catalogue of Lenin's quotes on the economic issues. His tiny room in a communal apartment was crowded with boxes of cards, quotes, and alphabetic lists. Every word Lenin had ever uttered on an economic subject was counted and accounted for, so accurate and pedantic an archivist he was. He stayed at home and worked on his catalogue, unsociable and lonely; he never meddled in anything—and that was how he preserved himself.

Once, Stalin needed Lenin's opinion on some obscure economic issue, for a report. Mekhlis, Stalin's efficient assistant, remembered about Suslov, his classmate at the Institute. He rushed to Suslov, and Suslov found what was needed in a flash. Stalin, who knew the extent of Mekhlis's theoretical knowledge all too well, asked him how he had managed to find the quote that quickly. Mekhlis told Stalin about Suslov, and thus began Mikhail Andreevich's rise through the ranks. He ended up a member of Politburo. This was the version of Suslov's career that was told in Moscow at that time.

His comments were petty; the novel would not have been much different if I took these comments into account. I did not object. I just thought, "What is it that they are doing, those leaders of ours? As if there are no more pressing issues to be dealt with in this country? Why do they think they have the right to meddle with the writer's vision?"

This is not too interesting. Another official showed me a much more interesting letter from one professor, who had proven convincingly that *Heavy Sand* was a Zionist novel. "It is not a coincidence," the professor wrote, "that the novel's protagonist was born in Basel, where the Zionist congress took place, exactly in the city where a certain Herzl proposed his idea to create a Jewish state in Palestine."

I put the editorial resolution from *Oktiabr'* on the official's desk: I had Zurich, they told me to replace it with Basel; with what do you want me to replace Basel now? And, could I have it replaced after thousands of people had already read the novel?

The official, to his credit, understood the absurdity of this situation and let the matter go.

26.

Heavy Sand was a success. Readers—Jews, Russians, Ukrainians, and Belarussians—sent numerous letters; those who wrote to me were people who survived the extermination camps, the ghettos, and captivity; they were the children who lost their parents, the parents who lost their children ... Horrendous fates ... "You wrote about me, about my family, about my town..." And the letters from the young people: "Having read your novel, I embraced my Jewishness."

In the West, the publication of *Heavy Sand* was perceived as "Kremlin's turnaround in the Jewish question." Of course, it was no turnaround. I just assessed the situation in *Oktiabr'* correctly and used it to my own advantage. Furthermore, the novel's publication coincided with a relative weakening of the Jewish emigration ban, right after the Helsinki Agreement.

Soviet press hushed the novel. Some critics gave me their approving reviews, however. Here is how it happened.

One prominent critic runs across me in the Writers' Union:

"I cried, and my wife cried, and my wife's mother cried in Minsk, and my mother in Kiev, she just wept, she was saying that you described her hometown of Sarny, you know, there is this town in Ukraine …"

"Very well then, write a review of the novel."

"It won't be appropriate. They'd say, here's a Jew praising a novel about Jews."

"I'm Jewish as well, yet I wrote the novel and didn't restrict myself in this way."

"Would they print this review, though? I doubt it."

"I was not sure they'd print my novel either, yet I wrote it."

"I have to think about it. But the novel is superb. I cried, my wife cried, her mother in Minsk cried, and my mother in Kiev, she wept remembering Sarny."

Of course, this critic hasn't written anything. Now he is considered a progressive; he goes around condemning the dead writers for their conformism.

Once, Vasia Aksenov approached me at the Central House of Literary Workers.

"There is this Reuters reporter, Bob Evans—do you know him?"

"No."

"He's a good guy. He wants to meet you. Can I give him your phone number?"

"Of course."

Bob Evans indeed turned out to be a good guy and a talented journalist. A big admirer of *Heavy Sand*, he did a lot to promote the novel in Britain.

I would ask a single question of all of the reporters who would call me during those days: "Have you read *Heavy Sand*?" I would grant interviews only to those who had. This was how Craig Whitney of *New York Times*, a talented man, ended up in my study. Only Samuel Rakhlin, a Danish radio and TV reporter, got an extra question from me: I wondered whether he was a relative of our famous conductor, Natan Rakhlin, People's Artist of the USSR, who was mentioned in *Heavy Sand*. The day before, I received a very sweet letter from him about the novel: "I was born and spent my childhood in this nice, wonderful town, and I remember the large Rybakov family well."

It turned out that yes, he was a distant relative. Samuel's father lived in Kaunas; a businessman, he went to Denmark in 1935, and met a girl in

Copenhagen; he married her and took her to Kaunas. In 1940, Lithuania joined the USSR, and Rakhlins were exiled to Yakutsk as "socially alien elements." Paradoxically, their lives were saved this way, because during the war the Germans exterminated all of the Lithuanian Jews. Yet, the Germans did not manage to exterminate the Danish Jews: at nights, the Danes transported them to the neutral Sweden by boats. Among those saved were the parents of Samuel's mother, Rachel.

In 1946, Rachel learned from newspapers that the Danish Embassy was open in Moscow. She wrote to the Ambassador and told her story. Iakov Ivanovich Klimov, director of an agricultural selection station, where Samuel's father worked, journeyed to Moscow and managed to leave a letter with the Embassy. In 1946! Under Stalin! He risked his life, and yet he did it! The Ambassador found Rachel's relatives in Copenhagen; a correspondence ensued, emigration petitions followed, dragging on for ten years, until the Prime Minister of Denmark, Hansen, came to Moscow and personally asked Khrushchev to let the Rakhlins go. They left for Denmark that same year. Samuel was born in Yakutsk, went to school there, he was brought up as a Russian and spoke Russian. After he graduated from a university in Copenhagen, and, afterwards, from Columbia University in New York, he came to Moscow as a reporter for Danish radio and TV. He worked there for seven years, and made several brilliant films, including the one about Vladimir Vysotskii's funeral.

Sam and his wife, Annette, would often come to visit us at Peredelkino, as would Bob Evans with Evgenia and Craig Whitney with Heidi. They were young, fun, and beautiful: it was a pleasure to have them at our place. We became friends. Rarely do foreign journalists understand Russia, but these guys did, probably because they loved Russia and knew the language. Tanya would buy a leg of veal at the market, she would bake potatoes, and everyone would sit in the veranda around the wooden table, casting glances out to the yard—there, the children of our friends would play in the snow by the porch.

Incidentally, Samuel's parents wrote and published a book in Copenhagen, titled *Sixteen Years in Siberia*. It went on to become a bestseller and came out in more than ten editions.

Heavy Sand was translated into many languages. The All-Union Copyright Agency (VAAP) managed the translation contracts. The biggest contract was with the Anglo-American publishing house, Penguin. The British translated the novel quickly, released it and asked Tanya and me to attend the release reception in London on June 2, 1981.

The trip to London did not happen.

On June 3, a London newspaper, *Evening Standard*, reported:

"Russian writer, Anatoly Rybakov, cancelled his visit to England in the last moment for the reasons that remain unclear. The goal of Rybakov's visit had been to promote his new book, *Heavy Sand*. The Soviet literary agency sent a telex to the publishers last night, notifying that the visit is cancelled … 'We do not know why Rybakov is not coming, nor whether he is planning to come later,' a perplexed representative of the publishers said."

My reason to cancel the trip would become clear from my letter to the Central Committee's Secretary, M. V. Zimianin:

> Dear Mikhail Vasil'evich,
>
> In conjunction with the release of my novel, *Heavy Sand*, in Britain, my wife and I were invited to London. Yet, before the departure, I received a phone call from VAAP, and was informed that I must go alone, without my wife …
>
> Should I have gone without her? How would I have explained it? Would I have to tell them that I was allowed to go when my wife was not? I did not wish to disgrace myself and my country in this way, and of course, refused to go alone.
>
> My novel, *Heavy Sand*, is under contracts in many countries of the world. It is likely that I will be invited to attend more promotional events, and it is likely that my wife, too, will be invited: the Western publishers believe that the promotional activities garner more respect if spouses attend. One could disagree with this belief, but it is impossible to ignore it.
>
> In any case, I would not like to find myself in situations like this in the future. I am over seventy, and my refusals to come receive undesirable publicity, which is why such developments are highly objectionable.
>
> *Anatolii Rybakov.*

There was no reply. Yet, after I wrote this letter, I was allowed to go abroad with Tanya.

The nerve the state had to humiliate us! And it did not make any sense: it was only deleterious to the state. The writer would receive only a minuscule part of the royalties, the rest was taken by the VAAP (they had a 25% commission!) and by the state (in the form of hard currency tax). I was never in London, the book received little promotion and thus fewer copies were sold, so the country got less money. Only because some official wanted to flex his muscles: well, he'll go alone, nothing special, he'll survive! They would not even consider a possibility that someone might not obey. After I said that I would not go anywhere without my wife, they had been calling me on the phone every hour, they tried to reason with me and threatened me that they would never let me go anywhere again. I said: "I will not have my wife humiliated like that. Her dignity is much more important to me than all of your prohibitions and refusals."

After that, I could not help but smile when I read an article in *Jyllands Posten*, a Danish newspaper. The article came out when *Heavy Sand* was presented in Copenhagen and was titled "A Soviet Writer in Attack of His Charm":

"Is it a coincidence that Rybakov, unlike many other Soviet writers, was able to go on a book tour like this? Can it be a coincidence that his wife, T. Rybakova, accompanied him? Many cases of a completely opposite nature necessarily make one suspicious. As we have grown accustomed to the fact that no Soviet initiative is coincidental, we grew wary."

This was the way we lived. In our homeland, we were suspected of the desire to defect; abroad, we were suspected of spying.

Heavy Sand was published in 26 countries. It sold well. It received a lot of attention from the press. I would just mention several titles of newspaper articles from different countries: "The Novel Transforms the Soul"; "Long Silence Broken"; "A Breath of History"; "A Jewish Family Saga"; "A Song of High Love"; "A Family Chronicle To Continue an Old Russian Tradition"; "A Powerful Solitary Cry"; "An Unprecedented Depiction of Jewish Suffering and Heroism"; "The Soviets Like the Jewish Saga."

The most comprehensive analysis of the novel was given in an article by Eli Wiesel, a Nobel Laureate, which was published in French and American newspapers.

In the USSR, *Heavy Sand* was published only in Russian. They did not allow its publication in any other language.*

Let us not rake over old ashes. Let us turn to the present …

---

* It was published in Yiddish in *Sovetish heymland*, nos. 4,5, and 6, 1979.

Only fifty years ago, the most horrible war in the history of mankind ended. The Soviet Union lost 27 million lives in this war. There is not a single family in the country that had not received a notice that their sons, husbands, brothers, fathers were killed in battle. Millions of people who lived through the war are still alive. They are disabled war veterans, people who survived the horrors of occupation and the wartime hunger and cold. Not all of the victims are yet found; not all bodies of the dead soldiers are yet buried. The extermination camp furnaces still emit putrid odor, while our own homegrown Fascists already march in the streets of Russian cities. They wear boots and black shirts and shoulder belts, praising Hitler, praising the traitors and the betrayers. A swastika has spread its spidery tentacles on the walls, and the antisemitic calls to pogroms are heard from rostrums and newspaper columns. These calls are inspired by writers who are already called "the nation's consciousness."

More than half a century passed since Hitler killed six million Jews, opening an eternal, never-healing wound in the heart of the Jewish people. The memory of this innocent blood is kept sacred by the state of Israel.

Tania and I were in Israel twice. First time we went on Shimon Peres's invitation. During the second visit, I was awarded an Honorary Doctorate from Tel Aviv University.

Shimon Peres invited us to a Seder—a traditional Passover dinner. It was an ordinary apartment in an apartment complex; a guard was sitting on a staircase landing. It was a united, close-knit family: the children, the grandchildren, the daughters-in-law, and the son—a pilot with a friendly, steadfast face. At the head of the table was Shimon Peres, the host. Traditional Passover food was on the table, each person had a Haggadah in front of them, Tanya and I had it in Russian, and everyone read their part, taking turns ... My grandfather's house floated to the foreground of my memory: the same Seder, my grandfather at the head of the table, I, the youngest, next to him; I ask the traditional questions and my grandfather answers them in a singing voice. The Jews have observed this tradition for millennia, wherever they were, wherever they will be.

We traveled all over Israel. I have been to many countries, but this place amazed me. Palestine is the cradle of human spirituality. Here, among the stones of Jerusalem and the sands of Sinai, the major world religions were born. "The desert harks to God, and star with star converses."[8] These rocks, this sand, this sky, these stars—all of this is eternal, inscrutable, and all of this raises the man towards the heights of thought, compels him to search for truth.

It is to this land that the Jewish people returned after two thousand years of exile.

Great, large, and small migrations of peoples are known to history. These were the migrations from the native lands to the foreign lands. The Jews, on the other hand, were migrants to their own land. I repeat—I am a Russian writer, I was born in Russia and I will die in Russia, but I was happy to see the Jewish people in their own land. I, an old soldier who went from Moscow to Berlin, was deeply moved by the sight of the Israeli young men and women in their military uniforms, with automatic rifles in their hands. The persecutions, the humiliation, the oppression of the shtetl, the barbed wire of the ghetto—nothing could kill human dignity and national identity in these people.

I gave my *Heavy Sand* archive, including many thousands of readers' letters, to Tel Aviv University.

Notes

1. Translator's note: the author quotes the Goncourt brothers opinion on the Parnassians.
2. Translator's note: Evgenii Evseev (1932-1990) was a Soviet historian who was instrumental in mythologizing the term "Zionism" in the Soviet Union. Vladimir Begun was a Soviet historian who was arguably the first to justify the pogroms in Soviet historiography.
3. Translator's note: Shchors (known as Snovsk until 1935) is a town in Chernihiv region of Ukraine.
4. Translator's note: quoted here from Hermann Rauschning's *Hitler Speaks* (London, 2006, originally published 1939), 140-41. The quote was featured in the Document USSR-378 in the Nuremberg Trials and appeared in the Nuremberg Trials volumes published in the Soviet Union.
5. Translator's note: The Book of Joel 4:21. See also Mordehai Altshuler, "Deiatel'nost' evreev po uvekovechivaniiu pamiati o Kholokoste v Sovetskom Soiuze v epokhu Stalina," in *Iad Vashem issledovaniia* 1 (2009): 184.
6. Translator's note: *Metropol* was an independent literary almanac. Rybakov mentions the outcome of its publication below.
7. Job 6:3.
8. Translator's note: Rybakov quotes from Mikhail Lermontov's poem, "I go out on the road alone" (*Vykhozhu odin ia na dorogu...*), 1840.

Chapter 11

Afterword
Soviet Jews in World War II:
Experience, Perception and Interpretation[1]

Zvi Gitelman

Nearly seventy years after the Holocaust ended, we continue to be perplexed, horrified, pained, worried and fascinated by it. Unfortunately, genocides—the purposive killing of peoples because they *are* peoples—have continued to this day. However, neither the events in Rwanda-Burundi, nor the Balkans, nor Cambodia, nor Darfur occupy as much of the world's attention as does the Holocaust, perhaps for three reasons: first, the scale of the Holocaust is unparalleled. Second, its purposive, deliberate and industrialized design sets it apart from more spontaneous outbreaks of ethnic or racial rage and destruction. This was not a localized war between Hutus and Tutsis; Serbs, Croats, and Muslims; or one group of Cambodians or Sudanese against another. Third, it was designed and largely perpetrated by a nation that was considered among the most civilized in the world. The Germans were the main culprits, but significant numbers of Dutchmen, Belgians, Frenchmen, Romanians, Hungarians, Austrians, Lithuanians, Estonians, Latvians, Ukrainians, and others participated in the crimes collectively known as the Holocaust. It is the Germans who have been the most willing to confront themselves and their crimes. Some of the others did so only long after the events, and still others maintain to this day that it was not their hands that spilled blood.[2] In the face of undeniable facts and evidence, some of which continue to be literally unearthed, explanations have been sought for denial or silence. In Eastern Europe, the most common rationale is that the Jews had betrayed the states in which they lived by collaborating with the Soviet Communists. Maybe not all Jews were Communists, it is said, but we can understand why people oppressed by Stalinist totalitarianism believed they were. Debates over culpability, responsibility, justice and retribution will undoubtedly go on for years. These are only in part debates about facts; mostly they are arguments from different perspectives.

About half a century elapsed before scholars could study the Holocaust in the Soviet Union and related subjects such as Soviet policies during the war, evacuation of civilians to the Soviet rear and the representation of the varied experiences of the war in Soviet and post-Soviet literature and the arts. As this volume makes clear, during and after the war the Soviet government, Soviet peoples and even Soviet Jews saw the annihilation of the Jews in a very different way than it has been perceived in the West and Israel, and they continue to do so. For most non-Soviet Jews, the crux of the events is the calculated murder of a third of the worldwide Jewish people. For most Jews from or in the Former Soviet Union (FSU), what should be emphasized is the heroic struggle of Soviet Jews against the Fascists. Of course, for non-Jews in the FSU the story is that of the sacrifice and heroism of the Soviet people, and, as Stalin put it in his toast in the Kremlin on May 24, 1945, above all of the Russian people, whom he called "the most outstanding nation of all the nations who belong to the Soviet Union."

The conference from which this book derives had three goals: first, to present new information; second, to demonstrate how and why Soviet Jews and non-Jews have different perspectives on the Holocaust than those dominant in the West; and, third, to explore some contemporary issues in former Soviet territories that emanate from the Holocaust. We wanted to open up a subject that is largely unknown in the English-speaking world, that is, the role of Soviet Jews as combatants in the Soviet forces that bore the brunt of the fighting against the Nazis. Most chapters in this book have as their evidentiary base largely unknown materials—documents, literature and oral history. This book should raise awareness of the subject, especially among English speakers; increase our understanding of Soviet Jewry during WWII, even while complicating it; and stimulate more research and greater understanding.

The Setting

About half of all the victims of the Holocaust were Soviet citizens at the time they were killed. In the USSR, perhaps 2.7 million Jews were killed, constituting 55 percent of the entire Jewish population of the country in June 1941, as

Soviet Jews in World War Two: Experience, Perception and Interpretation

Oleg Budnitskii points out in his chapter. The reason we know less about the Holocaust in the USSR than we know about how it occurred in other countries is that Soviet authorities—who controlled all mass media, publications, and curricula—while never denying that the Holocaust took place, chose not to have it commemorated, considered, or written about. Moreover, since the collapse of the USSR at the end of 1991, most of the original research done about the Holocaust in the former Soviet heartland has been published in Russian and Hebrew, closing it off to many.

What differentiates the Shoah in the Soviet Union from the deliberate and systematic murder of Jews in other places?

While the perpetrators of the Holocaust had the same general goal in all the areas they conquered, in the Soviet Union they declared the specific aim of eradicating Bolshevism as well as the Jews, which they equated. There was a prominent political dimension as well as a racial one to the attack on the Soviet Union. Second, the scale of human and material loss was enormous. The Soviet Union lost about 26-27 million of its citizens during the war, 8-9 million of them in combat. That country saw by far the most ferocious combat over a longer period of time than any other place in Europe, and perhaps in Asia. Losses on both sides were enormous. Of the over five million German soldiers who died in World War II, 52 percent (2,743,000) died on the Eastern Front, and 23 percent (1,230,000) in the final battles in Germany, in which the Red Army played a large role.[3] The Soviet Union played "*a*, if not *the*, decisive role in defeating Nazi Germany."[4]

Soviet losses have been reported differently over time, both for political reasons and because the information has become available slowly. Stalin announced in 1945 that 7 million had been killed, but a more recent estimate is that about 26 million Soviet citizens died during World War II, of whom about 8,668,400 were in the military. The Soviet Union suffered the third highest proportion of civilian deaths—12 percent of its population—if Soviet calculations are accurate.[5]

There were also significant losses in the Soviet Union by Germany's Romanian, Hungarian, Italian and other allies. Given the scale and intensity of the fighting, one could expect a great deal of what is euphemistically referred to as "collateral damage" in the USSR, including human and material losses. That was compounded by the Nazis' deliberate destruction of infrastructure and people, something they did not do in Western Europe. For example, if some villagers were suspected of contact with partisans, the whole village might be burned down, sometimes with all its inhabitants. There were many Lidices, many Oradours-sur-glane. Moreover, before World War II in the eastern parts of Europe brutality was the common experience of millions. There were revolutions in 1905 and 1917, the 1914-1918 world war, and a brutal civil war in Russia and Poland in 1918-21, which was largely face-to-face, all of which resulted in millions of civilian casualties. In 1928, Joseph Stalin launched the campaign to "collectivize" agriculture that resulted in the deaths of probably eight million peasants. The massive politically motivated purges between 1934 and 1940 cost tens of millions their lives, and other tens of millions their freedom. In territories annexed by the USSR in 1939-40—the Baltic states, eastern Poland and Bessarabia-Bukovina taken from Romania—there had been dictatorial and antisemitic regimes in power and much grass-roots anti-Semitism. These states barely tolerated and largely oppressed their ethnic and religious minorities, none more so than the Jews. Resentments and hatreds were simmering and needed only the sparks of war to burst into full flame, leading to multilateral ethnic wars that took place within the Second World War. Thus, Finns and Russians, Balts and Russians, Poles and Ukrainians, Romanians and Russians all fought each other in the context of the Second World War. Extreme and pervasive violence, often based on ethnic and religious rivalries, suffused the western peripheries of the USSR in a manner unparalleled in western Europe.

The Perpetrators' Perspective

The Nazis singled out Bolshevism as the most pernicious political doctrine and system. Already in 1930, Adolf Hitler described the Soviet regime as "on a Slavic-Tatar body is set a Jewish head."[6] General Von Manstein wrote that "The Jewish-Bolshevist system must be exterminated once and for all. The soldier must appreciate the necessity of harsh punishment of Jewry, the spiritual bearer of Bolshevist terror."[7] Russians, Belorussians and Ukrainians were regarded as scum, and it took less provocation to kill them than it did other Slavs. The Nazis flirted with nationalist Ukrainians oppressed under Polish rule who saw the Nazis as potential liberators and sponsors of Ukrainian independence, but fairly quickly the Nazis decided to forego the strategic opportunity to make an alliance that might have served them decisively.

The Holocaust in the USSR was also facilitated by the attitudes of the German troops and their allies. The "Eastern Front" was rightly regarded as a much tougher posting than anywhere else. In addition, German forces had been persuaded that they were not fighting against civilized people, such as the Dutch, French or Norwegians, but against primitive beasts. They also knew that surrender was a terrible option. The combination of resentment and fear at being in the East and the conviction that the lives they were taking were not worth living may have led the Eastern Front troops to greater acts of vengeance, brutality, and sheer cruelty than anywhere else in the war.

Perspectives of Collaborators

Collaboration with the Nazis was also different in the East from the West. In the West, most collaborators were either ideologues persuaded of Nazi doctrines or opportunists who saw collaboration as a means of survival and even making life reasonably comfortable for themselves. In the East, motivations were more complicated. Some saw the Nazis as liberators who afforded them the opportunity to take revenge on Soviet oppressors, whom they identified with the Jews. Many reasoned that "my enemy's enemy is my friend:" Baltic peoples who had enjoyed independence for only two decades before the Soviets annexed their countries; some Ukrainians who saw the Nazis as liberators from the yokes of Communism and Polish rule; and other Soviet citizens who bore deep resentments against a Bolshevik regime that had taken their property, their churches and the lives of their relatives. They had little compunction about taking Jewish lives (this was true even after the war) because they believed in the *Zydokomuna*—the "Kike-Commie Conspiracy"—and had seen Jews being murdered with impunity twenty years earlier during the Russian Civil War. Many were engaged in brutal wars, settling real or imagined scores between them and their neighbors. Life was highly uncertain and devalued. Killing was not a rare exception, nor was betrayal. Desperate people thought and behaved in ways that would have been unacceptable in "normal" times.

Wartime collaboration remains a fraught issue in post-Communist states, as it was for decades in France, Belgium and other countries. Whether to bring up the issue, how to address it, and whom it should affect are still debated in and beyond the region. The issue remains a sticking point between world Jewry and the State of Israel, on one hand, and several post-Communist states, on the other.

The Jewish Victims

The situation of Soviet Jews on the eve of the war was radically different from those elsewhere in Eastern Europe. Soviet Jews had no communal institutions, which might have provided some support in the initial phases of the Holocaust, because the Soviet government had dissolved them in the 1920s. They had no means of self-defense, no authoritative bodies or figures to turn to for succor or advice. Most had been shielded from knowledge of Nazi radical antisemitism by the curtain drawn over it by the Soviet media, though some got word in 1939-40 of what was happening to Polish Jews.[8] As several authors in this volume point out, many Soviet Jews remembered the Germans of World War One as decent, civilized people with no particular animus against Jews. Some in Ukraine began to feel at the outbreak of the war that they were more endangered by their Ukrainian neighbors than by the Nazis. Authors Estraikh and Zeltser show that many younger Jews had ceased to think of themselves as Jews, and firmly believed they were part of a new internationalist society where invidious distinctions based on ethnicity would no longer be made.

What set Soviet Jews apart from those of other conquered countries was that as individuals, not as a self-consciously Jewish group, hundreds of thousands were able to combat the Nazis and their allies. There were about half a million Jews in the Soviet military, the same number as in the American armed forces, except that in the Soviet Union about 140-180,000 of them were killed (30-36% casualty rate) whereas among the US personnel about 8,000 died out of a total number of war deaths of 480-500,000 (2%). We can deliberate over whether we would want to classify this as "Jewish resistance." Whatever we may think, my own impression from oral interviews with Soviet Jewish war veterans is that the great fought as patriotic Soviet citizens, not primarily as Jews. They fought to save themselves and their families, as all soldiers do, but also for their homeland, the USSR. They were not driven to save the Jewish people per se, and many say they were unaware of German intentions and actions when they first entered the service, and some, for quite some time after. Oleg Budnitskii arrives at the same judgment, though Mordechai Altshuler argues that the Jewish consciousness of many combatants was raised by their experiences. Both base their chapters on letters, oral histories and diaries. Of course, we do not know how many Jews hid their Jewishness during and after the war because what they saw convinced them there was nothing to be gained by being Jewish. That is, for some the war experience may have extinguished or diminished Jewish consciousness.

Perhaps we may think of the actions of Soviet Jewish combatants as resistance to the Nazi invasion by Soviet citizens who were Jews, rather than "Jewish resistance" to the Nazi Holocaust. Soviet Jewish *partisans*, on the other hand, were, for the most part, people who had escaped ghettoes and were fully aware of Nazi anti-Jewish atrocities. Their motivations for fighting were self-preservation, of course, sabotaging the general German war effort, a goal they shared with all Soviet combatants, but also explicitly saving as many Jews as possible.[9]

There was another important difference in perspective between two types of Jewish combatants, the so-called *zapadniki*, or freshly-baked Soviet citizens from the areas annexed in 1939-40, and the "real" Soviet Jews who had grown up under the new regime. The *zapadniki* had been Soviet citizens for two years, at most, when the Germans invaded their new country. Some had been Communists or Soviet sympathizers before they became Soviet citizens, and were probably as patriotic as Jews from the Soviet heartland. But the great majority had been Zionists, Bundists, Orthodox Jews, and those with no affiliation; they were not enthusiastic Soviet citizens. On the other hand, they had seen some Nazi atrocities first hand, and were strongly motivated to fight against them. Arkady Zeltser points out in his chapter that the Soviet Yiddish newspaper, *Eynikayt*, "stressed that the Jews were fighting both for the whole Soviet homeland and for themselves ... as [David] Bergelson put it, '*Far zayn foterland un zayn Yidishn folk*.'" *Eynikayt*'s mission was to rally foreign Jewish support for the Soviet war effort and the *Yidishn folk* idea was clearly designed for that purpose. In reality, it seems to me, generally speaking, the long-time Soviet Jews fought for *zayer foterland* and the *zapadniki*, *farn Yidishn folk*. Of course, there were *zapadniki* who expressed Soviet patriotism, and Soviet Jews who saw themselves as fighting for the Jewish people and the Soviet homeland.

The Soviet Government and the Holocaust

An issue that should be investigated further is what Soviet authorities knew about the Holocaust, to what ends that knowledge was put, and to which publics, if any, it was disseminated. We have to deduce Soviet policy from Soviet actions since no one has yet found written Soviet policy directives that would instruct people on how to deal with the mass murder of Jews on Soviet territory. The fate of many depended on snap decisions made by local officials who had no guidance from higher echelons. But by examining materials from Soviet archives, accessible at the US Holocaust Memorial Museum, the Yad Vashem archives, and elsewhere, and Soviet newspapers and literature of the time, we should be able to at least infer the calculus of Soviet policy toward the Shoah during the war itself.[10] Zeltser's and Joshua Rubenstein's chapters demonstrate the nuances and subtleties of that policy.

Three cautionary notes must be struck: 1) policy calculations are likely to have shifted over the course of the war, especially as the situation changed from catastrophic defeat to costly victory; 2) especially in the chaotic conditions of wartime, central controls may sometimes have been non-existent or ineffective, and so local authorities may have had more discretion than we know; 3) it is difficult and risky to impute motivation.

When considering Soviet policies toward the murder of their Jewish citizens, it is instructive to examine what the British and American governments, then fighting the Nazis, knew about the Shoah and what they did with that knowledge.[11] The British and American governments were very reluctant to publicize the atrocities they knew were occurring "in the East," especially in the early years of the war. Richard Breitman writes, "The American government was interested in broadcasting 'atrocity reports' only if they helped to mobilize the public and the outside world to win the war. Some allied officials thought that coverage of the Jewish plight hampered psychological warfare. Foreign Jews were not among the most popular groups in the United States, or, for that matter, in other parts of the world. Nazi ... propaganda ... [was] charging daily that the Allies were fighting this war only on behalf of Jews, and the American government did not want to seem to support this charge any more than Britain did."[12] Breitman concludes that the British, whose code-cracking operations gave them a great deal of information on the annihilation of the Jews even early in the war, "kept this irrefutable evidence secret" and "many State Department officials chose not to believe or to act on what evidence they had."[13]

Was Soviet policy any different?[14] Not very. My tentative hypothesis, based on research in progress, is that Soviet authorities uncovered a great deal of painfully detailed material about the Holocaust, especially after they liberated areas in which it had been perpetrated, but that they used the material very selectively.[15] They were intent on documenting German plunder of property, murder of Soviet POWs and of Soviet Jews as special categories, and the enslavement and deportation of Soviet citizens of many nationalities. The effort made to collect this material was likely aimed at presenting a reparations bill to the Germans after the war, and demonstrating to their allies that they had paid the greatest price for victory and therefore deserved the most compensation. But the question remains why they singled out Jews as particular victims. Perhaps they thought this would resonate with their allies, since the latter had evinced special concern for the Jews in January 1942.

The Jewish fate was not usually singled out in the media, though it was also not ignored. The press reported murders of Soviet Jews and, perhaps more often, of Jews in other countries. When extermination camps such as Auschwitz, Majdanek and Sobibor were liberated, the very high proportions of Jewish victims was not brought to light. Sometimes, published reports seem to have been deliberately ignored the ethnicity of Nazi victims.

Perspectives and Usable Pasts

Yesterday's events are often interpreted differently by those interested in them, turning them into issues of today. Even the names given to the same war differ: Is it World War II or the Great Patriotic Fatherland War; the Israeli War of Independence or the Palestinian Naqba (Catastrophe); the Yom Kippur War or the October War?[16] Obviously, how one stands on a war in retrospect depends on where you sit at present.

Second, the past is used for present purposes. As it was said in the Soviet Union, history is politics projected on to the past. For the Soviets, their victory in World War II, costly as it was, became the legitimating myth of the system. It justified its very existence and its policies. By the 1960s, the Revolution had passed from memory to history and lost its ability to stir the emotions. Ideology had become ritualized and stripped of its mobilizing power. The war served not only to promote a heroic image of the Soviet regime, but to excuse and forgive whatever sins Stalin, to whom the victory was attributed, may have committed. Eight million peasants were killed during the collectivization campaigns? "Perhaps, but Stalin led us to victory." The purges had terrorized the population and had decimated the most loyal Communists? "Maybe, but without Stalin we would have never won the war." Stalin's 1937 purge of the military leadership and his failure to prepare for a German invasion might have cost millions of Soviet lives? "Possibly, but Stalin planned the ultimate victory." Even after de-stalinization, the war served to justify the foundations of the system. Books, songs, musical compositions, films, paintings, posters, television and radio shows glorified the war and, either explicitly or by implication, the system that had not only survived it, but won it.

Some—not all—Jews, accepted that view. Tzesar Faytelson, born in Belorussia to a family that moved to Siberia so that he would not have to go to a Yiddish school, recalls that there was not much talk about the fate of Jews during the war, during which he served in the air force. He thinks that is a good thing. After all, they shared a fate with millions of other Soviet citizens. The main thing, he says, was to defend the Motherland.[17] Others are aware that, even in the midst of widespread atrocities against Soviet civilians, Jews suffered a fate shared by no other nationality. One Soviet author made so bold in the heyday of glasnost' to ask, "What about the victims of Dachau, Buchenwald, Auschwitz, Sachsenhausen, and Treblinka? Is it not time to count them among those who perished in the war?"[18] While he does not mention Jews specifically, the implication is clear.

For the Soviet government, the Holocaust was seen as an integral part of a larger phenomenon—the murder of civilians—whether Russians, Ukrainians, Belorussians, Gypsies, or other nationalities. It was said to be a natural consequence of racist fascism. The Holocaust, in other words, was but one of several reflexes of fascism, which was, in turn, the ultimate expression of capitalism. Thus, the roots of the Holocaust lay in capitalism, expressed in its most degenerate form. Racism was an outgrowth of capitalism.

In the West there is a vast body of literature that seeks to understand how and why the Shoah happened. There are many explanations: cultural, psychological, sociological, political and bureaucratic. I know of no book published in the USSR that sought to explain the Holocaust as *sui generis*. In a word, for the Soviets there was no mystery about the Holocaust, and none about German atrocities in general.

More recently an issue of competitive victimization has arisen. Not very long ago, most people preferred to be heroes and victors, rather than victims and losers. Today, it seems that many revel in the role of victims, or, more accurately, proxies for or heirs of victims. Earlier scorn for victims of prejudice and violence has been replaced in many quarters by a combination of sympathy and guilt, at least outwardly expressed, whether inwardly felt or not. Being a direct victim is a terrible thing; but claiming to be part of a victimized group may bring some rewards. In addition to sympathy, it may legitimize claims to compensation, preferential treatment and political and social support. Beyond concrete compensation and support, some groups resent it when their sufferings are not as widely recognized as those of others. Books have been written, for example, titled *Poland's Holocaust*, which is not about Polish Jews.[19] Well designed surveys taken in Poland have found that "the overall tendency" among Poles "is to claim that Poles and Jews suffered just the same during the Second World War." In 1992, "32 percent [of Poles] equated the suffering of Jews with that of Poles … 46 percent accepted the uniqueness of Jewish suffering." Ten years later, when the survey was replicated, the proportion of those equating Jewish with Polish suffering rose to 47 per cent and the proportion of those who thought the Jews had suffered more fell to 38 per cent.[20]

One can hardly expect an ordinary person to reflect on the fact that though millions of Poles and Jews were killed by the Nazis, the murdered Poles constituted perhaps ten percent of the Polish ethnic population, but over 90 percent of the Jews in Poland were murdered. Similarly, a Soviet or post-Soviet person, knowing that some 26-27 million of his or her compatriots died during the war, is unlikely to reflect upon the fact that Jewish losses were more than ten per cent of Soviet military and civilian losses, though Jews were only 2.5 percent of the population at the beginning of the war. It takes a certain degree of interest and sophistication to go beyond the huge numbers and appreciate that while there was suffering and death all around, it was *not* evenly or randomly distributed across all population groups.

Thus, we see that there can be many perspectives on the Holocaust, perhaps nowhere more so than in the Former Soviet Union. Similarly, there were many dimensions to the Shoah in the USSR. This volume explores several of them: persecution of Jews by their neighbors, and their confinement in ghettos; the activities of the Jews themselves: those who were evacuated or deported to the interior of the USSR, a unique experience in Europe; those who fought in the Soviet military; and how Jews and other have understood and represented their experiences during and after the war. The Holocaust is for many not history alone, but an issue with which we must continue to be grapple, as shown by several chapters.

We are under no illusion that this volume settles these issues. Rather, we hope it opens windows onto a variety of subjects, new perspectives, exciting possibilities, fresh ideas and, above all, greater understanding of that which, in the final analysis, has eluded human understanding for over sixty years.

Notes

1. Much of the research informing this chapter was done while I was a Shapiro Senior Fellow at the Center for Advanced Holocaust Study, United States Holocaust Memorial Museum in 2005-06.
2. It was only in 2009 that Romania, under pressure from the United States Holocaust Memorial Museum, Eli Wiesel, and others, erected its first monument to the Holocaust.
3. On the Einsatzgruppen, see Yitzhak Arad, Shmuel Krakowski and Shmuel Spector, eds., *The Einsatzgruppen Reports* (New York: Holocaust Library, 1989); Helmut Krausnick and Hans-Heinrich Wilhelm, *Di Truppe des Weltanschauungskrieges: Die Einsatzgruppen der Sicherheitspolizei und des SD 1938-1942* (Stuttgart: Deutsche Verlags Anstalt, 1981). I am grateful to Geoffrey Megargee of the United States Holocaust Museum for these references. He cautions that the Arad, Krakowski, and Spector book contains some poor translations.
4. Jeffrey Herf, "The Nazi Extermination Camps and the Ally to the East: Could the Red Army and Air Force Have Stopped or Slowed the Final Solution?" *Kritika* 4.4 (Fall 2003), 917.
5. Presumably, these figures include "natural" deaths, though what a "natural" death was under the Nazi occupation that brought disease, famine and other privations, is difficult to define. Soviet calculations are that 17.2 percent of the Polish population (including Jews and Poles), 12.7 percent of the German population, 11.5 percent of the Soviet population (which was 168,524,000 in 1939) and 10.9 of Yugoslav civilians died during the war.
6. Quoted in Alexander Dallin, *German Rule in Soviet Russia, 1941-1945*, 2nd ed. (Boulder, CO: Westview, 1981), 9.
7. Quoted in Matthew Cooper, *The Phantom War* (London: Macdonald and James, 1979), 171-73.
8. See Mordechai Altshuler, "Hamifgash bein lokhamim yehudim ba-tsava ha-adom la-shoah," *Dapim* 23 (2009): 1-27.
9. The categories of soldier and partisan cannot be neatly separated since some partisans were escaped POWs who were soldiers before they were partisans, and others were drafted into the Red Army after their areas had been liberated, so that they were partisans before they became soldiers.
10. I have written on the Soviet treatment of the Shoah in the post-war period in "Soviet Reactions to the Holocaust," in *The Holocaust in the Soviet Union*, ed. Lucjan Dobroszycki and Jeffrey Gurock (Armonk, NY: M. E. Sharpe; 1993), 3-28.
11. I am concerned with the governments, not with mass media, mass publics or Jewish organizations.
12. Richard Breitman, *Official Secrets: What the Nazis Planned, What the British and Americans Knew* (New York: Hill and Wang, 1998), 135-36.
13. Ibid., 229.

14 The British and Americans confronted an issue that the Soviets dealt with differently because the issue presented itself in different forms. Communist refugees from the Nazis had come to the USSR in the 1930s.

15 The first systematic reports came from "Military Commissions," which collected eye-witness testimonies very soon after an area was liberated. Somewhat later, information was gathered by the "Extraordinary State Commission to Examine and Investigate German-Fascist Crimes Committed by the Invaders and Their Accomplices on Soviet Territory" (*Chrezvychainaia gosudarstvennaia komissiia po ustanovleniiu i rassledovaniiu zlodeianii nemetsko-fashistskikh zakhvatchikov i ikh soobshchnikov*).

16 A comprehensive discussion of how wars are remembered and what significances are attached to them is T.G. Ashplant, Graham Dawson and Michael Roper, eds. *The Politics of War Memory and Commemoration* (London and New York: Routledge, 2000), Part One (3-86).

17 Visual History of the Shoah, ID: 11131. The interview was conducted in Los Angeles on January 25, 1996.

18 A. M. Samsonov, *Znat' i pomnit': Dialog istorika s chitatelem*, 1st ed. (Moscow: Izdatel'stvo Politicheskoi Literatury, 1988), 22.

19 Tadeusz Piotrowski, *Poland's Holocaust: Ethnic Strife, Collaboration with Occupying Forces and Genocide in the Second Republic, 1918-1947* (Jefferson, NC: McFarland, 1998).

20 Ireneusz Krzeminski, ed., *Antysemityzm w Polsce i na Ukraine, raport z Badan* (Warsaw, 2004), quoted in Hanna Kwiatkowska, "Antisemitism by Numbers," *East European Jewish Affairs* 36.1 (June 2006): 106-7.

Index

Abramovich, Aron 98
Adorno, Theodor 7, 154
air force 22, 65, 260
Akhmatova, Anna 131, 139
Aksenov, Vasilii 239, 245
Aleksandr Nevskii, 106, 108
Aleksandrov, Georgii F. 221
Aleksandrov, Grigorii V. 221, 224, 225, 228, 229
Aleksei Mikhailovich (tsar) 93
Alpert, Max 187, 189
America see United States of America 7, 8, 22, 23, 37, 39, 53, 95, 96, 109, 256, 258
American Federation of Ukrainian Jews 94
Anan'ev, Anatolii 241
Andreev, Andrei 227
antisemitism 13, 28-30, 54, 73, 75, 77-79, 90, 109, 112, 113, 115, 122, 181, 219, 220, 228, 232, 233, 254, 256
Antselovich, I. 195
Aramaic 19
Argentina 95
artillery 40, 64-68, 119
Auschwitz 7, 133, 162, 163, 184, 196, 259, 260
Austria 42, 45, 64, 251

Babel', Isaac 70, 89, 99, 141, 152
Babii Iar 25, 37, 54, 85, 133, 143, 153, 168, 169, 172, 177, 181-183
Babochkin, Boris A. 175, 176, 177, 180, 221, 223
Bagerovskii rov (ravine) 152
Bagritskii, Eduard 145, 152
Baklanov, Grigorii 241
Baltermants, Dmitrii 187, 190, 193-195
Baltic counties 11, 254, 255
Baltic Fleet 120
Baltic front 152
Bar Kochba 107, 116-119

Baraban, Elena 168
Bartal, Israel 89
Beethoven, Ludwig van 52
Belarus see Belorussia
Belgium 46, 255
Berkhoff, Karel 169
Bialik, Hayim Nahman 135, 140, 141
Belgium 46, 255
Belorussia 11, 46, 47, 49, 50, 76, 78, 97, 124, 141, 187, 233, 235, 244, 260
Belzhets 46
Belostok (Białystok) 39, 113
Berdiaev, Nikolai 139
Berdyshev, Matvei (Motl) 92, 97
Bergelson, David 7, 11, 98, 99, 105, 115, 119, 160, 161, 257
Berdichev 18, 30, 32, 39
Berlin 13, 16, 22, 24, 39, 43, 49, 50, 53, 132, 136, 193, 198, 203, 204, 250
Beskin, Izrail 119
Bessarabia 63, 254
Birobidzhan 10, 90, 93, 95, 107, 128
Birobidzhan State Yiddish Theater 107
Blavatnik Archive Foundation 6, 9, 60
Blum, Klara 114
Bobruisk 138, 141, 148
Bol'shakov, Ivan G. 174, 180, 182, 220, 221, 222, 225, 226, 229
Bolshevism 11, 77, 89, 91, 97, 106-108, 110, 125, 232, 253-255
Bolshoi Trostianets 46, 181
Borovoi, Saul 93, 94
Brest 50
Brezhnev, Leonid 36, 63, 203, 232, 233
Buchma, Amvrosii 178-181
Budapest 70, 196-205
Bulgaria 64
Bund 106, 124, 141, 257
Bykov, Vasyl' 58, 59, 82

Canada 95
Caruth, Cathy 155
Caucasus 21, 77, 97, 152, 157
Caucasus Mountain Jews 21, 33
Celan, Paul 142, 155
Central Asia 67, 77
Central Jewish Committee for the Relief of Victims of War 10
Chekhov, Anton 54, 108
Cherkassy 26, 35
Chernenko, Miron M. 168
Cherniavskii, Mikhail 120
Chernilovskii, Zinovii 58, 60
Chiaureli, Mikheil 224, 228
Chimkent 67
Chopin, Frédéric 54
Christianity 136, 138-140, 142, 150, 155, 158-160, 167, 173, 211
Chukhrai, Pavel 183
circumcision 145, 158
Civil War in Russia 86, 89-91, 98, 152, 188, 190, 232, 254, 255
collaboration with the Nazis 7, 29, 86, 87, 112, 157, 173, 174, 193, 203, 255
Cologne 51
Copernicus, Nicolaus 54
Cossacks 12, 23, 85-100, 120, 173
Crimea 40, 47, 88-90, 105, 124, 152, 155, 163, 231

Danzig 73
Degen, Iosif 150
Der Nister 100
Decembrists 106
Denmark 246
Derrida, Jacques 155
Diskin, Chaim (Efim) 105, 124
Dnepropetrovsk 64, 81
Dobrushin, Yehezkel 116, 117
Donbass 182
Donetsk 190, 191
Donskoi, Dmitrii 108, 144

Index

Donskoi, Mark S. 170-175, 177-179, 183
Dos Passos, John 62
Dostoevsky, Fedor 81, 139, 242
Dovator, Lev 98, 99
Dovzhenko, Aleksandr 110, 221, 225, 228
Dragunskii, David 8, 115
Drobitskii Iar 143
Druzhba narodov 241
Dubinskii, Il'ia 89
Dunaevskaia, Irina 62, 63, 66, 67, 72, 79, 81
Dyskin, Hayim 40

Eastern Europe 94, 116, 251, 326
Ehrenburg, Il'ia 9, 11, 12, 20, 30, 36-56, 57, 58, 70, 72, 112, 113, 118, 143, 147, 148, 177, 193, 196
Einstein, Albert 39, 105, 108, 225
Eisenstein, Sergei M. 172, 174, 179, 180, 183, 221, 224, 228
Ekaterinapol 47
El'kinson, Pavel 69
England *see also* Great Britain 37, 39, 56, 247
Epshteyn, Shakhno 105, 109, 112, 114-116, 121
Ermler, Fridrikh 219, 220, 223, 225, 226, 228
Erofeev, Viktor 239
Evtushenko, Evgenii 85, 185, 238
Eynikayt 7, 8, 10, 12, 98, 104-106, 109, 111-116, 118-122, 159, 196-198, 201, 202, 257

Fagelman, Lazar 96
Falikman, Ikhil 85
fascism 52, 54-57, 86, 92, 151, 228, 260
Fedin, Konstantin 239
Fefer, Itsik 12, 95, 105, 109, 113, 117, 118, 120-122, 159, 161

Feferman, Kiril 169
Feuchtwanger, Lion 90
Fink, Viktor 90
First World War 9, 57, 86, 98, 99, 116, 117, 139, 140, 188
Fisanovich, Israel 40, 120, 121
Forverts 94, 96
France 46, 56, 223, 255
Fridliand, Semen O. 189

Galaktionov, M. R. 176
Gekht, Semen 152
Gel'fand, Vladimir 61, 62, 76, 81
Geminder, Bedřich 112
Germany 9, 13, 22, 24, 37, 39, 50-53, 78-81, 86, 87, 92, 104, 130, 133, 196, 198, 201, 214, 240, 253
Gestapo 48, 157, 212
ghettos 17, 18, 41-45, 50, 80, 113, 119, 120-122, 161, 196, 197, 199, 201-203, 217, 235, 244, 250, 257, 261
Gitelman, Zvi 151, 204
Gladkov, Aleksandr 240
Glatstein, Yankev 136
Glazman, Boruch 89
Glinka, Mikhail 108
Godiner, Shmuel 91, 92, 117
Godunov, Boris (tsar) 145, 146, 147
Goebbels, Joseph 53
Goethe, Johann Wolfgang von 52
Golbshteyn, Motl 117
Golovnia, Anatolii 222, 223
Gomel 39, 41, 76
Gorbatov, Boris L. 169, 175
Gordon, Shmuel 88, 97
Gorky, Maxim 42, 44, 45, 63, 108, 171, 172, 190
Granovskii, Viktor 76
Great Britain *see also* England 95, 109
Great Patriotic War 7, 57, 63, 82, 86, 87, 99, 174, 242

Greenberg, Uri Zevi 140
Grinberg, Aleksandr 187
Grossman, Vasilii 9, 18, 196
Gudzenko, Semen 150
Gulag 16, 30

Ha'aretz 109
Halevi, Yehuda/Judah 108, 118, 130
Halkin, Shmuel 94, 105, 107
Hamsun, Knut 242
Hazman 20
Hebrew 9, 11, 19, 20, 21, 109, 135, 140-142, 145, 152, 200, 202, 233, 237, 238, 253
Heine, Heinrich 39, 105
Hemingway, Ernest 62
Hicks, Jeremy 168, 172, 184, 186
Himmler, Heinrich 53
Hitler, Adolf 11, 17, 36, 37, 39, 40, 46, 50-53, 55, 94, 116, 159, 161, 194, 216, 230, 232, 235, 249, 254
Hitlerjugend 72
Holland 46, 52
Hungary 64, 69, 196-198
Hus, Jan 54

Iakovlev, Aleksei 110
intelligentsia 104-124, 170
internationalism 13, 72, 144
Israel 7, 36, 81, 131, 204, 232, 233, 249, 250, 252, 255, 259
Ivan the Terrible 106, 134, 135, 180
Izvestiia 37, 38, 181, 196

JAC *see* Jewish Anti-Fascist Committee
Jewish Anti-Fascist Committee 7-10, 22, 30, 38, 42, 57, 85, 95, 97, 98, 100, 104, 119, 120, 159, 180, 198, 232
Jewish Colonization Society 10
Jewish Chronicle 95

Jewish identity 7, 11-13, 16, 31, 79-81, 104, 204, 250
Judaism 34, 173, 179

Kabbalah 130, 136
Kabo, Isaak 120
Kaganovich, Lazar 105, 107, 108
Kamenets-Podolsk 80
Kandava 152, 161-164
Kanev 18
Kaplun, Iosif 96
Kats, David 41
Katsnelson, Berl 141
Kaufman, David 62, 71, 77
Kaverin, Veniamin 152
Kazakevich, Emanuil 9, 90
Kazakhstan 27, 30
Kerch' 151-164, 193-196
Khaldei, Evgenii (Efim) A. 13, 22, 23, 187-205
Khalip, Iakov 190
Kharkov 17, 27, 29, 64, 143, 208, 209, 213-216
Khazan, Vladimir 131
Kheifits, Iosif 223, 225
Khelemskii, Iakov 17
Khlebnikov, Velimir 142
Khmelnytskyi, Bohdan 93-96, 109
Khrushchev, Nikita 85, 109, 203, 246
khurbn 7, 160
Kiev 10, 18, 25, 27, 37, 51, 64, 85, 120, 153, 160, 186, 189, 209-211, 215, 245
Kittel, Bruno 43-45
Kochetov, Vsevolod 241
Koltsov (Fridliand), Mikhail 188, 189
Komskii, Boris 62, 67-69, 71, 77, 78, 81
Komsomol 26, 65
Koreans 90
Korneichuk, Aleksandr 94
Kornilov, Boris 239
Korzhavin, Naum 150
Kostyrchenko, Gennadii 198
Kotliar, Leontii 96
Kozintsev, Grigorii 223, 225, 226, 228

Krasnaia zvezda 36, 40, 152, 196
Krasnodar 152, 156, 157
Krasnograd 216, 217
Kreizer, Iakov 96, 119
Kron, Aleksandr 238
Kryzhopol 16
Kulbak, Moyshe 107
Kul'chitskii, Mikhail 147
Kunnikov, Tsezar 104
Kuprin, A.I. 179
Kursk 17, 67, 69
Kushnirov, Aron 114, 117
Kutuzov, Mikhail 108, 114
Kvitko, Leyb 92, 105, 120

Lander, Olga 190
Langman, Eleazar 189
Latvia 17, 152, 161, 251
Latvian Division 11
Lee, Malka 89
Lekert, Hirsh 106, 107, 139
Lenin, Vladimir 23, 108, 211, 243
Leningrad 24, 41, 53, 63-66, 73, 78, 81
Leningrad Blockade 63, 66, 73
Lesiuchevskii, N.V. 238
Leskov, Nikolai 150
Lev, Mikhail 8, 85
Levitan, Isaac 42
Levitan, Yurii 9
Liady 19
Lille 51
Lipkin, Semen I. 239
Lisnianskaia, Inna 239
Literaturnaia gazeta 182, 238
Lithuania 20, 41-45, 246
Lithuanian Division 11, 105
Lobachevskii, Nikolai 54
London 53, 55, 95, 247, 248
Lotman, Yurii 131
Lvov 49, 74, 81
Lyotard, Jean-Francois 155

Maccabees 107, 116, 117, 118
Madrid 117
Maimonides 108, 130

Majdanek 45, 52, 54, 80, 162, 163, 173, 184, 196, 259
Malenkov, Georgii 224, 227
Mandelshtam, Osip 131, 145
Mariánské Lázně International Film Festival 182
Mariupol 25, 153
Mark, Ber 20, 21
Markish, Peretz 11, 38, 94, 105, 115, 159, 161
Markov-Grinberg, Mark 187, 189
Marshak, Samuel 92
Marx, Karl 105, 108
Mekhlis, Lev 243, 244
Melamud, Khaim 86, 88, 90, 92, 93, 97
Mendeleev, Dmitrii 54
Mezhirov, Alexander 150
Mexico 95
Mikhoels, Solomon 38, 42, 95, 98, 115, 171
Minin, Kuzma 106, 108
Minsk 10, 34, 39, 46, 121, 181, 235, 245
Molotov, Viacheslav 36, 108, 153, 242
Molotov-Ribbentrop Pact 10, 133, 149
Moscow 26, 36-38, 40, 64, 65, 107, 138, 141, 148, 168, 187, 188-193, 198, 203, 220-222, 227, 228, 233, 234, 236
Moscow Institute of Philosophy, Literature and History 62, 105
Moscow State Yiddish Theater 95, 107
Mosfilm 219, 221, 222
Mozhaysk 40
Munich 55
Mussolini, Benito 55

Nancy 51
Nathans, Benjamin 91
nationalism 54, 85, 108, 110, 113, 115, 116
Nazi propaganda 29, 76, 79, 109, 122, 123, 258
Nekrasov, Viktor 58

Nicholas I (tsar) 119
Nikolaev 28, 189
Nikulin, N.N. 59
Northern Fleet 120
Novozlatopol (Nayzlatopol) 87, 88, 90, 92
Novy Dvor 46
Novyi mir 238, 240, 243
Nuremberg Trial 42, 153, 169, 178, 193, 199, 205, 235
Nusinov, Isaac 94

Odessa 28, 62, 64, 93, 98, 141, 189, 211
Ogonek 188, 189, 193-195
Okhlopkov, Nikolai P. 175, 178-180
Oktiabr' 241, 242, 243, 244
Organization for Rehabilitation through Training 10
Ortenberg, David 198
Osherowitch, Mendel 94
Oyslender, Nokhem 116, 117
Ozerskii, Israel 194, 195

Radziechow 19
Paris 39, 55
Paris Peace Conference in 1946 193, 199
partisans 8, 11, 18, 26, 42-45, 48, 78, 88, 100, 111, 113, 119-122, 153, 161, 170, 173, 236, 237, 253, 237
Passover 20, 140, 249
Pasternak, Boris 139
Patriotic War of 1812 108, 116
patriotism 8, 53, 54, 65, 106-109, 114-117, 120, 122, 257
Paulus, Friedrich von 86
Pentateuch 135
People's Volunteer Corps 63-65, 208
Peredelkino 231, 235, 238, 239, 246
Pereiaslav 93, 96
Peres, Shimon 249
perestroika 58

Peretz, I. L. 115, 127, 128, 159, 167
Perm' 17
Persov, Shmuel 98, 105, 119, 120
Peter the Great 42, 106
Piatnitskii, Osip (Iosif) 97
Piatnitskii, Vladimir 97
Podoksik, Efim 97
Pokrovskii, Mikhail 106
Polyanker, Hershl 97, 121
Pomerants, Grigorii 75, 80, 81
Ponary 43, 46, 47, 49, 235
Ponovich 24
Popov, Evgenii 239
Popov, Khaim (Efim) 98, 120
Pozharskii, Dmitrii 106, 108
POWs: German 45, 72, 85; Soviet 26, 46, 87, 168, 208, 259
Prague 46, 175
Pravda 37, 42, 45, 51, 169, 170, 181, 183, 189, 196, 199
Priestley, J.B. 62
Pudovkin, Vsevolod 221, 222, 224
Pugachev, Emel'ian 106
Pushkin, Alexander 39, 90, 108, 145, 146
Pyr'ev, Ivan A. 174, 178, 219-221, 223, 224, 226

Rabochaia gazeta 189
Raizman, Iuli 219, 220, 223, 225, 226
Rava Russkaia 46
Razin, Stepan 106
Red Army: Jewish combatants of 16, 21, 22, 24, 28, 31, 57, 60, 64, 96, 97, 105, 112, 114; volunteers to 16, 28, 40, 64, 66, 98, 121
Redkin, Mark 193-195
Reichstag 13, 22, 188, 192, 193, 198, 199, 204, 205
Repin, Il'ia 42, 44
Ricoeur, Paul 131
Riga 17, 43, 51
Rolland, Romain 42

Romania 16, 22, 63, 64, 80, 254, 262
Romm, Mikhail I. 174, 175, 177, 178, 185, 219-228
Roosevelt, Franklin 170
Rosenshield, Gary 99
Rosin, Shmuel 117
Roskies, David 134
Rostov-on-Don 90, 93, 189, 214
Russian State Historical Museum 203
Russianness 147, 150, 178, 222
Rybak, Natan 96
Rybakov, Anatolii 13, 22, 86, 99, 230-250

Samoilov, David 62, 150
Satunovskii, Ian 150
Savchenko, Igor A. 174, 176, 177, 223
Savitsky, Mikhail 233
Seekers of Happiness (film) 93
Seidman, Naomi 160, 167
Sel'vinskii, Il'ia 12, 151-164, 193
Shaikhet, Arkadii 187, 189
Shcherbakov, Aleksandr 112, 227
Shefer, A. 113, 116
Shimoni, David 141
Shmidt, Dmitrii (Gutman, David) 89
Shnaider, Eli 119
Sholem Aleichem 44, 88, 93, 105, 108, 116, 117
Sholokhov, Mikhail 87, 97, 126
Shostakovich, Dmitrii D. 175, 185
Shpayer, Lev 41
Shtern, Sholem 94
Shulman, Moyni 98
Shumelishskii, Mark 61, 62, 65-67, 74
Shvartsman, Moisei 26
Shvartsman, Osher 117
Simferopol 152, 189, 230, 233

Index

Simonov, Konstantin M. 174, 175, 187
Sito, Faivel 121
Skorzeny, Otto 86
Slutskii, Boris 12, 13, 96, 130-149, 208-218
SMERSH (Death to Spies) 62
Smolensk 18, 20, 26, 44
Snovsk (Shchors) 233, 234, 236, 237, 250
Sobibor 46, 259
Sobolev, Aleksandr 29
Society for Health of Jews 10
Solzhenitsyn, Aleksandr 243
Sovetish heymland 8, 85, 86, 160, 248
Sovetskii Pisatel' (publishing house) 85, 239
Soviet propaganda 8, 21, 38, 59, 70, 86, 91, 104, 106, 109, 111, 112, 115, 116, 118, 155
Soviet Writers' Union 10, 239
Sovinformburo, Soviet Information Bureau 8-10, 43, 112
Spinoza, Baruch 105, 108
Sprintson, Ruvim 41
Stalin, Iosif/Joseph 10, 36-38, 60, 65, 81, 85, 94, 97, 98, 107-110, 118, 144, 150, 159, 199, 203, 220, 225, 230-232, 242-244, 252-254, 259
Stalin Prize/Award 170, 228, 239
Stalingrad 17, 30, 41, 49, 73, 85, 119, 147
Stalino 190, 192, 195, 196
Stampfer, Saul 94
Sudak 230
Suris, Boris 62, 67, 72, 76, 77, 81
Suslov, Mikhail 243, 244
Sutzkever, Abram 41-45
Suvorov, Aleksandr 108, 114, 118

Sverdlov, Iakov 105, 108
Switzerland 230, 242

Taganka Theater 240
Talmud 130
Tarantino, Quentin 161
Tartakovskii, Boris 67, 73, 74, 80, 81
Tashkent 24, 40, 98, 190, 211, 221, 226, 228
TASS 192, 196, 198, 199
Tatars 110, 114, 124, 130, 143-146, 193, 195, 254
Tchaikovsky, Petr 54, 108, 118
Tevekelian, Diana 238, 240, 241
Tolkatchev, Zinovii 173, 184
Tolstoy, Lev 38, 39, 42, 44, 54, 108
Torah 109
Transnistria 80
Trauberg, Leonid 219, 220, 223, 225, 226, 228, 229
Treblinka 45, 52, 54, 162, 260
Trifonov, Iurii 239, 240
Trostianets *see* Bolshoi Trostianets
Trud 181, 199
Tsetlin, Vladimir 98
Tsimlianskaia 87, 90-92
Tsymbal, Vassily 63
Turovskii, Semen 89
Tuwim, Julian 39, 42, 54
Tvardovsky, Aleksandr 238

UFA Studios 43
Ukraine 11, 16, 18, 27, 39, 52, 80, 87, 89, 90, 93, 94, 97, 109, 157, 170, 187, 190, 214-216, 245, 256
Uman 24
United States of America 95, 98, 227, 232, 239, 258
Uritskii, Moisei 108
Uzbekistan 30

Vainrub, Matvei 96
Vecherniaia Moskva 181

Vengeroff, Pauline 141
Venice Biennale 169, 182
Vergelis, Aron 86
Vienna 46, 198
Vilna/Vilnius 20, 41-46, 49, 50, 106, 235
Virgin Mary 155
Vlasovites 78, 217
Volchek, Boris 222
Voroshilov, Kliment 92

Wahl, Victor von 106
Wandering Jew 140, 171, 174, 179
Warsaw 48, 55, 56, 113, 122, 197
Wehrmacht 37, 38
Weiner, Amir 151, 164
Weinper, Zishe 94
Western Europe 37, 161, 253, 254
Wiener, Meir 117
Wiesel, Eli 169, 248, 262
Wittenberg, Yitzhak 43, 45

Yablokoff, Herman 89
Yad Vashem 38, 258
Yeisk Pedagogical College 63
Yiddish writers 11, 44, 85, 86, 99, 105, 116, 160
Yom Kippur 18, 259
Yugoslavia 54, 64
Yutkevich, Sergei 228

Zabolotsky, Nikolai 239
Zhabotinskii, Vladimir 140
Zalgaller, Viktor 64-66, 71, 73, 78-81
Zaporozh'e 64, 73, 81
Zarkhi, Aleksandr 223, 225
Zelmanovitch, Georgii 190
Zhdanov, Andrei 227
Zhmerinka 80
Znamia 156, 159
Zuskin, Veniamin L. 168, 180-182
Zyuk (Nekhamkin), Mikhail 89
Zionism 74, 141, 232, 250

www.ingramcontent.com/pod-product-compliance
Lightning Source LLC
Chambersburg PA
CBHW051113230426
43667CB00014B/2562